CHANGING POPULATIONS
CHANGING SCHOOLS

CHANGING POPULATIONS
CHANGING SCHOOLS

Ninety-fourth Yearbook of the
National Society for the Study of Education

PART II

Edited by

ERWIN FLAXMAN AND A. HARRY PASSOW

Editor for the Society
KENNETH J. REHAGE

19  95

Distributed by THE UNIVERSITY OF CHICAGO PRESS • CHICAGO, ILLINOIS

The National Society for the Study of Education

Founded in 1901 as successor to the National Herbart Society, the National Society for the Study of Education has provided a means by which the results of serious study of educational issues could become a basis for informed discussion of those issues. The Society's two-volume yearbooks, now in their ninety-fourth year of publication, reflect the thoughtful attention given to a wide range of educational problems during those years. In 1971 the Society inaugurated a series of substantial publications on Contemporary Educational Issues to supplement the yearbooks. Each year the Society's publications contain contributions to the literature of education from more than a hundred scholars and practitioners who are doing significant work in their respective fields.

An elected Board of Directors selects the subjects with which volumes in the yearbook series are to deal and appoints committees to oversee the preparation of manuscripts. A special committee created by the Board performs similar functions for the series on Contemporary Educational Issues.

The Society's publications are distributed each year without charge to members in the United States, Canada, and elsewhere throughout the world. The Society welcomes as members all individuals who desire to receive its publications. Information about current dues may be found in the back pages of this volume.

This volume, *Changing Populations/Changing Schools*, is Part II of the Ninety-fourth Yearbook of the Society. Part I, published at the same time, is entitled *Creating New Educational Communities*.

A listing of the Society's publications still available for purchase may be found in the back pages of this volume.

Library of Congress Catalog Number: 94-069014
ISSN: 0077-5762

Published 1995 by
THE NATIONAL SOCIETY FOR THE STUDY OF EDUCATION

5835 Kimbark Avenue, Chicago, Illinois 60637

First Printing

Printed in the United States of America

iv

Board of Directors of the
National Society for the Study of Education
(Term of office expires March 1 of the year indicated.)

Contributors to the Yearbook

v

Acknowledgments

The co-editors of this volume, Erwin Flaxman and A. Harry Passow, have been deeply involved in issues relating to diversity in the schools. Their years of experience with these issues made it possible for them to develop plans for a Yearbook that brings various perspectives to bear on problems that confront schools because of changing populations. In addition to conceptualizing the plan for the Yearbook and working with authors in the development of their essays, both editors have contributed chapters to the volume. With great gratitude, the National Society for the Study of Education acknowledges its debt to the editors.

The Society also appreciates the contributions of the several authors who responded to the invitation to prepare chapters for the Yearbook. Their respective essays have enriched the volume in ways that are possible only when authors are knowledgeable about their subject and aware of the broad implications of the issues about which they write.

Professor Margaret Early of the University of Florida at Gainesville and a former member of the NSSE Board of Directors, has again helped with the editing of this volume by painstakingly reading each chapter and making most helpful suggestions.

Robert Mehler, assistant in the NSSE office, has prepared the name index.

NSSE is pleased to have this volume as part of its 94th Yearbook.

KENNETH J. REHAGE
Editor for the Society

Table of Contents

Section One
Changing Demographics

Section Two
Strategies for Educating Changing Populations in the Schools

Section One
CHANGING DEMOGRAPHICS

Introduction

In one way or another all contributors to this Yearbook try to explain the reasons for the poor "fit" between schools and poor, immigrant, linguistically different, and racial minority students. Part way through his history of the efforts to educate such student populations, W. Norton Grubb pauses to review the common explanations for the failure of the schools to educate these students adequately. They do poorly in school because they are mentally defective or lack character, motivation, or self-esteem; their families are deficient in some ways and so they do not develop their children's readiness to do school work; schooling generally is insufficiently differentiated to accommodate their very different interests and abilities; students' cultural backgrounds are different from the culture of the schools; and the students inevitably fail because the schools mirror or re-create the inequities of the larger society. Grubb argues that our preoccupation with these explanations has so blinded us that we do not recognize that the conventional method of instruction in the schools—"skills and drills," as he calls it—has contributed to the educational failure of many lower-class, immigrant, and minority students. Such an instructional method, he contends, does not prepare these students to meet the demands of today's rapidly changing and complex society in which they must live and work.

Grubb acknowledges that many social forces sustain this instructional method—efficiency, bureaucratic regulation, social control, and the absence of resources to teach any other way. He maintains, however, that educators have paid too little attention to the deleterious effects of this pedagogy and have tracked students out of academic opportunities and meaningful learning that could lead to profitable employment. In the past, the content of the curriculum and the methods

1

of instruction for the nontraditional student have worked because they satisfied society's need for vocationally skilled youth with an adequate set of life skills. But Grubb argues that we now need a *differentiated curriculum and pedagogy* for students to meet *undifferentiated demands and standards*. In his terms, such curriculum and instruction would be individually "meaning making" and responsive to the demands of the larger society. What is more, this way of educating in the twentieth century would meet the nineteenth-century educational ideal of moral and intellectually meaningful schooling for all.

Aaron Pallas, Gary Natriello, and Edward McDill also argue that student outcomes depend on the social, political, and institutional nature of schooling, not just on the characteristics of individual students and their families. The current trend toward greater accountability, the changing patterns of centralization and decentralization, and the "routinized" and institutionalized school structures may impede, although unintentionally, the academic and social development of students from nontraditional backgrounds. According to these authors, we clearly can no longer locate school failure in students alone; success or failure in school is a consequence of the way students function in a complex organization.

Pallas, Natriello, and McDill argue that schools have deliberately differentiated among students by grouping them on the basis of ability, disability, age, and interest. They conclude that while such differentiation may be a rational response to diversity and the uncertainty of outcomes—especially with so many special interests to satisfy—homogeneous grouping may not be the only way to group students for instruction. Despite diversity in student populations, there may be commonalities among them that can point to mechanisms for organizing schooling that will transcend differences.

Differences and differentiating mechanisms are also a subject of A. Harry Passow's chapter. In reviewing the nation's efforts to provide equitable support to talented and gifted children in all cultural and socioeconomic groups and in all human endeavor, he points to an essential educational dilemma. In the current environment of educational reform, should curriculum and instruction and related educational experiences remain differentiated for gifted and talented students (inclusively defined)? Or, should all tracking be eliminated in the belief that the exemplary education provided for the gifted and talented student can be used as the basis of education for every student and thus provide all students with equal access to a quality education?

All the authors of chapters in the following section agree that the success of immigrant, poor, linguistically different, and racial minority students can be affected by the school's institutional policies, but how these policies should be changed to ensure this success is not so clear.

CHAPTER I

The Old Problem of "New Students": Purpose, Content, and Pedagogy

W. NORTON GRUBB

Current discussions of education often begin by invoking what we might call the "new demographics." The student body is changing, this argument goes. There is more poverty, and so more poor children. There is more immigration from Asian and Latin American countries, and so more children who do not speak English. Because of immigration and natural population increases, there are more non-white students, especially in some states like California the harbinger, which will soon become "majority minority." There are advances in medical care, but these have left us with more handicapped children, and crack and other forms of substance abuse have exacerbated the problem. In higher education a similar litany points out the numbers of "nontraditional" students, particularly in community colleges and nonelite four-year colleges, who are older than other students, often have employment and family responsibilities, are likely to have mediocre academic records, are likely to be nonwhite, and often have parents lacking higher education. Behind this rhetoric is a sense of urgency. Schools and colleges have never done well by these groups, who are often called "new students" because educators have always considered them different in some way from those previously enrolled. Yet their numbers are growing.

But so what? What should educators do? Is sensitivity to the problem—the awareness gained from rehearsing the figures over and over—sufficient? If not, what responses are necessary? And why should anyone think that this problem, an old one in the history of American education, can be resolved this time around simply by resolving to do better? Without clear answers, the familiar litany of figures serves little purpose.

W. Norton Grubb is Professor in the School of Education at the University of California, Berkeley. He is also a site director for the National Center for Research in Vocational Education located at the University of California, Berkeley.

Given the enormity of the problem, it may be helpful to look at the historical record. Alarm about "new students" flooding into the schools is hardly new, after all: concern about lower-class and minority children is a persistent strain, and in a nation of immigrants each wave of arrivals has led to various efforts to cope with them. Not surprisingly, the dominant responses have been contradictory. On the one hand there have been powerful efforts to include "new students," to provide access, and to find new resources for them. The other response has been to accommodate "new students" through differentiation by developing new purposes for schooling and by varying its content for groups of students with supposedly different needs and interests. The result is that access to schooling for all students has been preserved, though "schooling" means very different things for different students.

But in all these debates one aspect of schooling has rarely been examined: the conventional pedagogy of instruction. Indeed, as Cuban has pointed out so clearly,[1] teaching methods have been quite resistant to calls for reform, particularly in high schools. Yet there are reasons to suspect that very little will change for the majority of "new students" unless there are serious reforms in approaches to teaching, the dominant forms of which contain special problems for low-income students. At the very least, reshaping pedagogy represents a response which has rarely been tried, one consistent with other currents of reform and with substantial promise for the old problem of "new students."

The Promise of Access and the Search for Resources

What has been done with "new students" in the past—with the successive waves of immigrants, with newly freed slaves migrating to the north after the Civil War, with the low-income children who sought entry into the high school around the turn of the century? One consistent response—the common school, with its inclusionary impulse and its promise of access for all—developed in the early nineteenth century. It represented a significant departure from European systems, where it was more usual to argue that lower-class children should be excluded from schools lest a little education should prove dangerous. In this country, education was to be the bulwark against rebellion, the way of socializing all into a common political and moral culture.

In the early nineteenth century, the conditions of life in the large cities—the places that increasingly defined the institution building of the United States—were changing markedly. The relative equality of the countryside was being replaced with the greater inequality of early capitalism: employers and employees became increasingly differentiated, differences in incomes and poverty grew, and Jefferson's one-class society of independent farmers and craftsmen was being displaced by an increasingly complex (and "modern") class structure. Immigration continued, especially from Ireland and Italy, increasing the numbers of lower-class families. And their children were labeled as poorly reared, a threat to the stability of society. The dominant view, emerging from the religious convictions of yet an earlier period, was that such children lacked "character," that is, the moral standards and behavior appropriate for a stable, democratic society.[2] The response was the creation of the common school, a publicly supported system of education whose sole purpose was the moral and political development of the young in an institution common to all. As the Free School Society of New York declaimed in 1821, the public schools

are rapidly extending the benign influence of moral principles, inspiring self-regard, creating respect for the laws, diminishing the sources of pauperism and crime, and preparing for usefulness a large portion of what must soon compose our future active population, who might otherwise grow up in idleness, remain a burden on the community, and become victims to every species of vice and profligacy incident to extensive and populous cities.[3]

Ever since then the public schools have at least tried to keep up with the flood of "new students" in an effort to provide access that has been labeled the genius of American education.[4] One mark of that effort has been the persistent concern with high school dropouts. As early as the late nineteenth century, educators began noticing the high rates of high school dropout, which was a thorn in their sides because low-income students were most likely to drop out despite the claim that the schools were for rich and poor alike.[5] With the scientific fervor of the age, educators began to study the causes of dropout and "retardation" and to devise cures such as enforcement of compulsory attendance laws and child labor laws and the development of differentiated curricula (like vocational education) to appeal to the "interests" of the new students. In a sense, the *angst* over dropouts seems curious: high school enrollments were booming and the schools had all they could do to accommodate those who were coming to the doors. But the concern for dropouts revealed anxiety about social stability, as much as a concern about the future prospects of those individuals who dropped out.

Ever since, the problem of dropouts has been one that every generation of educators has rediscovered. In the 1920s arguments about the "money value of education," first popularized during the movement for vocational education, reappeared as a way of persuading students to stay in school. In the 1930s, Roosevelt's Advisory Commission on Education complained again about dropouts, despite the fact that enrollments were increasing anyway as the lack of employment drove adolescents into the schools. After the hiatus of World War II, the problem of dropouts burst forth again in the 1950s, especially as part of the alarm over juvenile delinquents; the leitmotif of the period was James Bryant Conant's image of "social dynamite" accumulating in urban ghettos, reflecting the concern with social cohesion. In the 1960s concern with dropouts focused more on the individual rather than social benefits: only by preventing dropouts would it be possible to guarantee access to employment for black students and other low-income students. Since then there has been a virtually constant rumble about dropouts, continuing today with the recognition that the economic differences between dropouts and high school graduates has been growing.

In the waves of interest in keeping students in school, one common response has been fiscal—the effort to find additional curricular resources to support low-income students.[6] From the turn of the century, various educators noted that low-income children were more likely to be in schools with low levels of resources, and the attempts to equalize resources began—first through state aid programs that attempted to establish a minimum educational "foundation" for each student, and then through increasingly elaborate formulas and guarantees. To be sure, these efforts were only partially successful, and so a series of lawsuits during the 1970s and 1980s—beginning with the well-known *Serrano* case in California—has attempted to do through litigation what was difficult to do through legislation. Still another fiscal tactic began during the 1960s, as funding special-purpose programs for low-income students became part of President Johnson's War on Poverty. The funding for compensatory education through Title I (later Chapter 1) and through Head Start (and the parallel efforts in higher education to fund grants and loans for low-income students) began a pattern that was followed with funding for bilingual education, for disabled children, for dropout prevention programs in high schools and middle schools, and for special services funded through job training efforts like the Job Training Partnership Act.

Again the results may have been inadequate. In a recent critique, Jonathan Kozol ripped the schools for "savage inequalities" within them, almost twenty-five years after he had first criticized the ineffectiveness of urban schools for the children of the poor.[7] But of course the fiscal response to the advent of "new students" is one that has been forced to take place within the political arena. It has consistently faced the limits of funding for equalization within a society committed to limited government, individual freedoms, a relatively unbridled form of capitalism, and the persistence of inequality.

The other dominant response to "new students" and dropout problems—and one which has been more nearly within the control of educators—has been curricular. Repeatedly, the response to dropout problems and to "new students" has been to change the purposes of schooling and to differentiate the curriculum, in part to appeal to their supposed "needs" and "interests." The result has been a system in which all students have access to education, but where "education" means different things for different students.

Rhetoric and Response: The Differentiation of Purpose

When the common schools were established in the nineteenth century, there was only one overriding purpose for formal schooling: the moral training of the young to provide them the behavioral norms, the "character," necessary for a heterogeneous society. This moral education had political purposes too, since it was important to prepare students to be citizens in a political structure that could work for a cohesive society. The curriculum to support these moral and political purposes was the classical liberal curriculum—Latin, Greek, and mathematics—joined over the course of the nineteenth century by modern languages and "modern" subjects like science and history. But while some battles were fought over what was to be included and excluded, there was not much choice: the purpose of the common school was, after all, that all students should receive a similar education. When the National Education Association's Committee of Ten defined the high school curriculum at the end of the century it recommended four curricula—the classical, the Latin-scientific, modern languages, and English. The curricula varied in the amounts of science and of modern versus ancient languages, and they allowed for more choice (based on "the different capacities and powers," and the likes and dislikes of students) than most high schools then offered. But mental discipline and moral development were still the only purposes of schooling, and the report argued against differentiation by denying any differences between college-bound and non-college-bound students: "Every subject which is taught at all in a secondary school should be taught in the same way and to the same extent to every pupil as long as he pursues it, no matter what the probable destination of the pupil may be."[8]

At the turn of the century, however, moral purposes gave way to more explicitly occupational purposes. Part of this change came from higher education. Professional schools at the collegiate level, particularly in business, engineering, medicine, and law, began requiring high school diplomas and choosing students based on their high school records, making high school a necessary prerequisite to professional and managerial careers which previously had not been the case. At the same time, educators noted the continued influx of immigrant and lower-class students into the high school. G. Stanley Hall spoke of the "great army of incapables" storming the doors, and the president of the National Education Association lamented in 1897: "Whether agreeable or not, we must recognize the fact that it is the children of the plain people, in city and country, who are crowding our schoolrooms today, and these will always be in the majority. The children of the masses and not of the classes will rule us."[9]

For these students, the solution was vocational education within the high school—a form of preparation not for the professional and managerial careers associated with college going, but for lower-level craft jobs, manual occupations, farming, and the increasing numbers of secretarial and clerical positions of the expanding corporations. Thus the development of occupational purposes for formal schooling led directly to a new form of differentiation, one based, as Charles Eliot declared in 1897, on the "evident and probable destinies" of students. Since occupations were so different, it no longer made sense to follow the advice of the Committee of Ten that "every subject . . . should be taught in the same way . . . to every pupil."

As a result, the vocational differentiation of the high school was a corollary of its expansion.[10] As the high school continued to grow, educators noted the "invasion" of schools by less capable students, or lower-class students, or immigrants. Almost universally, the response was to call for more vocational education. As one educator said during the 1930s of the students who stayed in school because of the lack of work: "In past years many of those who could not meet high school standards were able to find some sort of work. Now these pupils are forced to remain in school. The crying need of this group is vocational education."[11]

However, the adoption of vocational purposes for schooling ran into yet another difficulty as the high school continued to expand. While vocational education prepared students for jobs requiring some technical skills, the fact was that many jobs in the economy required virtually no preparation—a fact that became especially clear during the Great Depression. In 1937, the American Youth Commission of the American Council on Education summarized its work in a volume entitled *What the High Schools Ought to Teach*, which noted the tremendous increase in the student population "from every level of society," a circumspect way of describing what another Commission report called "the new pupil of lesser academic ability." Vocational education was only a partial solution to the problem of what to do with these students because many individuals would not need vocational skills:

Much of the work provided in vocational classes fails to meet the needs of pupils because it is quite as specialized as were the traditional preprofessional courses. The unit-trade courses which have been organized in many technical secondary schools are, in reality, aimed at the cultivation of skills of a high order in particular trades. For such skills, there is, in the industrial world, only a limited demand. The fact is that a large proportion of the workers in America are engaged in routine jobs that require relatively little skill or training.[12]

The solution was a program of general education—the development of the general track, neither academic nor vocational—emphasizing reading, work experience, and social studies as a means of citizenship training. Roosevelt's Advisory Committee on Education also recommended "a well-planned program of general education" emphasizing "useful habits and basic traits roughly included in the term 'character' " rather than specific trade training. And after World War II, the Educational Policies Committee of the National Education Association called for a core curriculum including "civic competence, health, family life, and the cultural heritage—a program of life skills" necessary for all students. Only some students needed to take a more academic program to prepare for college, while a few others enrolled in vocational programs for the trades.

A few years later, this tripartite division was enshrined in the movement for life adjustment education:

It is the belief of this conference [on "Vocational Education in the Years Ahead"] that the vocational schools of a community will be better able to prepare 20 percent of the youth of secondary school age for entrance upon desirable skilled occupations; and that the high schools will continue to prepare another 20 percent for entrance to college. We do not believe that the remaining 60 percent of our youth of secondary school age will receive the life adjustment training they need and to which they are entitled as American citizens—unless and until the administrators of public education with the assistance of the vocational education leaders formulate a similar program for this group.[13]

Thus a response to the continued growth of the high school, and to the continuing influx of "new students," was to add yet another purpose to the school—a purpose which can be described as providing "life skills" for those destined for unskilled jobs. While life adjustment education itself died out in a conservative backlash of the 1950s, it lives on in the general track, in courses like "Social Living" and "Family Life," and in the tendency of some teachers in the "shopping mall high school"[14] to turn their social studies and English courses into explorations of students' personal interests.

Yet another elaboration of purpose has come from efforts to wrestle with the material deficiencies of poor students. One of the earliest manifestations of this emerged in the settlement house movement at the turn of the century. In trying to provide for the "whole child," settlement houses and the schools they sponsored, especially kindergartens, tried to provide food and clothing as well as instruction. The notion that children could not learn when they are hungry was finally institutionalized in the school lunch and breakfast programs started during the 1960s. Rudimentary health care—check-ups and immunizations—was a routine part of schools (at least, elementary schools) through the 1960s, when budget problems began to eliminate positions for school nurses. At a more ambitious level, Head Start represents an effort to view an educational program as a comprehensive social service center as well, providing not only food and health care but also parent education, counseling to parents, and other support services.

Other social services within schools (especially high schools) have been responses to various kinds of "crises," many of them predominantly problems of low-income students: the efforts to provide sex education and school clinics to prevent teen pregnancy, venereal disease, and now AIDS; drug abuse courses and counseling; and crisis counseling for various personal problems, often the responsibility of counselors or school psychologists whose primary duties are quite different. More generally, there has been a perennial call to use the schools for comprehensive social services, with the argument that the public schools bring together all children in a way that makes the delivery of comprehensive services both convenient and universal. By and large, however, these efforts have not been realized. Battles over turf, the lack of funding (especially crucial in the low-income school districts where social problems are concentrated), and the inability of schools to respond to the multiple pressures on them have made it impossible to realize the vision of the schools as comprehensive, "one-stop" service centers.[15]

Thus the basic purposes of public education have been shaped, in large part, by the challenges of "new students," low-income, minority, and immigrant. Over time, purposes have piled up rather than being superseded, and so now the moral and political enculturation of the nineteenth century common school coexists with occupational purposes dating from the turn of the century, with the efforts to provide "life skills," and some limited social services. Each of them now has its own history and claims to legitimacy, and each is reinvented as new social challenges and new population groups appear. Together, they have managed to demolish the nineteenth-century notion of a unitary purpose for schooling and the ideal that "mental discipline"—or as we would say now, "intellectual development"—should be the sole focus of schools.

At the same time, there has been a persistent undercurrent of suspicion that the drift of purposes has been detrimental, both to the schools as a whole and more particularly to low-income students. The low status and unsophisticated intellectual demands in many forms of vocational education, the frivolity of what has passed for life skills education, and the inappropriateness of social services in what are supposed to be educational institutions have all come under attack at different periods and in different ways, particularly in the 1950s, with the revulsion against life adjustment education and the focus on science and mathematics after the Sputnik crisis, and in the 1980s with the "New Basics" fostered by *A Nation at Risk* and other commission reports. Current strands of such thinking include the followers of Adler's *Paedeia Proposal* and of the Coalition of Essential Schools, the latter a movement with elements of essentialism and conservatism in its return to a unitary ideal of intellectual development ("using minds well"). But Pandora's box has been opened. Now that purposes other than intellectual development have been accepted for the public schools, especially the vocational purposes that are almost impossible to ignore, every proponent of a unitary ideal must fight against the presumption that it is archaic, irrelevant, and elitist.[16]

The Differentiation of Content

A related response to the influx of "new students" has been the differentiation of the content of schools—particularly of the high school. To be sure, the differentiation of content has been part of the elaboration of purposes. In particular, the advent of vocational education meant that some students have followed an academic curriculum to prepare them for college, while others studied business, or agriculture, or some craft. The tripartite division of students into academic, vocational, and "general" has placed the lowest-performing students in "life skills" classes, and the provision of social services has similarly drawn some students out of the conventional academic program.

But the differentiation of content has taken other forms, too. One was ability grouping—the tendency to sort students into different classes according to their abilities. Several trends within schools supported ability grouping, including the efficiency movement which required identifying different types of students and treating them accordingly. As Lewis Terman, father of intelligence tests, wrote in 1922 about the "mental defectives": "They clog the educational machinery. . . . They consume a disproportionately large part of the regular teacher's energy. They pull down the standard of achievement for other children."[17] But, of course, those considered mental defectives were disproportionately to be found among low-income and immigrant and minority students. As Terman described the "feeble minded," who, he claimed, included 80 percent of immigrants:

Their dullness seems to be racial or at least inherent in the family stocks from which they come. The fact that one meets this type with such extraordinary frequency among Indians, Mexicans, and negroes suggests quite forcibly that the whole question of racial differences in mental traits will have to be taken up anew. . . . There will be discovered enormously significant racial differences . . . which cannot be wiped out by any scheme of mental culture.

Children of this group should be segregated in special classes. . . . They cannot master abstractions, but they can often be made efficient workers.[18]

While ability grouping was a way of meeting a variety of educational goals—individualizing instruction, reducing the "clogging" of classes by "misfits" unable to keep up, reducing dropouts by allowing some students to progress at different rates—there were unmistakable vocational strains as well. As Terman's comment illustrates, the assumption that low-ability students would become low-level workers meant that students of low ability levels needed a different education—not the kind that would prepare them for college and the professions, but the kind to fashion them into "efficient workers." As a result, ability grouping, at whatever level it was practiced, came to be justified by vocational rationales as well as those related to efficiency.

Still another form of curricular differentiation has affected the content of particular courses. Beginning in the 1920s, reformers began to subject the curriculum to a utilitarian scrutiny, and the old academic curriculum was found wanting. Critics objected that too many students were still in academic subjects, "poorly adapted to the needs of students." Latin came under fire as "useless," of course, and slowly passed from many high schools; but the standard academic subjects were also transformed. English became differentiated as educators, stressing the "hordes of students who have little genuine interest in *anything purely intellectual*," introduced modern literature in place of the classics and personal skills in place of writing and reading. History remained because of its link with political education, but was often transformed into civics or social studies. The conventional mathematics sequence began to develop variants like general mathematics, and science became general science. The curriculum debates of the 1920s gave the curriculum a new fluidity, a heterogeneity consistent with the increasing heterogeneity of the school population.

The trend continued during the 1930s when a movement for curriculum revision developed to make the content of the high school "modern" and "dynamic" and more in line with the supposed needs of students, thus decreasing the numbers enrolled in college preparatory courses and increasing those which looked like life skills.[19] Life adjustment education during the 1940s and 1950s and the search for "relevance" during the 1960s continued these impulses. The result was the "horizontal curriculum" of the shopping mall high school, where any particular subject was in practice modified to fit the needs and interests of students. In a high school where Advanced Placement science coexists with general science and calculus with remedial arithmetic, there is a superficial commitment to providing the conventional academic subjects to all students. But the practice shows how flexible that commitment has been. As long as the "children of the plain people"—now labeled "at risk" or "educationally disadvantaged"—are thought to have different needs and interests, the curriculum itself winds up highly differentiated.

To be sure, like the differentiation of purpose, the transformation of content has come under attack from two quite different sources. Those interested in the "traditional" or "academic" curriculum have consistently inveighed against the accumulation of trivial courses, or trivial versions of academic subjects; and those interested in greater equity have also pressed for the replacement of "watered down" versions of academic courses with greater content. Currently, for example, the movement to eliminate tracking and another movement to replace the general track with a more demanding curriculum are attempting to reverse these particular kinds of differentiation. But they must fight against a well-established pattern in which student motivation, needs, and interests (especially those thought to be rooted in different class and racial backgrounds) form the basis for adjusting the curriculum accordingly.

The Neglect of Pedagogy

The dominant responses to the various waves of "new students," then, have been changes in purpose and curricula. But evidently these have not been successful. Poor children continue to do much worse than middle-class children on every dimension of education including persistence, test performance, and attainment. The inequalities of the 1960s have been rediscovered in the 1990s, and the "new demographics" of increasing poverty, continued immigration, and ever larger numbers of minority students are as frightening now as they were a century ago. There are, to be sure, ways of minimizing the bleakness of these facts. One way is to shout the good news: American students do well in comparison with students in other countries. And various inequalities have converged somewhat as is true for test differences among black, white, and Hispanic students, as well as high school dropout rates, some spending differences, and access to schools for handicapped children.[20] Another is the "moving target" argument: that the schools confront an escalating set of demands, with new problems not of their own making (new immigrant groups with yet more languages, new crises like drugs or AIDS, new levels of violence in the central city) coming along before schools have had a chance to cope with old ones. Still another is the resource argument: educators have tried hard, but society has not provided them with sufficient resources to undertake the changes that are necessary. All of these are partly true, but none is particularly helpful. The good news is not good enough, the differences among students grouped by class and race are still enormous, the moving targets are likely to continue moving, and there is not much hope at this point of increasing resources massively.

A different direction is to determine if some potential change has been neglected in the many waves of reform—one which would help schools respond more appropriately to "new students," and perhaps even to the not-so-new students who sometimes complain that the emphasis on resources for the poor and on compensatory programs and bureaucratic initiatives to ensure equal treatment have degraded their own education. In searching for such a path, it is useful to review in a different category the dominant approaches to "new students" who do not fit the common mold of schools. As Cuban and Tyack review the historical record, there are five common ways of explaining the "mismatch" between schools and certain kinds of students who fit poorly.[21]

• Students who do poorly in schools are themselves responsible for the problem—because they lack "character" (in the nineteenth century), or are mentally defective (as Terman called them), or are lazy or unmotivated, or (in the latest twist on this theme) lack self-confidence or self-esteem. The building of "character" through moral education, the differentiation of high-ability from low-ability students and the total or partial exclusion of low-ability students, the efforts to shore up the incentives of grades with yet more tests (or competency measures or skill standards) are all responses. Providing self-esteem "classes" might be another.

• The families of students who do poorly are deficient in some ways. The efforts to provide compensatory education in various ways (and the earlier the better, as years of discussion about early childhood programs show) quite explicitly compensate for parental deficiencies. Parent education, parental involvement, and family literacy programs are others, designed more directly to shore up the family's ability to reinforce school-based learning. In an earlier era, child removal policies—programs to take children from the harmful environment of their families and relocate them in healthier, often rural environments—were often proposed, but now this idea lives on only in the Job Corps, and perhaps in some boarding schools run by the Bureau of Indian Affairs.

• The school is insufficiently differentiated to accommodate the range of abilities and interests of its students. Unlike the two previous explanations, this one locates the fault in schools themselves. Schools should change by differentiating their purpose and content so as to find a place for everyone.

• Some students fail because their cultural backgrounds are so different from the culture of the schools. One response to this "mismatch" has been to introduce multicultural elements into schools that represent a dominant white, middle-class culture. Multicultural education, for example, or truly bilingual education (not English as a Second Language), or more black and Hispanic teachers can be interpreted as efforts to shift culture. Efforts to sensitize teachers to their hidden biases, especially to the "Pygmalion effect" where teachers' assumptions about their students' capacities become self-fulfilling prophecies, are other examples. Community-based schools during the 1970s, presumably more consistent with the culture of children from the surrounding community, and community control of schools have been still other responses, emphasizing governance mechanisms rather than classroom practices. The current efforts at restructuring could be viewed as recent versions of community control, for in theory restructuring returns governance to the school level, where it might be used to make any of a number of changes consistent with local preferences. In many of these cases, "culture" is interpreted in purely racial or ethnic terms. The culture of schools is defined by the race of those who run them, and changing the racial composition of the staff and of school boards is equivalent to changing the "culture." In a different vein, a cynic might note that the efforts to replace the print-based culture of the schools with more video (particularly in lower-track classrooms) and video-based computer materials are attempts to bring the culture of the schools closer to the common television culture.

• Some children fail because schools reproduce the inequalities of the larger capitalist society. In an unequal society only relatively few students can succeed, and the schools are structured so that the successes tend to be white, middle-class, and male. Responses to this critique have been few and far between, since it implies that school reform must await the transformation of society. However, there are many ways in which schools can combat inequality, including reforms to promote greater equity in resources and to develop compensatory programs of great variety. In addition, efforts to promote greater sensitivity to the needs of low-income children—for example, by eradicating cultural insensitivity and the "Pygmalion effect"—are at least consistent with efforts to counteract the ways in which larger inequalities affect schools. But these approaches cannot be very successful either since if inequalities pervade our culture, they are difficult to remove from our thinking and impossible to eliminate from conventional politics.

There is a symmetry in these five ways of assigning blame: two of them blame "new students" and parents; two blame schools; and one blames the larger society. But none of these responses has done much to change the dominant approach to teaching in the schools. Teaching methods have been almost impervious to reform, though there have been some innovations (usually short-lived), more in elementary schools than in middle schools or high schools. The approach to school reform which is closest to pedagogical change—the efforts to change the culture of schools to make them more consistent with the culture of low-income students—has generally neglected teaching approaches because "culture" has been interpreted as a product of the people who work within the schools (too often white, for example), or as a product of a curriculum that neglects black or Hispanic accomplishments, or that results from a governance structure that gives control to far-off bureaucrats. But these are not the most crucial aspects of school culture, and so such changes—adding more minority teachers, say, or adding multicultural courses or units or textbooks—has never done much to change what schools are like.

Instead, with the constant comings and goings of "new students," school reform generally has failed to grapple with changes in pedagogy. The nature of the interactions between teachers and students has stayed the same as other reforms have come to the schools. The dominant approach to teaching—called by such terms as "skills and drills," "teacher-centered instruction," "top-down approaches," "skills development," "conventional wisdom," and "passive learning"—is composed of several distinct but consistent assumptions and practices about the structure of the classroom, the nature of learning, the roles of teachers and students.[22] Complex competencies—the ability to read, for example, or the ability to use mathematics in various forms—are broken into smaller discrete skills such as the ability to decode words, or to recognize the point of a three-sentence paragraph, or to add two-digit numbers with carrying. Students drill on each of these subskills until they have mastered them. The teacher's main responsibility is to implement the curriculum, which is embodied in textbooks, workbooks, or computer programs. By and large, these curriculum materials are generated specifically for teaching purposes, rather than coming from life outside the schools; they are decontextualized, rather than being part of a culture of practice within which students live. They are "school activities," contrived and lifeless, unconnected to the flow of normal activities outside the schools.

Within skills and drills, "individualization" means that a teacher determines a student's achievement level within the hierarchy of skills; then the student begins working at the level which he or she has not mastered, progressing to the next skill only when he or she has mastered the previous skill. By and large, individualization does *not* mean that the content is modified related to the interests and experiences of individual students, or that the method of teaching is changed to fit the learning preferences of individuals. Students are therefore defined in terms of what they are unable to do—their deficiencies within a rigid hierarchy of skills. School is therefore a long process of discovering a student's deficiencies and overcoming them—a process which is inevitably fraught with the sense of failure. Furthermore, skills and drills approaches *assume* motivation on the part of the student, since the drills themselves are not meaningful or particularly interesting. If a student wavers in his or her commitment or fails to see the connection between drills and any other goal, nothing in the skills and drills approach will supply motivation.

The approach of skills and drills is fraught with problems for many students—perhaps for the vast majority of students. One kind of evidence, for example, is that available from the National Assessment of Educational Progress (NAEP), which indicates that many students fail to retain many of the simple facts taught them. But a more devastating critique is that large numbers of students pass through schools without understanding much of what they are learning, and they therefore apply even the simplest knowledge (decoding, arithmetic, knowledge of facts in science or social studies) in a haphazard manner. Evidently, the kind of decontextualized and didactic instruction typical of many schools is not especially effective for either form of learning. Many current efforts at reform attempt to reshape instruction (as in Henry Levin's Accelerated Schools, Theodore Sizer's Coalition of Essential Schools, schools following the Foxfire approach, the movements to create interdisciplinary curricula and to integrate academic and vocational education) by replacing some or all of the practices of skills and drills.

The most serious problem with skills and drills instruction for low-income students is motivation. Children who do not have well-educated parents who can demonstrate the value of formal education, and who can help interpret the meaning of what are otherwise meaningless rituals, frequently are viewed as unmotivated. The major motivation of conventional schooling—the threat of low grades or the disapproval of teachers—means literally nothing if the promise of further schooling means nothing to a student. The dominant motivation in vocational schooling—the promise of access to good jobs later on—may be too distant and too uncertain for students who cannot see much connection between schooling and success in the lives of their parents and other adults. Some students—minority and immigrant children in particular—may believe that there is no connection.[23] They may be wrong, but there is nothing in their direct experience to correct their misinformation. Ever since Joseph Mayer Rice ridiculed the schools in the 1890s,[24] a persistent critique has noted the boredom and profound disengagement of many students, a result of the "irrelevance" of instruction, more so for lower-class than for middle-class students.

Similarly, in a decontextualized system of instruction, middle-class parents can provide the context—their own occupations and lives, their knowledge of current events and the wider world—to make sense of skills and drills instruction, but lower-class parents are less likely to be able to do that. The culture of the school may be strange to a poor child, or to a black or Hispanic or immigrant child, but there are fewer ways for their parents to mitigate its strangeness—its reliance on symbolic representation in language and mathematics, for example, or its emphasis on print culture in a society which has largely moved away from text. Managers and professionals almost by definition move in a culture of text, of abstraction, of abstracted or depersonalized relations with other people in other places, and their lives are filled with school-like activities; they overwhelmingly report that they use what they have learned in their work.[25] But these aspects of school culture are more likely to be missing from the families and communities of working- and lower-class students. Their parents tend not to learn the skills they need for work in schools; abstraction and text are less common parts of their work lives, and reading materials are less common in the home. The school culture is more likely to be foreign, but its difference relates less to racial or ethnic backgrounds of teachers (though these differ too, of course) than to the fact that tasks encountered in school are quite different from those encountered in life.

Yet another problem comes from the treatment of error and failure in conventional instruction. In skills and drills, the goal is error-free performance on routine drills. Errors result in lower grades, and begin a process of sorting where "able" students (more error-free) are distinguished from "less able" students. Unlike the opposing tradition of what I call "meaning making,"[26] there is little effort to understand and profit from errors. Conventional schooling is therefore a passage through a thicket of opportunities for making mistakes, and the sense of failure and shame or low "self-esteem" often associated with school comes in part because of the conventional treatment of errors. Unfortunately, the experience of deficiency comes earlier and more frequently to lower-class children either because they have not learned from their parents the "school skills" (letters, numbers, simple reading that are prerequisites to doing well in the early grades) or the school-appropriate behavior of their middle-class peers. Or teachers may treat them as if they are unlikely to do well. Within a system built on a hierarchy of skills, a student's weak performance at early levels (reflected in errors, low grades, placement in lower tracks) virtually guarantees weaker performance later on, and so early failures are magnified rather than redressed over time.

The personal relations of the classroom may also contribute to the problems of "new students." In conventional instruction, the teacher is an authority figure and purveyor of knowledge, and motivation in conventional classrooms depends on students accepting this authority relation. But Eckart and others have argued that this kind of hierarchical relationship contradicts those in working class communities, where learning from peers is more common and figures of authority are more likely to be distrusted. These observations are consistent with the "resistance" theories, which note that lower-class students, and boys more than girls, and students with experiences of failure may decide to resist educational authorities, allowing them to maintain their sense of self but at the cost of intractably poor school performance.[27] This analysis suggests another reason why the extrinsic motivation of the conventional classroom, depending on the authority of the teacher, may work less well for many "new students."

Finally, conventional instruction incorporates a peculiar vision of student "needs" and "interests." On the one hand, at least since G. Stanley Hall and John Dewey, there has been a convention that schools should respond to a child's needs and interests; indeed, statements about what poor children "need" have been common in the conclusion that they need vocational rather than academic education, or "useful" approaches to English or mathematics. But schools conventionally *assume* what children need, rather than asking them; the generations of parents who have resisted the lower track assignments for their children have been testimony to this problem. And conventional instruction makes no provision for a child's interests or background. The material is set by the teacher and often by the textbook, providing no way for student preferences and experiences to modify the curriculum, or redirect the nature of reading, or provide the context for subsequent content. Because there has been a greater consistency between the experiences of native-born middle-class students and the overt content of the curriculum, the failure to incorporate student interests in any way is less of a problem for them. But for other students, constant references to student "needs" and "interests" in the context of teacher-centered instruction has only masked the fact that their preferences are rarely consulted.

My argument, then, is that a complex interaction between family background and the dominant kind of school instruction is responsible for the persistently poor performance of many lower-class, minority, and immigrant students. In the terms that Cuban and Tyack have set out, virtually every viewpoint is "right" in some sense: lower-class students are "deficient," their parents do prepare them "inadequately" for schools, and the "culture" of the school does differ from the culture of many children. It is foolish to argue that there are no differences in the preparation of children for school; there are real differences, and they are rooted in the nature of parent and child experiences, values, expectations, and the like. But it is important to understand that deficiencies and inadequacies are defined by the nature of conventional instruction. The differences among students of different class and racial backgrounds have such profound effects largely in the context of instruction based solely on "skills and drills," which assumes the kinds of motivation, background knowledge, values, and personal relations which lower-class children are likely to lack. Some children can and do learn from skills and drills methods; after all, some students emerge from even the most conventional schools having learned a great deal, even with their "self-esteem" intact. But they are likely to be from middle-class families and communities that can compensate in many ways for the limitations of skills and drills instruction, and do so consistently over the long years of elementary and secondary schooling.

The obvious implication is that alternatives to skills and drills—the approach to instruction I describe as "meaning making," which reverses many of the assumptions of skills and drills—would be especially beneficial to "new students." Indeed, this is precisely the conclusion of a recent review of remedial programs for low-income students: the "conventional wisdom" stressing the deficits of disadvantaged students and emphasizing sequential mastery of discrete subskills often works poorly, and needs to be replaced with an alternative vision.[28] Such a vision is exemplified in the approach taken by certain other celebrated schools hoping to improve the learning of low-income students, including Deborah Meier's changes in New York City and Henry Levin's "Accelerated Schools." However, this approach has never been taken when waves of "new students" crowd into the schools. If anything, the dominant response for them has been to further rigidify instruction, presenting smaller and simpler bits of information under increasingly detailed motivational structures (as in mastery learning), while middle-class students have greater access to the kinds of student-centered, discussion-based, problem-solving approaches associated with meaning making.

From the perspective of current practice, a recommendation for new approaches to instruction requires much more detail about what these practices would look like, what teacher preparation is required, and what other existing practices need to be changed to accommodate such reforms—a process that is only barely underway. From a historical perspective, however, such a recommendation begs for an explanation of why conventional pedagogy has been so rarely challenged. Here, too, my answers are preliminary because the relations between classroom-level practices and the larger social, economic, and political forces affecting the history of schooling have so rarely been examined. However, some of these influences are relatively obvious: the legacy of an authoritarian religious tradition, a preoccupation with control and order in the classroom (especially for the "children of the plain people"), the fixation on efficiency in the schools, the need for an instructional method conducive to bureaucratic oversight and regulation, the lack of resources for smaller and truly student-centered classes, the rigidity of teacher certification, the expectations of parents about what "school" entails, biased conceptions of what "new students" can do, the fragmentation of disciplines. The social forces keeping skills and drills methods in place are so numerous, and so mutually reinforcing, that it is no wonder that experiments with alternatives have been so few, so evanescent, and so largely confined to middle-class students.

The Prospects for Reform

Attention to pedagogy, then, has always been the missing element in the response to "new students" in the schools. Indeed, the dominant responses—the differentiation of purpose and curricula—have often worked to their disadvantage, providing them curricula (like the general or vocational tracks) and material (like that in watered-down versions of nominally academic classes) that have denied them access to the real paths of upward mobility, especially important in a vocational schooling system. But even these modifications have been ineffective; a differentiated curriculum within a standardized method of instruction has presented low-income students with simplified material that still remains inaccessible. They have had the worst of both worlds: content that is unsophisticated and instruction that is especially ineffective for them. Small wonder, then, that the gap between them and their middle-class peers tends to grow as schooling progresses.

In another vision, the schools would incorporate *undifferentiated demands* but *differentiated pedagogy*.[29] That is, all students would be held to roughly the same expectations for certain high-level competencies: reading and writing in a variety of voices, understanding and applying mathematics, knowing both the content and the method of scientific disciplines, appreciating the insights of history and the social sciences for civic purposes, mastering the generic skills required in a variety of work settings, and the like. But the teaching methods associated with meaning making cannot be uniform because they need to start with the experiences and interests of students and incorporate their preferences in more active ways. In a highly differentiated society, this means that instruction will look quite different from classroom to classroom, with content presented in different order, with teachers (rather than state curriculum committees and textbook publishers) developing curriculum locally in collaboration with their peers.[30]

What are the reasons to think that this approach stands any chance of being adopted in the schooling system, when the historical record suggests how difficult this has been? One reason for optimism now is that the demands from outside the schools have changed. Current trends in employment are to undo this pattern. The development of more integrated production and of flatter hierarchies in which there are fewer levels of supervision and more responsibilities for production-level workers[31] have reduced the separation of management and execution, of academic and vocational. As a result, the business community has spent the past decade calling for workers with higher-order thinking skills, communications skills, problem-solving abilities, greater independence and initiative. These are not the kinds of capacities which conventional instruction can instill, and the "New Basics" of the 1980s have failed to change the demands for reforms in education. Only new approaches to teaching can respond successfully to these pressures.

But demands from outside the schools, and top-down reforms, have never been especially effective. So another reason for optimism is that external pressures for reform are consistent with internal motivation—with the desires of teachers themselves to be professionalized in the sense of retaining (or gaining) greater control over the "stuff" of teaching, over curriculum and pedagogy. Reforms which lead by giving more responsibility to teachers must grapple with their uneven acceptance of new approaches, of course, but they are likely to have more effect than are changes imposed upon unwilling teachers, who can then thwart anything they want to within the classroom.

At the same time, several other reform movements are roughly consistent with turning to more active instruction. The efforts at "restructuring" return greater control to the school level, again with the argument that teachers and local administrators, closer to students and the problems of teaching and learning, must be in control. "Authentic assessment," the movement to replace intrinsically meaningless measures of learning like multiple-choice exams with more intrinsically valuable indicators (exhibits, the results of substantial projects, portfolios of accomplishments), is also more consistent with contextualized teaching, project-based learning, and the like. And choice mechanisms, which seek to give more choice to students (or their parents) over the schools they attend, can be implemented by giving students within public schools choices among alternative foci or contexts, for example, among different occupational clusters, or different subjects for magnet schools, making them more active participants in defining their "needs" and "interests."

Finally, several ways of institutionalizing changes in instruction provide some hope that current changes might not be blown away by the next round of reforms. In the past changes in teaching methods have often been idiosyncratic, limited to particular teachers (usually in elementary schools) and vulnerable to their personal commitment. Interdisciplinary courses have also been fragile, readily replaced by conventional disciplinary courses once a few teachers lose interest in teaching them. But the institutional structures that have developed in the last decade—academies and other schools-within-schools, magnet schools (or "focus schools") with particular themes or teaching approaches, the development of clusters, majors, or houses within a school—are potentially more enduring ways of changing instruction. They include larger numbers of teachers and administrators rather than being dependent on a crucial one or two. They can develop identities and cultures of their own, which are then useful in recruiting students and socializing new teachers. They can therefore perpetuate themselves in ways that individual teachers, or courses, cannot. They provide a very different image of what a school should look like, thereby institutionalizing changes in both the curriculum of the schools and their pedagogy.

There is a final reason for optimism in turning to pedagogical reform on behalf of "new students." The dominant efforts to help the poor in this country have created special programs for them—welfare programs, compensatory education, compensatory early childhood programs, dropout prevention programs, and the like. Even when those operating such programs have not wanted to assume that the poor are deficient, the segregation of "new students" in special programs has labeled them as different, out of the mainstream, and has inevitably created stigma out of such segregation—a problem that Minow has called the "dilemma of difference."[32] In response, the demand has arisen for mainstreaming rather than "pull-out" programs, and for universal programs rather than categorical efforts targeted on the poor. Changing the nature of teaching is consistent with universal approaches—a shift that would benefit all students, even as it would develop a pedagogy better suited to the varying conditions of low-income students.

Every generation of educators since the early nineteenth century has been forced to grapple anew with the problems of serving "new students." It is a tribute to the egalitarian impulse of the common schools that we have not given up on the goal of including all students. But the responses of the past—differentiating the purposes of schooling and the curriculum, while maintaining a relatively uniform pedagogy—have been more effective in providing all students access than in providing them all with a real education, that is, with the competencies that matter outside the schools. To complete the promise of the common schools will require greater attention to the aspect of schooling that has always been the least considered even as it remains the heart of the enterprise—the nature of teaching.

NOTES

1. Larry Cuban, *How Teachers Taught: Constancy and Change in American Classrooms, 1880-1920,* 2d ed. (New York: Teachers College Press, 1992).

2. See especially Larry Cuban and David Tyack, "Mismatch: Historical Perspectives on Schools and Students Who Don't Fit Them" (Unpublished paper, Stanford University, April 13, 1989).

3. Quoted in Carl Kaestle, *The Evolution of an Urban School System, 1750-1850* (Cambridge, MA: Harvard University Press, 1973), pp. 112-113.

4. See Lawrence Cremin, *The Genius of American Education* (Pittsburgh: University of Pittsburgh Press, 1965); Patricia Graham, "What America Has Expected of Its Schools over the Past Century," *American Journal of Education* 101 (February 1993): 83-97.

5. For the history of the high school and of curriculum developments, I rely especially on Edward Krug, *The Shaping of the American High School, 1880-1920,* vol. 1 (Madison: University of Wisconsin Press, 1969); Daniel Tanner and Laurel Tanner, *History of the School Curriculum* (New York: Macmillan, 1990); and Herbert Kliebard, *The Struggle for the American Curriculum, 1893-1958* (Boston: Routledge and Kegan Paul, 1986).

6. Another response, the legal effort to enforce compulsory attendance and child labor laws, essentially ran its course during the Progressive Era.

7. Jonathan Kozol, *Savage Inequalities* (New York: Crown, 1991).

8. National Educational Association, *Report of the Committee of Ten on Secondary School Studies* (New York: American Book Co., 1894), p . 17.

9. Krug, *The Shaping of the American High School,* vol. 1, p. 175.

10. This pattern of expansion of a level of education along with a greater vocational purpose also occurred in the college at the turn of the century, in the community college during the 1960s and 1970s, and in publicly supported four-year colleges in the 1960s.

11. Edward Krug, *The Shaping of the American High School, 1920-1941,* vol. 2 (Madison: University of Wisconsin Press, 1972), p. 219.

12. American Youth Commission, *What the High Schools Ought to Teach* (Washington, DC: American Council on Education, 1940), p. 10.

13. U.S. Office of Education, *Life Adjustment Education for Every Youth* (Washington, DC: U.S. Government Printing Office, 1948), p. 15, n. 2.

14. See Arthur G. Powell, Eleanor Farrar, and David K. Cohen, *The Shopping Mall High School: Winner and Losers in the Educational Marketplace* (Boston: Houghton Mifflin, 1986).

15. For a review of the issues, see Robert Crowson and William Boyd, "Coordinated Services for Children: Designing Arks for Storms and Seas Unknown," *American Journal of Education* 101 (February 1993): 140-179.

16. See also Kliebard, *The Struggle for the American Curriculum,* which portrays three schools of thought—social efficiency, developmentalist, and social meliorist—as all battling against the older humanist ideals.

17. Paul Chapman, "Schools as Sorters: Testing and Tracking in California, 1910-1925," *Journal of Social History* 14 (Summer 1981): 703.

18. Lewis Terman, *The Measurement of Intelligence* (Boston: Houghton Mifflin, 1916), pp. 91-92.

19. Diane Ravitch, *The Troubled Crusade: American Education, 1945-1980* (New York: Basic Books, 1983), pp. 45-47.

20. One summary of the "good news" comes in a series of "Bracey Reports." See Gerald Bracey, "The Third Bracey Report on the Condition of Public Education," *Phi Delta Kappan* 5 (October 1993): 104-117. Bracey acknowledges, however, that schooling for poor students is dreadful, despite any modest convergence in performance and persistence.

21. Cuban and Tyack, "Mismatch."

22. See W. Norton Grubb et al., *Readin', Writin', and 'Rithmetic One More Time: The Role of Remediation in Vocational Education and Job Training Programs* (Berkeley, CA: National Center for Research on Vocational Education, 1991); Kenneth Goodman, *What's Whole in Whole Language?* (Ontario, Canada: Scholastic Books, 1986); Michael Knapp and Brenda Turnbull, *Better Schooling for the Children of Poverty: Alternatives to Conventional Wisdom*, vol. 1: *Summary* (Washington, DC: U.S. Department of Education, 1990); M. S. Knowles and Associates, *Andragogy in Action: Applying Modern Principles of Adult Learning* (San Francisco: Jossey-Bass, 1980); Cuban, *How Teachers Taught*.

23. See in particular John Ogbu, *Minority Education and Caste: The American System in Cross-Cultural Perspective* (New York: Academic Press, 1978).

24. Lawrence Cremin, *The Transformation of the School* (New York: Vintage Books, 1964), ch. 1.

25. Norman Bowers and Paul Swain, "Education, Training, and Skills" (Unpublished paper, Bureau of Labor Statistics, U.S. Department of Labor, 1992).

26. For a more detailed description of meaning-making, see Grubb et al., *Readin', Writin', and 'Rithmetic One More Time*. I refer to this tradition as meaning-making because of its similarities to interpretation and the creation of meaning in other spheres as outlined in Jerome Bruner, *Acts of Meaning* (Cambridge, MA: Harvard University Press, 1990). This approach is referred to by others as learning-centered instruction, active learning, the "holistic" approach, or simply as the alternative to conventional wisdom. See references in footnote 22.

27. Penny Eckart, *Jocks and Burnouts: Social Categories and Identity in the High School* (New York: Teachers College Press, 1989); Paul Willis, *Learning to Labor: How Working Class Kids Get Working Class Jobs* (Hampshire, England: Gowan House, 1977). There are problems with this analysis. In particular, another literature following Melvin Kohn, *Class and Conformity* (Homewood, IL: Dorsey Press, 1969) has argued that lower-class parents are more likely to socialize their children for obedience and middle-class parents for independence, contradicting the notion that families contribute to defiant versus obedient behavior of children from different backgrounds. A more complex and complete analysis would worry about the balance of obedient and independent behavior with respect to different kinds of authority figures.

28. The evidence presented in this study is not as extensive as my argument requires. It is limited to remediation for low-income students, and most of the evidence comes from the elementary grades rather than the entire K-12 system. In addition to Knapp and Turnbull, *Better Schooling for the Children of Poverty*, vol. 1, see also Michael Knapp and Patrick Shields, *Better Schooling for the Children of Poverty: Alternatives to Conventional Wisdom*, vol. 2, *Commissioned Papers and Literature Review* (Washington, DC: U.S. Department of Education, 1990), and Michael Knapp et al., *What Is Taught, and How, to the Children of Poverty: Interim Report from a Two-Year Investigation* (Washington, DC: U.S. Office of Education, 1991).

29. To continue the oversimplification, currently we have differentiated demands, with less asked of and provided to low-income students, and an undifferentiated pedagogy particularly inappropriate for low-income students. Or, more precisely, we have had the worst teaching in the skills and drills tradition for the low-income students for whom it is least appropriate, while at least some middle-class students have benefitted from more innovative pedagogy.

30. For a more general argument about the merits of decentralized rather than centralized approaches to school reform, see William Clune, "The Best Path to Systemic Educational Policy: Standardized/Centralized or Differentiated/Decentralized?" *Educational Evaluation and Policy Analysis* 15 (Fall 1993): 233-255.

31. See Sue Berryman and Thomas Bailey, *The Double Helix of Education and the Economy* (New York: Institute on Education and the Economy, Teachers College, Columbia University, 1992); W. Norton Grubb et al., *Betwixt and Between: Education, Skills, and Employment in Sub-Baccalaureate Labor Markets* (Berkeley, CA: National Center for Research in Vocational Education, 1992); Secretary's Commission on Achieving Necessary Skills (SCANS), *What Work Requires of Schools* (Washington, DC: U.S. Department of Labor, 1991).

32. Martha Minow, *Making All the Difference: Inclusion, Exclusion, and American Law* (Ithaca: Cornell University Press, 1990).

CHAPTER II

Changing Students/Changing Needs

AARON M. PALLAS, GARY NATRIELLO,
AND EDWARD L. MCDILL

This volume is concerned with the relationship between schools
and the students who attend them. Our intent in this chapter is to
explore one particular aspect of this relationship through a sociological lens. We contend that a key element for understanding the complex, interdependent relationship between schools and students is the
social, political, and institutional context of schooling. This broader
context of schooling shapes the ways in which schools are organized,
which in turn shape students' experiences in school. The changing
population of students, we argue, is an important dimension of the
social, political, and institutional context of schooling, but it is by no
means the only dimension. Thus, the changing population of students
will not have simplistic or deterministic consequences for schools and
schooling. Rather, the implications of the changing population of students for the way schools work are contingent on other dimensions of
the context of schooling. In the case of students and schooling,
demography is not destiny, but it is the first defining step in a journey
of many miles.

We begin by describing the context of contemporary American
schooling. We then examine the consequences of this context for the
social organization of schools and schooling, drawing on organizational theory to help us understand the relationship between schools
and their external environments. Next we consider the consequences
of context and school organization for students' experiences in
schools, focusing particularly on the ways in which schools attempt to
resolve the quintessential American dilemma of creating citizens who
are at once individual and different on the one hand, and unified and

Aaron M. Pallas is Associate Professor of Educational Administration at Michigan
State University. Gary Natriello is Associate Professor of Sociology and Education at
Teachers College, Columbia University. Edward L. McDill is Professor of Sociology at
The Johns Hopkins University. All specialize in the sociology of education.

equal on the other hand. We conclude by exploring some of the tensions of this dilemma in school context, school organization, and student experiences, and we speculate on the likely consequences for schools of the future.

The Context of Contemporary American Schooling

In this section we attempt to map the social, political, and institutional forces that form the context for contemporary schooling in the United States. Our approach is selective, not exhaustive, and there are other important contexts for schooling that we shall not consider. The factors that we emphasize are, we believe, especially important for understanding how schools are currently organized and how they might be organized in the future. In particular, we consider the changing mix of students our schools are expected to serve; the changing conceptions of U.S. citizenship; the changing goals and demands that society has placed on these schools; the higher levels of performance to which schools are being held; the continuing weak technologies available for actually meeting these performance levels; and the changing social and political contexts for schooling.

THE CHANGING STUDENT POPULATION

The demographic changes observed over the last two decades are likely to reverberate through much of the next century. America has become a more diverse society in its racial, social, and ethnic make-up. Elsewhere we have projected that, if recent fertility and migration trends are a guide, over the next thirty years there will be a dramatic shift in the racial/ethnic composition of the school-aged population.[1] We expect the number and proportion of Hispanic children and youth to more than double, the number of Asian and African-American children to rise and the proportion of non-Hispanic white children to decline. These changes will result in a school-aged population with a racial, ethnic, and cultural configuration distinctly different from that of today.

Race and ethnicity are coarse proxies for other aspects of children's lives. Nonwhite children are more likely than white children to live with only one parent; to live in poverty; to have a mother who has not completed high school; and to speak a primary language other than English. Thus, assuming that the social conditions of various racial and ethnic groups remain stable, as the number and proportion of nonwhite children increases over time, so too will the number and proportion of children with these characteristics. While we do not mean to minimize the direct discrimination, in school and out, that many children experience solely because of the color of their skin, we view the social correlates of race and ethnicity as a greater challenge for schools and schooling than the racial/ethnic make-up of the school population. This is because these correlates are more direct measures of the social and educational resources available to children that may affect their schooling experiences and outcomes.

In addition to the growing proportions of nonwhite children in the U.S. population, there are other changes in the social conditions in which majority children live. We have come a long way from the days when a typical child came from a two-parent family in which the father earned an adequate salary to permit the mother to remain at home and see to the various and unpredictable needs of growing children. Even in those situations in which the economic status of families is substantial, the access that children have to the social capital of their parents may be diminished. Increasingly, students from all levels of society come to school with needs that are less likely to be addressed at home.[2]

These demographic and social changes in the school-aged population imply an increasingly diverse student population with increasingly diverse needs. Schools confront two important kinds of differences that are likely to become more pronounced in the future. First, the school-aged population is increasingly heterogeneous. That is, children and youth differ from one another in more profound ways. Perhaps more important, schools are no longer permitted to overlook student diversity, to reduce it, or to use it as an excuse for vast differences in educational performance. Second, the school-aged population is increasingly different from a conception of the ideal student. Public schools in the United States have historically been organized to concentrate their attention on children and youth who have an adequate and stable set of social and educational resources in their family and community environments. Moreover, it is this group with whom schools have been most successful. The current and future school-aged populations are fundamentally different from the idealized image of the white middle-class suburban family where dad earns an adequate wage and mom is a housewife. As greater proportions of the student population have departed from this pattern, there has been *decreasing* pressure on students to meet the demands of schools and *increasing* pressure on schools to meet the needs of students.

DIVERSE AND CONFLICTING GOALS OF SCHOOLING

One of the key legacies of the industrial revolution has been the changing configuration of education. In the preindustrial era, education was primarily a private process taking place in the family, rather than a public process taking place in schools. The knowledge, skills, and values needed to become a competent adult could be transmitted within the family, in large part because the family was the locus of production and children inherited their occupational positions from their parents. With the advent of the industrial revolution, production moved outside the home, and families were less able to provide the necessary socialization experiences. Moreover, the expansion of the state and nation-building that relied on the extension of citizenship to more and more individuals also required a public socialization mechanism. Public schooling expanded for these and other reasons.

While the current configuration of education can be traced to these historical pressures, there are contemporary conditions that also shape the goals of schooling. Like Cremin,[3] we view schools and schooling as part of a configuration of education that locates a set of educating institutions in relation to one another. Whereas families and communities once were strong educating forces, both of these social institutions have weakened considerably in post-World War II America. In many cases, schools have been called upon to fill the void left by the breakdown of the family and of the community, especially in central cities.[4]

In consequence, public schools have had an array of responsibilities thrust upon them, frequently without an appreciation of the level of resources needed to meet those responsibilities. Among the many goals that we expect schools to meet are the successful teaching of basic skills and the skills of responsible citizenship; preparing young people for the world of work, for further education, and for adult family responsibilities; and promoting personal and social development. Yet, this list barely scratches the surface. Even if educators knew how to do all these things well—and even the most talented and dedicated among them would dispute that they do—the constraints on human and fiscal resources would create tensions among competing goals.

Moreover, American public schools, no less than other American institutions, are confronted with the competing demands of creating a unified citizenry with equal rights as well as enabling each individual in the society to realize his or her unique potential. Thus schools must be responsive to both society's demands and the needs of individuals.

INCREASED SOCIETAL DEMANDS

In the past, when schools were charged with balancing the demands of society for a unified citizenry and the needs of individual students, one of the coping mechanisms employed was educational triage—investing resources only in those students who were deemed likely to succeed, or at least to benefit from the investment. This kind of "creaming" was apparent at all levels of the education system, and was legitimated either through a functional ideology (schooling is a rational means for choosing the best individuals to fill important positions) or through a conflict ideology (those students who receive the largest share of resources are entitled to them by virtue of their station in life).[5] Regardless of which ideology was invoked, society as a whole agreed that the fact that some students succeeded in school and others failed was not especially noteworthy. Pressure to respond to the needs of students for personal development was mitigated by the broader social consensus that only some in society would achieve individual success. The fact that only some would achieve the highest levels of success in school was not particularly troubling in an era when jobs were plentiful, especially ones that did not require skilled labor. During this same period, the public schools showed evidence of tangible progress toward assuring an educated or at least a "schooled" citizenry by graduating increasing numbers and proportions of students at all levels.

But as the position of the United States in the world economy has changed, the skill needs of the labor force have also shifted. Fewer and fewer unskilled factory jobs are available, and many newly created jobs require a broad repertoire of skills and high levels of competencies. School dropouts and high school graduates who do not pursue postsecondary education are at particular risk of finding themselves in dead-end jobs or on the outside of the labor market looking in. And, in a new twist, schools are being held accountable for the performance of these dropouts and minimally competent graduates. This is a turnaround from the historical pattern in which the locus of school failure was held to be in the student, not in the school.

The standards to which schools are held have been ratcheted upward. American public schools are being pressured along three dimensions. First, in response to the weakening of the family and the community as nurturing environments for children, the goals of schooling have broadened, thereby straining the existing mix of human and fiscal resources and forcing educators to make difficult choices in deploying those resources to meet expanding goals. Second, the level of performance has simultaneously increased, so that lackluster performance on virtually any goal is no longer acceptable. Third, the focus has shifted from judging schools in terms of their most successful graduates to judging them in terms of their least successful graduates and even the dropouts.

A WEAK TECHNOLOGY FOR EDUCATING CHILDREN AND YOUTH

While the goals of schooling and the performance levels associated with those goals have created heightened demands on schools and schooling, the technology for meeting those goals has not kept pace. Classrooms continue to be organized much as they were decades ago, with seatwork and lecturing to the whole class still the dominant instructional forms. Teachers still rely on textbooks, and there is a steady demand for chalk and chalkboards, duplicating machines, and roll books. Computers, one of the few demonstrable advances in educational technology, continue to be little more than a curiosity in the array of instructional tools on which teachers draw.

It is tempting to interpret this stability in the organization of instruction as evidence that educators know what works and are sticking with it. While there can be little doubt that most educators have personal theories about the nature of teaching and learning, a dispassionate observer would be hard-pressed to conclude that these theories "work." In fact, teaching and learning are remarkably unpredictable, sometimes in uplifting and serendipitous ways and other times in disappointing and maddening ways. Teachers often must make decisions about what to do in the classroom in the face of competing or contradictory goals[6] and limited knowledge about what their students already know[7] and they typically lack theories of pedagogy specific enough to provide guidance about how to proceed.

This is not to say that teachers do not attempt to routinize their activities in the classroom. Most teachers develop routines and repertoires of teaching behaviors on which they draw, and many are quite comfortable in applying these activities in the classroom. The fact that some teachers express a sense of certainty about what they are doing, however, seems more a reflection of the need for a sense of purpose than of a powerful theory of teaching and learning.

The uncertainty expressed by individual teachers is paralleled by the uncertain and inconsistent effects of the organization of instruction at the school and/or district level. Ability grouping and tracking,

for example, have different effects on students' experiences and outcomes in different educational settings,[8] and we have yet to develop a
body of evidence from research that specifies the conditions under
which a particular organizational innovation is likely to have particular
consequences.

In light of these uncertainties, we contend that the uncertainties of
instruction, coupled with weak technologies, form an important context for understanding the condition of contemporary American education. We add parenthetically that these uncertainties are especially
great with regard to the education of traditionally disadvantaged populations, since what works for middle-class majority populations will
not necessarily transfer to the education of different kinds of students.
Our schools have had less experience in attempting to educate minority populations, and the "knowledge base" of what works in those situations is weaker. Since teaching and learning are greatly influenced by
the knowledge and experiences that children bring to the classroom,
the different patterns of knowledge and experience of minority populations are an additional unknown with which teachers must contend.

THE CHANGING SOCIAL AND POLITICAL CONTEXTS

The final context we consider is the changing social and political
context for public schooling in the United States. We note three
trends: greater accountability, changing patterns of centralization and
decentralization, and a changing institutional context for schooling. We
believe that these trends have complex consequences for how schools
organize themselves, which in turn determine the ways in which students experience school and their likelihood of school success.

Accountability. In recent years, various stakeholders—including parents, the business community, and government officials—have
attempted to hold schools more accountable for their performance.
Part of this movement appears to stem from a broader effort than
heretofore to subject public schools to market forces, on the theory
that market pressures can compel particular schools to change or fail.[9]
The trend toward greater accountability also can be attributed to the
widespread perception that schools are failing, and that holding
schools responsible for their performance is necessary to turn the tide.
This accountability sometimes takes the form of "outcomes" accountability, in which schools are held responsible for the performance of
the students they serve (often assessed through standardized test
scores), and in other instances can be characterized as "process"

accountability, in which schools are held responsible for the processes they use to educate children and youth (often assessed through the presence of particular curricula or school improvement plans).

From an organizational standpoint, greater accountability reflects a tighter coupling between schools and their external environments. Although the control of public schools is a right reserved for the states in the Constitution, it has been local governing bodies and citizens that have had the most continuing interest in schooling. But in the postwar period, first the federal government and then the state governments have made schools more salient in their deliberations. Interest in education has moved beyond the local community level during this time, just as it moved beyond the family at the dawn of the industrial age, because the two primary problems that education has most recently been asked to address, the need for equity and the need for competitive performance in the world marketplace, cannot be addressed at the local level, just as the need to prepare industrial workers could not be addressed within the family.

But if the most prominent demands placed upon the public schools motivate forces at the state and national levels, the demands posed by the changing student population motivate forces at the most local levels. As the school population becomes more diverse culturally, the explicit and implicit demands placed on schools by their students become increasingly local, oftentimes even more local than in the area represented by local units of civil government. School districts with lines taken from the local governing unit may increasingly find themselves having to respond to multiple and diverse constituent groups within their boundaries. Thus increasing pressures for accountability at the state and federal levels are not accompanied by corresponding decreasing pressures for accountability at the local and neighborhood levels.

Centralization/Decentralization. The multilevel accountability movement has been accompanied by contrasting trends toward centralization and decentralization. In many locales, educational policy reforms have consisted of tightening accountability for student performance while simultaneously decentralizing the authority for organizing to meet standards or student performance. This decentralization has taken many forms and can include building-level budgeting and resource allocation, greater control over textbooks and other instructional resources, and greater control over school and classroom policies and regulations. Often, decentralization leads to the sharing of decision making between administrators and teachers.

In effect, policymakers are saying to local school personnel, "We don't care how you meet these standards, as long as you do in fact meet them." The combination of greater accountability and decentralized decision making has been met with mixed feelings on the part of local educators. On the one hand, decentralization has freed individual schools (and, in some cases, school districts) from bureaucratic regulations that constrained the ability of school staff to do what they felt was in the best educational interests of their students. Decentralization, which often includes shared decision making, also holds the promise of improving the working conditions of educators. But the greater accountability attached to this decentralization is threatening, particularly under the conditions of uncertainty created by the social and demographic changes noted earlier. Schools freed from regulatory strictures sometimes flounder because there is no clear pathway of techniques to travel to meet high standards, and no clear mechanism on gaining consensus within increasingly diverse communities and buildings on how to pursue that objective.

Whereas the movement for greater accountability has most recently turned to decentralization as an inducement for cooperation and participation, accountability sometimes is accompanied by increased centralization. This is evident in the goals and objectives embedded in the National Education Goals originally agreed to by the fifty governors and President Bush in 1989 and the voluntary national standards that continue to emerge from the National Education Goals Panel. It is also apparent in the proliferation of statewide and regional accreditation programs for elementary and secondary schools as well as in the increasing volume of state regulations governing schools.

Institutional context. Finally, we note the institutional context of schooling. We argue that our society's perceptions of what schooling is are changing, and that these changing beliefs about the nature of schooling affect the internal processes of schools, especially their capacity to foster a sense of commitment on the part of the school's clients, particularly its students. Following Meyer and Rowan,[10] we refer to these beliefs as "myths," acknowledging their status as powerful symbols that guide social action. Myths do not have to be true to have consequences; rather, the fact that individuals believe them is what makes them potent.[11] Two central myths associated with public schooling in the United States have come in for increasing questioning in recent times: the myth of opportunity and the myth of rationality.

Americans have historically viewed schools as the central mechanism for social mobility. This has been particularly true for traditionally disadvantaged populations such as immigrants, minorities, and the poor, who could not rely on social inheritance to assure them access to valued positions in the social and economic structure. American schools have been relatively open to all comers, as the school system in the United States has been less stratified and more permeable than the systems of many other countries.[12] The key beliefs associated with the image of schools as the great equalizers are that schooling is meritocratic and that schooling provides access to good jobs for all who take the time and make the effort to participate. As long as most people believed that this was true, schools could count on high levels of commitment from students, parents, and others who make up their proximal environments.

In fact, however, in recent years schooling has not been wholly successful in removing the social disadvantages suffered by immigrant, poor, and minority youth for at least three reasons. First, education is now more a mass institution than an elite institution.[13] A high school diploma once signified a rare level of accomplishment to be followed quite naturally by successful experience in the workplace. Moreover, the lack of a high school diploma offered an explanation for the failure to find satisfactory work. Since attending and completing high school is now commonplace, the diploma, while remaining a necessary condition for workplace success, is no longer a sufficient condition for achieving that success.

The simple fact of the expansion of education is not, however, the whole story. A second and perhaps even more important reason for the diminished impact of schooling as a vehicle for opportunity among immigrant, poor, and minority youth is the loose coupling of schooling and the economy. Although individuals who obtain more schooling are more likely to be employed, and to work in jobs that provide more rewards, obtaining a high school or even college degree is no guarantee of a good job. There is, in fact, little evidence that schooling leads to jobs. This is in contrast to the situation at the beginning of the twentieth century when immigrants entered a population in which basic labor was in relatively short supply for the growing industrial system and education appeared to operate as a key entry point into the workplace. In the very different economy of the end of the century, it has become clear that the education system and the economy move to different rhythms, particularly at the level of local communities. The experience of recent cohorts of youth has contributed to the erosion of the myth that schooling is a guarantor of socioeconomic success.

The third and most telling blow to the myth of opportunity comes from the experiences of racial and ethnic minorities, precisely the group we have indicated is likely to expand over the coming decades. The dissolution of this myth is reflected in the split between the concrete expectations and the abstract aspirations of minorities[14] and in the development of culturally based opposition to schooling, wherein students from lower socioeconomic groups and students from minority groups define success in school as the exclusive prerogative of middle-class whites, and define their own social identities in ways that devalue scholastic success.[15] This pattern differs from the experience of immigrant minorities in the early decades of this century, in part due to differences in the structural conditions faced by minorities then and now, and also due to differences in the nature of minority status. Ogbu has described important differences between what he terms voluntary minorities, such as European immigrants, and caste-like minorities, such as American blacks, Native Americans, and Mexican-Americans.[16] Caste-like minorities have experienced structural constraints on the opportunities available to them. Moreover, these constraints persist across generations, whereas voluntary minorities often have been assimilated into mainstream society over the course of one or two generations. Thus, while the myth of the capacity of schooling to grant access to desired status has weakened, it has dimmed especially among the population with the greatest stake in its central claim: racial and ethnic minorities and the poor.

The second myth that is central to understanding how schools work is the myth of rationality. Our society believes that schools, like other organizations, have goals and objectives, and that schools are organized in a rational manner to achieve those goals and objectives. A consequence of this myth is that the internal operations of schools are rarely scrutinized directly or subjected to critical analysis. Rather, what Meyer and Rowan term the "logic of confidence"[17] is used to legitimate what schools do. Teachers are assumed to know how to teach, and to organize instruction in the classroom to enable students to learn, and administrators are assumed to engage in rational management practices.

Because the myth of rationality legitimates the internal structures and processes of schooling, many educational practices are reproduced without direct evidence of their effects. Perhaps the most striking example of this is the literature on the effects of ability grouping and tracking. For decades, these practices were employed without careful regard for their consequences for children's academic and social development. Even today, the arguments for detracking and the abolishment of homogeneous ability grouping rest more on ideology than on evidence. These practices have persisted because educators, but even more importantly the general public, viewed them as rational ways of organizing instruction, even though some children were placed in the high groups and tracks and others were mired in the low groups and tracks.

The myth of rationality, however, has suffered the same fate as the myth of opportunity in the contemporary period. As schools have come to be viewed as less effective in meeting the demands of society and the needs of the changing student population, the assumption that they operate in rational and appropriate ways has diminished. Increasingly, the activities of schools are questioned, and increasingly schools are open to charges that they operate to maximize the interests of groups other than students and the community at large. The same bureaucratic structure that was once perceived as providing even-handed treatment of students is now perceived as guarding the benefits of established labor groups. This change in perception has led to calls for the restructuring of schools, the introduction of market forces through school choice, and more intensive assessment of schooling outcomes, each in part the result of the decline of the myth of rationality.

In this section, we have attempted to provide a context for examining the schooling experiences of disadvantaged children and youth as we move into the twenty-first century. We have argued that there are several important changes that have consequences for how schools are organized. These include the changing composition of the school-aged population; the diverse goals of schooling; the heightened demands for school success; the weak technology of schooling; and the changing social and political context for schooling. In the next section, we look at the implications of these changes for how schools are organized.

Consequences of Context for School Organization

Schools and schooling are shaped by their social contexts. While there are many social forces that have exerted an effect on how schools are organized, we shall highlight those we have mentioned in the preceding section. Our analysis leads to a curious paradox: We have organized schools as if they are carrying out a routine, standardized set of activities, even in the face of evidence that the task of educating children and youth is uncertain and anything but routine. And, as we shall see later, the attempts to make the process of schooling as rational as possible have set in place an array of structural features of schooling that sometimes have the unintended consequence of impeding the academic and social development of all children, but especially those from nontraditional backgrounds.

SCHOOLING AND UNCERTAINTY

We take as axiomatic the belief that organizations are interdependent with their environments. Organizational contexts shape the structure of those organizations and the processes that go on within them, and, at times, organizational structure and process can influence the organizational environment, too. But not every organizational structure will be successful in every environment. Rather, effective ways of organizing are contingent on the organizational context.[18] For example, an organization that has a stable environment might have a different structure from one that has a turbulent and constantly changing environment. Similarly, an organization producing many outputs might be organized differently from one producing a single product. When we consider schools as organizations, we see some evidence that the organization of schools differs according to the environmental context. Elementary schools are smaller and more decentralized than secondary schools,[19] in part because of differences in their goals and clienteles, and public high schools are organized differently than Catholic high schools.[20] But, it also is the case that current school environments are much more varied than school organizational structures. This suggests that, while school organization could be shaped by the school's environment, it is not always clear that the school's organizational structure has in fact responded to that environment or to changes within it.

Like Galbraith[21] we believe that a key feature of an organization is the uncertainty of the basic task being performed by the organization. Some organizations carry out a small set of routine tasks, while others have multiple inputs and outputs and unpredictable work processes. When an organization has a small number of raw inputs and outputs and a highly predictable set of tasks, there is little uncertainty involved in the production process, and the work can be planned in advance. Conversely, when there are many different inputs and outputs, and an unpredictable set of tasks, advanced planning is unlikely to be helpful because so much of the actual process is uncertain.

Our contention is that schools are currently organized as if teaching and learning are predictable and routine, when in fact these activities are fraught with uncertainty. In an earlier era, American schools had a constrained set of goals, a relatively homogeneous student population, and more modest expectations for schooling outcomes. While waves of immigration and the mobilization of ethnic minority groups served to diversify the school-aged population during the first half of this century, there still was little pressure on schools to be successful with most students. Moreover, schooling was defined primarily in terms of basic skills and concrete knowledge. The teaching and learning of basic skills and "facts" were widely regarded as routine by most societal members.

More recently, in response to the social forces we have adumbrated, American schools are facing increasingly diverse student populations, both with respect to students' social and cultural backgrounds and to the knowledge, skills, and values they bring with them to the school and classroom. And, as both private and public social institutions in our society have weakened, an increasingly ambitious agenda, characterized by diverse, ambiguous, and contradictory goals, has been superimposed on American schooling. Part of this agenda involves the teaching and learning of higher-order thinking skills and problem solving, activities that are, by most accounts, much more difficult than the teaching and learning of basic skills.

In sum, we see American schools being faced with increasing levels of uncertainty as they carry out their fundamental activities. This uncertainty is reflected in the social and academic diversity of students, their families, and their communities, in the diversity of the goals to which schools are being held accountable, and in the more difficult tasks that schools are attempting to carry out with only incremental changes in the technology of teaching and learning.

ORGANIZING FOR INCREASINGLY ELUSIVE CERTAINTY

Despite, or perhaps because of, the evident increase in the uncertainty connected to the tasks of schooling in contemporary society in the United States, schools continue to be organized as if they were carrying out routine teaching and learning activities with a homogeneous student population. The structure of most American schools resembles nothing so much as a machine. The imagery of schools as machines portrays schools as rational, technical organizations that process raw inputs (students) in batches to produce homogeneous outputs[22]—in particular, minimum levels of student competency.[23] Teachers and administrators plan their work, organizing students into different grade levels, programs of study, classes, and instructional groups within classes. Teachers are expected to have detailed lesson plans specifying what all of the students in a class will do and learn during a particular class period, and the aggregate plans specify competencies to be mastered during a term or academic year.

Like most machines, schools typically are organized through a bureaucratic or instrumental rationality in which job positions are distinguished through a clear definition of functional responsibilities. Teachers teach; administrators manage; students are the clients; school board members are stewards. Typically, a mathematics teacher will not teach French, nor a science teacher social studies, especially at the secondary level. Even at the elementary level, where teachers are more likely to be "generalists," their responsibilities are circumscribed by their classrooms and the students assigned to them. Mr. Whitaker will have few responsibilities for Ms. Pemrose's students, whether these two teachers are assigned to the same grade level or not. While teachers have great discretion in the classroom and what they actually do there is rarely inspected directly, they nevertheless are expected to adhere to a set of common overarching goals and develop plans to meet those goals. Their discretion is constrained by the organizational structure, and the linkages between grade levels and curricular sequences. The first grade teacher is expected to prepare children for second grade, the English II teacher is expected to prepare students for English III, and so on.

In addition to these traditional bureaucratic constraints on the roles of teachers, schools are organized so as to create at least the perception of homogeneous instructional groups. That is, the traditional solution to the problem of managing differences among students is to group them into more homogeneous units, either by age, grade level, subject matter, or ability level. The creation of homogeneous subunits within schools and classrooms is widely seen as more efficient for teaching and learning purposes than is grouping students in ways that do not recognize the differences among them. Moreover, the assignment to these various instructional groups of specially certified personnel armed with specially targeted instructional strategies adds to the impression that the learning needs of students are being addressed rationally.

But, like the constrained bureaucratic roles in schools, this kind of differentiation within schools may present obstacles to learning for some or all students. Some group placements are associated with differing access to school resources, and others are stigmatized in various ways. The next section of this chapter reviews the literature on differentiating processes within schools that stem from their organizational structure, noting especially the likely consequences of such differentiating mechanisms for the changing student population.

Students' Experiences in Schools: Varieties of Differentiation

Changes in the context of schooling mean new challenges to the enduring organizational form of schooling. The context in which schools operate is increasingly differentiated in various ways that place great strains on the school as a site for assembling for the purpose of education. At the same time the organizational form of schooling has been arranged to maintain the myths of opportunity and rationality that are necessary for continued popular support. Thus formal schooling is at a stage in which the forms necessary to maintain public confidence are becoming increasingly dysfunctional. This dilemma is particularly salient when we consider the experiences of at-risk students in schools.

Throughout much of this century schools have instituted explicit policies and practices designed to enhance their ability to educate their increasingly diverse populations. The bases for this intentional separation of students are frequently biosocial characteristics such as ability and age, which are believed to affect the efficiency and effectiveness with which students can be educated. Here we consider five types of deliberate differentiation of students in contemporary schools.

CURRICULUM TRACKING

For more than six decades schools have employed tracking and ability grouping. Studies of curriculum tracking over the past twenty-five years have concentrated on (1) the evolution of tracking practices;[24] (2) the differential access to knowledge offered to students in different tracks;[25] (3) the processes by which students are assigned to tracks;[26] (4) the amount of mobility among tracks;[27] and (5) the effects of tracking on a host of outcomes such as school performance, standardized test scores, educational plans, college attendance, educational attainment, occupational plans and attainment, intellectual orientations, attitudes toward school, and psychosocial development (self-concept and locus of control).[28]

The first focus of research, the evolution of tracking practices, has revealed that tracking practices developed in response to the enormous growth of increasingly diverse students enrolling in secondary education between 1910 and 1940.[29] The sociodemographic heterogeneity of the student population was reflected in curriculum differentiation in that all students were admitted to the high school but channeled to different curricula.

The second focus of research, the differential access to knowledge, has been concerned with the content, pace, and duration of teaching different curricula in tracked schools.[30] Students in the college preparatory program move at a faster rate, have more access to knowledge in subjects such as mathematics and science and are exposed to more higher-order thinking skills than those in lower tracks.[31] Gamoran and Berends cite a range of ethnographic studies which indicate that teachers of lower-track subjects reduce the pace and complexity of instruction and that such differences are reinforced by the assignment of more experienced and more competent teachers to the higher tracks.[32]

Researchers, educational policymakers, and judicial authorities have been concerned with the third component of research on tracking, the links among track assignment and students' performance and background characteristics. This is a contentious topic of research, with contradictory evidence being presented. In a thorough review of this literature, Oakes, Gamoran, and Page[33] conclude that prior achievement is the best predictor of future performance, with family socioeconomic background having some explanatory power. Useem recently specified and documented some of the processes which produce the substantial correlation between parents' education and children's placement in the "fast" track: college-educated parents were knowledgeable about children's placement; they were immersed in parental information networks; they intervened in school decisions about their children's placement; and they influenced their children's decisions regarding placement.[34] These findings have been reinforced by Riehl, Natriello, and Pallas, who found that parental intervention was one of the most important determinants of track placement.[35]

Evidence concerning the fourth component of the literature on tracking, the amount of movement of students across tracks, has shown that such mobility is rather modest and that it is mostly downward from the academic program to the vocational or general track.[36]

Without question, the fifth issue is the most frequently addressed in the literature on tracking, that is, the extent to which tracking enhances academic achievement and related socioemotional variables such as educational and occupational aspirations and plans and attitudes toward schooling. As noted by Oakes, this large body of literature is quite uneven in quality, producing conflicting conclusions.[37] In general, the more rigorous studies reveal differences in academic growth which favor students in the higher tracks.[38]

ABILITY GROUPING

Slavin has systematically reviewed the literature on ability grouping in elementary schools and concluded that the practice takes several fundamental forms, which have different cognitive as well as affective outcomes.[39] Two major types of grouping are between-class and within-class. Our focus here is on within-class ability grouping at the elementary level in order to maximize the distinctions between it and tracking at the high school level. Ability grouping of this type is widely practiced in the middle school, and is even employed in junior and senior high schools.[40] Slavin defines within-class grouping as "the practice of assigning students to homogeneous subgroups for instruction within the class."[41] Each subgroup is taught at its own aptitude level and progresses at its own rate. Ability grouping thus differs from curriculum tracking in high schools in two important ways. First, it involves dividing the time of a teacher among two or more homogeneous groups, which sacrifices quantity of instruction in an attempt to enhance its quality[42] by permitting the teacher to tailor instruction to the similar needs of smaller groups of students. Second, ability grouping does not separate students by classrooms. Instead it permits students of each group to observe all students in the class with respect to the allocation of differential services across the homogeneous groups.

Within-class grouping poses a challenge to the teacher not found in between-class grouping, namely, the problem of managing two or more groups, because while the teacher is instructing one group, the remaining group(s) typically engage(s) in seatwork activities which can be of limited academic utility.[43]

Much of the research on this type of deliberate differentiation of students can be subsumed under one or both of the following two headings: (1) differences in the quality of the curriculum and instruction and the relationship of assignment processes to the social background of students; and (2) the effects of grouping on student achievement and affective variables such as interpersonal relationships and attachment to school.

Concerning the first category, the more recent literature reveals that students of lower socioeconomic backgrounds and/or minority status are not victims of assignments to lower ability groups when the students' prior achievements are controlled.[44] This finding conflicts with Rist's widely cited study which revealed that elementary school teachers were biased in their assignment of poor students to lower ability groups.[45]

Concerning the studies of effects of within-class grouping on students' learning, Slavin states that a sizeable segment of the literature is methodologically flawed.[46] However, he concludes that the systematic studies consistently show a positive effect on achievement for students in grouped classes, with the effects being larger for low achievers than for average or higher achievers. He also specifies the conditions under which the effects of grouping are more pronounced: when the grouping is limited to specific subjects (especially mathematics); when the grouping mechanism reduces heterogeneity in the specific skill or subject being taught; when group assignments are flexible and are assessed frequently; and when teachers adapt the level and pace of instruction to students' needs. While Hallinan agrees that grouping has positive effects on learning rates of students, she argues that the practice is more beneficial to high-ability students and explains the disparity in terms of the way in which grouping conditions three major factors affecting learning (opportunities for learning, instructional climate, and student aptitudes), factors that favor students in the high-ability groups.[47]

DISABILITY GROUPING

Three principal forms of this generic type of deliberate differentiation of students discussed are here—compensatory education, special education, and bilingual education. Each form is based on a separate rationale in terms of the needs of the students, and each leads to separate schooling experiences for them. Compensatory education rests on the premise that the social and economic liabilities handicap poor, ethnic, and racial minority children at the time they enter school and need to be compensated for by enriched academic experiences.[48] Special education is rooted in the belief developed during the first half of this century that students handicapped or disabled by mental, physical, or emotional problems were often rejected in regular classrooms and could be better educated in small, homogeneous classes using specially trained instructors.[49] The primary goal of bilingual education is to enable students with limited English proficiency (LEP) to obtain knowledge and skills through their native language and simultaneously to learn English. It is assumed that LEP students can make more progress in acquiring academic knowledge and skills by initial instruction in their native language.[50]

Although each of these three forms of disability grouping has sometimes been offered in regular classroom settings, more often students classified in one or more of these three categories are separated for delivery of educational and social services. However, in the past two decades a spate of federal and state laws, buttressed by judicial authority, has required that handicapped children be placed in the "least restrictive educational environment." Nevertheless, some critics of disability grouping have questioned the bases on which students are assigned to these programs, arguing that nonuniversalistic criteria, such as race, ethnicity, or socioeconomic background, play a disproportionate role in students being selected for such programs.[51]

The studies attempting to assess the academic consequences of these programs in various settings, ranging from segregated to integrated, have often been methodologically flawed.[52] The more systematic studies suggest that students in compensatory education,[53] special education,[54] and under specified conditions[55] for certain subjects in bilingual education[56] profit from participation in regular classes. However, there are conflicting findings from some other studies.[57] It may be that the institutional setting for students grouped by disabilities or handicaps is less important than the nature of the instructional process.[58]

There is also disagreement regarding the effects on the social adjustment of disabled students when they are placed in regular classroom settings. Meyen and Altman[59] cite several studies indicating that disabled students fare poorly in regular classes with respect to social adjustment, but Cole and Meyer[60] and Madden and Slavin[61] conclude that such placement procedures lead to higher self-concept and social competence and to more prosocial behavior and attitudes toward school.

AGE GROUPING

In most Western school systems students are not only differentiated horizontally by practices such as ability grouping and tracking, but also vertically by age.[62] Kett has documented that age grading did not emerge in American schools until very late in the nineteenth century as part of a "new culture of childhood."[63] Nongraded plans are defined as grouping practices in which grade levels are eliminated in favor of flexible cross-age groupings for different subjects.[64]

Slavin (1989) and Gutierrez and Slavin (1992) have synthesized the literature on the effects of nongraded plans in elementary schools on students' achievement.[65] They found the effects of such plans to be inconsistent but generally positive. Most of the studies that failed to show positive results were in laboratory schools or in regular schools where the plans were not implemented with fidelity.

Evidence on the impact of nongraded plans on students' social adjustment to school is very rare. Guarino found that students in an ungraded school matched with a comparable graded school had a higher level of self-concept and a lower level of anxiety.[66] Much more research is needed before any firm conclusions can be drawn regarding the relationship between nongraded plans and students' socioemotional development.

INTEREST GROUPING

Finally, students may be separated into groups by their academic interests or choices. Magnet schools are a prominent example of the parental and student choice movement of the past three decades. Such schools, or specialized programs within schools, are characterized by open enrollment and specialize in one field or a limited number of fields such as the performing arts, computer science, or criminal justice. The original impetus for magnet schools came from policy initiatives in the late 1960s to aid in school desegregation. These efforts were reinforced by public dissatisfaction with the perceived low quality of the pedagogy, curricula, and social climate of schools in the 1960s.

Most efforts to evaluate systematically the academic and affective outcomes of magnet schools are handicapped by the problem of self-selection or "creaming" of the more academically competent and positively oriented students into them. Nevertheless, some studies use rigorous methods to minimize the biasing effects of self-selection. For example, Driscoll compared the achievement and attitudes of eighth grade students in 66 choice schools with those of a sample from 66 matched schools.[67] She discovered essentially no meaningful difference between the two samples. Crain, Heebner, and Si compared students who were admitted to choice schools in New York City by lottery with a group who applied but were not admitted,[68] thus avoiding the bias of self-selection. These students were followed from junior high into high school, and the investigators found that students admitted to the choice schools had higher reading scores, earned more course credits, and were less likely to drop out than students in the comparison group who were not admitted.

These results suggest that those magnet schools which match students' interests with curriculum and pedagogy are likely to increase students' motivation and identification with the school. This hypothesis is compatible with Toch's conclusion that choice schools engender a sense of common purpose or positive ethos.[69] It is also compatible with empirical research on school climates,[70] which shows that schools with environments that place a strong emphasis on learning, that create a caring community that values students intrinsically, and where parents who are deeply involved in the performance and social behavior of their children and who are committed to the welfare of the institution, have higher levels of achievement and more prosocial behavior than schools lacking such characteristics.

Conclusions

We have argued that the relationship between students' needs and their school experiences must be placed in a broad context that locates schooling in a set of societal expectations and in a web of linkages among social institutions. Viewing schooling in this way helps us to understand how school contexts affect the internal organization of schooling and thus influence students' experiences and educational outcomes. In particular, we have pointed to the pressures that the changing demography of the school-aged population have created for schooling as an institution. While American schools have always tried to adapt to the changing mix of students they serve, the process of adaptation is complicated by other simultaneous changes in the social, political, and institutional contexts of schooling.

As we approach the turn of the century, we observe that schooling has taken on an increasingly diverse and conflicting set of goals, and can no longer mediate among these goals by focusing on the subset of the school-aged population that is easiest to educate. These heightened demands have been accompanied by changing patterns of school governance and a weakening of the historic connections between schooling and the economy, but few changes have occurred in the technology of schooling or in the ways schools are organized. We have suggested that this changing context defines schooling as an increasingly uncertain activity, and that we can understand the ways schools are organized as a reflection of the uncertain environment in which schools operate. One of the most important ways that the structure of schooling has responded to environmental uncertainty is to differentiate and separate students into groups in ways that are seen as rational. Deliberate differentiation mechanisms such as ability grouping, tracking, age grading, and disability grouping have resulted in increasingly fragmented and stratified experiences for students.

These differentiating mechanisms within schools are not going to go away easily. One need not resort to dark conspiracies pitting the more advantaged members of society against the less advantaged to understand why this is so. Rather, the persistence of differentiating mechanisms that impede students' learning and/or increase inequalities in the success students achieve can be linked to at least two features of school context.

First, differentiation within schools has been institutionalized as a rational means for dealing with diversity and uncertainty. While parents, educators, and students may not like the idea of the homogeneous grouping of students for instruction, they see few alternatives to it. There is no vocabulary to describe other visions of how to organize complex teaching and learning tasks.

Second, a great many parents, educators, and students *like* the idea of homogeneous grouping. This is reflected in the attempts of more affluent parents to maintain programs for gifted and talented students, even while they decry tracking and ability grouping as ways of organizing instruction. More generally, the politics of special interest groups is a strong force for the maintenance of differentiated educational experiences for children and youth who are labeled in particular ways. There are powerful advocacy groups acting on behalf of exceptional children, children with limited English proficiency, emotionally impaired or mentally retarded children, gifted and talented children, and children receiving compensatory education services, to name but a few. These advocacy groups often have measured their success in terms of the dollars or services that are directed at a specific subset of children in a school. Because the inclusion movement, which calls for ending the physical segregation of children labeled as exceptional from "mainstream" children and "mainstream" classes, appears to run counter to the historic pattern of influence, inclusion remains more a matter of rhetoric than reality. And proponents of the inclusion movement have not been outspoken on the issue of differentiation within mainstreamed classrooms.

If, as we have argued, differentiating mechanisms within schools are here to stay, what is to be done? We suggest three avenues of research, development, and policymaking. First, it is important to recognize that, while differentiating mechanisms are not likely to disappear from American schools, such mechanisms need not be as pervasive as they have been in the past. It is well worth experimenting with ways of organizing instruction that are not dependent on groups of students who are similar in age, ability, or disability. Any such experiments must, however, be sensitive to the institutional inertia and political forces that prop up existing differentiation mechanisms. If evidence on the negative consequences of common differentiating mechanisms were to emerge as stronger and more problematic in the eyes of the public and the education community, it is conceivable that some of these institutional barriers to alternative ways of organizing instruction might weaken.

Second, we might devote greater attention to how it is that differentiating mechanisms increase inequalities among students, to the detriment of students who are most in need of help if they are to succeed in school. Without a firm grasp of the processes by which specific differentiating mechanisms affect students, it is difficult to formulate policies that might mitigate the negative effects of differentiation. Some differentiating processes influence students' opportunities to learn; others shape students' identities, motivation, and self-concept; while still others are deeply embedded in the national consciousness in ways that are hard to unearth. The extent to which we understand the ways in which differentiating mechanisms work will influence our ability to design research and development projects that might soften their impact on students' experiences and, hence, their academic and social development.

Third, we might, as Natriello suggests, pay as much attention to unifying processes in schools as to differentiating processes.[71] While differentiating mechanisms pull students apart by marking them as different from one another in ways that lead to unequal treatment at the hands of teachers, peers, and others, unifying mechanisms bring students together. It is conceivable that the presence of strong unifying mechanisms could offset the pernicious effects of differentiating mechanisms. But the evidence on this hypothesis is highly speculative, as we have never devoted as much attention to issues of commitment, bonding, and school membership as we have to issues of difference.

Differences are important, especially in the context of the uniquely American individualism that permeates our society and our schools. But commonalities are important too, and the tension between differentiating and unifying mechanisms in schools has only recently emerged as an issue for both researchers and practitioners.[72]

This chapter was prepared under the auspices of the Center for Research on Effective Schooling for Disadvantaged Students at Johns Hopkins University, supported as a national research and development center by the Office of Educational Research and Improvement, U.S. Department of Education (Grant Number R117R90002). The opinions expressed are ours and do not necessarily reflect the position or policy of either organization.

NOTES

1. Gary Natriello, Edward L. McDill, and Aaron M. Pallas, *Schooling Disadvantaged Children: Racing against Catastrophe* (New York: Teachers College Press, 1990).

2. James S. Coleman and Thomas Hoffer, *Public and Private High Schools: The Impact of Communities* (New York: Basic Books, 1987); Ernest L. Boyer, *Ready to Learn* (Princeton, NJ: Carnegie Foundation for the Advancement of Teaching, 1991).

3. Lawrence A. Cremin, *Traditions of American Education* (New York: Basic Books, 1977).

4. William J. Wilson, *The Truly Disadvantaged: The Inner City, the Underclass, and Public Policy* (Chicago: University of Chicago Press, 1987).

5. Christopher Hurn, *The Limits and Possibilities of Schooling* (Boston: Allyn and Bacon, 1985).

6. Magdalene Lampert, "How Do Teachers Manage to Teach? Perspectives on Problems in Practice," *Harvard Educational Review* 55, no. 2 (1985): 174-194.

7. Robert F. Floden and Christopher M. Clark, "Preparing Teachers for Uncertainty," *Teachers College Record* 89, no. 4 (1988): 505-524.

8. Adam Gamoran, "The Variable Effects of High School Tracking," *American Sociological Review* 57, no. 2 (1992): 812-828; Robert E. Slavin, "Achievement Effects of Ability Grouping in Secondary Schools: A Best-Evidence Synthesis," *Review of Educational Research* 60, no. 3 (1990): 471-499.

9. John E. Chubb and Terry M. Moe, *Politics, Markets, and America's Schools* (Washington, DC: Brookings Institution, 1990).

10. John W. Meyer and Brian Rowan, "Institutionalized Organizations: Formal Structure as Myth and Ceremony," *American Journal of Sociology* 83, no. 2 (1977): 340-363.

11. William I. Thomas, "The Relation of Research to the Social Process," in *Essays on Research in the Social Sciences* (Washington, DC: Brookings Institution, 1931).

12. Richard Rubinson, "Class Formation, Politics, and Institutions: Schooling in the United States," *American Journal of Sociology* 92, no. 3 (1986): 519-548.

13. Martin Trow, "The Second Transformation of American Secondary Education," *International Journal of Comparative Sociology* 2, no. 2 (1961): 144-165.

14. Roslyn Mickelson, "The Attitude-Achievement Paradox among Black Adolescents," *Sociology of Education* 63, no. 1 (1990): 44-61.

15. Paul Willis, *Learning to Labor: How Working Class Kids Get Working Class Jobs* (New York: Columbia University Press, 1977); Signithia Fordham and John Ogbu, "Black Students' School Success: Coping with the 'Burden of Acting White,'" *Urban Review* 18, no. 3 (1986): 176-206.

16. John Ogbu, "Diversity and Equity in Public Education: Community Forces and Minority School Adjustment and Performance," in *Policies for America's Public Schools: Teachers, Equity, and Indicators*, edited by Ron Haskins and Duncan MacRae (Norwood, NJ: Ablex, 1988), pp. 127-170.

17. John W. Meyer and Brian Rowan, "The Structure of Educational Organizations," in *Environments and Organizations*, edited by Marshall W. Meyer and Associates (San Francisco: Jossey-Bass, 1978): 78-109.

18. Paul R. Lawrence and Jay W. Lorsch, *Organization and Environment: Managing Differentiation and Integration* (Boston: Graduate School of Business Administration, Harvard University, 1967).

19. Roger B. Herriott and William A. Firestone, "Two Images of Schools as Organizations: A Refinement and Elaboration," *Educational Administration Quarterly* 20, no. 4 (1984): 41-57.

20. Anthony S. Bryk, Valerie E. Lee, and Peter B. Holland, *Catholic Schools and the Common Good* (Cambridge, MA: Harvard University Press, 1993).

21. Jay Galbraith, *Designing Complex Organizations* (Reading, MA: Addison-Wesley, 1977).

22. Gareth Morgan, *Images of Organization* (Beverly Hills, CA: Sage, 1986).

23. Charles E. Bidwell, "The School as a Formal Organization," in *Handbook of Organizations*, edited by James G. March (Chicago: Rand McNally, 1965).

24. Paul D. Chapman, *Schools as Sorters* (New York: New York University Press, 1988); Jeannie Oakes, *Keeping Track: How Schools Structure Inequality* (New Haven: Yale University Press, 1985).

25. Aaron V. Cicourel and John I. Kitsuse, *The Educational Decision-Makers* (Indianapolis: Bobbs-Merrill, 1963); Adam Gamoran, "The Variable Effects of High School Tracking," *American Sociological Review* 57, no. 6 (1992): 812-828; Carolyn Riehl, Gary Natriello, and Aaron Pallas, "Losing Track: The Dynamics of the Student Scheduling Process in High Schools" (Paper presented at the Annual Meeting of the American Sociological Association, Cincinnati, 1992); Elizabeth L. Useem, "Middle Schools and Math Groups: Parents' Involvement in Children's Placement," *Sociology of Education* 65, no. 4 (1992): 263-279.

26. Jeannie Oakes, Adam Gamoran, and Reba N. Page, "Curriculum Differentiation: Opportunities, Outcomes, and Meanings," in *Handbook of Research on Curriculum*, edited by Philip W. Jackson (New York: Macmillan, 1992).

27. James E. Rosenbaum, *Making Inequality* (New York: Wiley, 1976); Maureen T. Hallinan, "Track Mobility in Secondary School" (Paper presented at the Annual Meeting of the American Sociological Association, Miami, 1993).

28. Barbara Heyns, "Social Selection and Stratification Within Schools," *American Journal of Sociology* 79, no. 4 (1974): 1934-1951; Karl L. Alexander and Edward L. McDill, "Selection and Allocation Within Schools: Some Causes and Consequences of Curriculum Placement," *American Sociological Review* 41, no. 6 (1976): 47-66; Adam Gamoran, "The Stratification of High School Learning Opportunities," *Sociology of Education* 60, no. 3 (1987): 129-143; Adam Gamoran and Robert D. Mare, "Secondary School Tracking and Educational Inequality: Compensation, Reinforcement, or Neutrality," *American Journal of Sociology* 94, no. 5 (1989): 1146-1183; Robert M. Hauser, William H. Sewell, and Duane F. Alwin, "High School Effects on Achievement," in

Schooling and Achievement in American Society, edited by William H. Sewell, Robert M. Hauser, and David L. Featherman (New York: Academic Press, 1976): 309-341.

29. Trow, "The Second Transformation of American Secondary Education."

30. Maureen T. Hallinan, "Ability Grouping and Student Learning," in *The Social Organization of Schools*, edited by Maureen T. Hallinan (New York: Plenum Press, 1987): pp. 41-69.

31. Beth E. Vanfossen, J. D. Jones, and J. Z. Spade, "Curriculum Tracking and Status Maintenance," *Sociology of Education* 60, no. 2 (1987): 104-122; Oakes, Gamoran, and Page, "Curriculum Differentiation: Opportunities, Outcomes, and Meanings."

32. Adam Gamoran and Mark Berends, "The Effects of Stratification in Secondary Schools: Synthesis of Survey and Ethnographic Research," *Review of Educational Research* 57, no. 4 (1987): 414-435.

33. Oakes, Gamoran, and Page, "Curriculum Differentiation."

34. Useem, "Middle Schools and Math Groups: Parents' Involvement in Children's Placement."

35. Riehl, Natriello, and Pallas, "Losing Track: The Dynamics of the Student Scheduling Process in High Schools."

36. Rosenbaum, *Making Inequality*; Hallinan, "Track Mobility in Secondary School."

37. Jeannie Oakes, "Tracking in Secondary Schools," in *School and Classroom Organization*, edited by Robert E. Slavin (Hillsdale, NJ: Lawrence Erlbaum, 1989).

38. Karl Alexander, Martha Cook, and Edward L. McDill, "Curriculum Tracking and Educational Stratification: Some Further Evidence," *American Sociological Review* 43, no. 1 (1978): 47-66; Alexander and McDill, "Selection and Allocation Within Schools"; Gamoran, "The Stratification of High School Learning Opportunities"; idem, "The Variable Effects of High School Tracking"; Gamoran and Mare, "Secondary School Tracking and Educational Inequality: Compensation, Reinforcement, or Neutrality"; Alan Kerckhoff, "Effects of Ability Grouping in British Secondary Schools," *American Sociological Review* 51, no. 6 (1986): 846-858.

39. Robert E. Slavin, "Ability Grouping and Student Achievement in Elementary Schools: A Best-Evidence Synthesis," *Review of Educational Research* 57, no. 3 (1987): 293-336.

40. Oakes, "Tracking in Secondary Schools."

41. Robert E. Slavin, "Grouping for Instruction in Elementary School," in *School and Classroom Organization*, edited by Robert E. Slavin (Hillsdale, NJ: Erlbaum, 1989), p. 167.

42. Hallinan, "Ability Grouping and Student Learning."

43. Linda M. Anderson, Nancy L. Brubaker, Janet Alleman-Brooks, and Gerald G. Duffy, "A Qualitative Study of Seatwork in First Grade Classrooms," *Elementary School Journal* 86, no. 2 (1985): 123-140.

44. Emil J. Haller, "Pupil Race and Elementary School Ability Grouping: Are Teachers Biased against Black Children?" *American Educational Research Journal* 22, no. 4 (1985): 465-483; Emil J. Haller and Sharon A. Davis, "Does Socioeconomic Status Bias the Assignment of Elementary School Students to Reading Groups?" *American Educational Research Journal* 17, no. 4 (1980): 409-418; Aage Sørenson and Maureen T. Hallinan, "Race Effects on the Assignment to Ability Groups," in *The Social Context of Instruction: Group Organization and Group Processes*, edited by Penelope L. Peterson, Louise C. Wilkinson, and Maureen T. Hallinan (New York: Academic Press, 1984), pp. 85-103; Gamoran, "Rank, Performance, and Mobility in Elementary School."

45. Ray C. Rist, "Student Social Class and Teacher Expectations: The Self-fulfilling Prophecy in Ghetto Education," *Harvard Educational Review* 40, no. 3 (1970): 411-451.

46. Slavin, "Ability Grouping and Student Achievement in Elementary Schools"; idem, "Grouping for Instruction in Elementary School."

47. Hallinan, "Ability Grouping and Student Learning."

48. Natriello, McDill, and Pallas, *Schooling Disadvantaged Children.*

49. Edward Meyen and Rubin Altman, "Special Education," in *Encyclopedia of Educational Research*, vol. 4, edited by Harold E. Mitzel (New York: Free Press, 1982), pp. 1739-1749; James G. Carrier, *Learning Disability: Social Class and the Construction of Inequality in American Education* (New York: Greenwood Press, 1986).

50. James Cummins, "The Entry and Exit Fallacy in Bilingual Education," *Journal of the National Association for Bilingual Education* 4, no. 3 (1980): 25-29; Doris V. Gunderson, "Bilingual Education," in *Encyclopedia of Educational Research*, vol. 1, edited by Harold E. Mitzel (New York: Free Press, 1982): 202-211.

51. Carrier, *Learning Disability*; Hugh Mehan, Alma Hertweck, and J. Lee Miehls, *Handicapping the Handicapped: Decision Making in Students' Educational Careers* (Stanford, CA: Stanford University Press, 1986).

52. Meyen and Altman, "Special Education"; Nancy A. Madden and Robert E. Slavin, "Mainstreaming Students with Mild Academic Handicaps: Academic and Social Outcomes," *Review of Educational Research* 53, no. 4 (1983): 131-138.

53. Gaea Leinhardt and Allan Pallay, "Restrictive Educational Settings: Exile or Haven?" *Review of Educational Research* 54, no. 4 (1982): 409-425; Natriello, McDill, and Pallas, *Schooling Disadvantaged Children.*

54. George Calhoun and Raymond Elliott, "Self-Concept and Academic Achievement of Educable Retarded and Emotionally Disturbed Children," *Exceptional Children* 43, no. 6 (1977): 379-380; Gaea Leinhardt and William Bickel, "Instruction's the Thing Wherein to Catch the Mind that Falls Behind," in *School and Classroom Organization*, edited by Robert E. Slavin (Hillsdale, NJ: Lawrence Erlbaum, 1989), pp. 197-226; Meyen and Altman, "Special Education."

55. Malcolm N. Danoff, *Evaluation of the Impact of ESEA Title VII Spanish/English Bilingual Educational Program: Overview of Study and Findings* (Palo Alto, CA: American Institutes for Research, 1978); J. David Ramirez, Sandra D. Yuen, Dena R. Ramey, and David J. Pasta, *Final Report: Longitudinal Study of Immersion Strategy, Early-Exit and Late-Exit Transitional Bilingual Education Programs for Language Minority Children* (San Mateo, CA: Aguirre International, 1990).

56. Shelley L. Olson, "Long Term Effects of Bilingual Education on a National Sample of Mexican-American Sophomores: A Component Analysis," *Resources in Education* (November 1989) ED 307803.

57. Kevin N. Cole, Paulette E. Mills, Philip S. Dale, and Joseph R. Jenkins, "Effects of Preschool Integration for Children with Disabilities," *Exceptional Children* 58, no. 1 (1991): 36-45; Ann C. Willig, "A Meta Analysis of Selected Studies on the Effectiveness of Bilingual Education," *Review of Educational Research* 55, no. 3 (1985): 269-317.

58. Leinhardt and Pallay, "Restrictive Educational Settings: Exile or Haven?"

59. Meyen and Altman, "Special Education."

60. David A. Cole and Luanna H. Meyer, "Social Integration and Severe Disabilities: A Longitudinal Analysis of Child Outcomes," *Journal of Special Education* 25, no. 3 (1991): 340-351.

61. Madden and Slavin, "Mainstreaming Students with Mild Academic Handicaps."

62. Philippe Aries, *Centuries of Childhood* (New York: Vintage Books, 1962); Joseph Kett, "The History of Age Grouping in America," in *Youth: Transition to Adulthood*, edited by James S. Coleman (Chicago: University of Chicago Press, 1974), pp. 9-29.

58   CHANGING STUDENTS/CHANGING NEEDS

63. Joseph Kett, "The History of Age Grouping in America," in *Rethinking Childhood*, edited by Arlene S. Skolnick (Boston: Little Brown, 1976).

64. John I. Goodlad and Robert H. Anderson, *The Nongraded Elementary School* (New York: Harcourt Brace and World, 1963); Slavin, "Grouping for Instruction in Elementary School."

65. Slavin, "Grouping for Instruction in Elementary School"; Roberto Gutierrez and Robert Slavin, "Achievement Effects of the Nongraded Elementary School: A Best-Evidence Synthesis," *Review of Educational Research* 62, no. 4 (1992): 333-376.

66. Anthony Guarino, "An Investigation of Achievement, Self-Concept, and School Related Anxiety in Graded and Non-Graded Elementary Schools," *Dissertation Abstracts International* 43, 08-A (University Microfilms No. AAD83-01577).

67. Mary E. Driscoll, "Choice, Achievement, and School Community," in *School Choice: Examining the Evidence*, edited by E. Rasell and Richard Rothstein (Washington, DC: Economic Policy Institute, 1993).

68. Robert Crain, Amy Heebner, and Yiu-Pong Si, *Career Magnets: Interviews with Students and Staff* (Berkeley, CA: National Center for Research in Vocational Education, 1992).

69. Thomas Toch, *In the Name of Excellence* (New York: Oxford University Press, 1991).

70. Edward L. McDill and Leo C. Rigsby, *Structure and Process in Secondary School: The Academic Impact of Educational Climates* (Baltimore, MD: Johns Hopkins University Press, 1974); Michael Rutter, Barbara Maughan, Peter Mortimore, and Janet Ouston, *Fifteen Thousand Hours: Secondary Schools and Their Effects on Children* (Cambridge, MA: Harvard University Press, 1979); Bryk, Lee, and Holland, *Catholic Schools and the Common Good*.

71. Gary Natriello, "Coming Together and Breaking Apart: Unifying and Differentiating Processes in Schools and Classrooms," in *Research in Sociology of Education and Socialization*, vol. 10, edited by Aaron Pallas (Greenwich, CT: JAI Press, forthcoming).

72. Ibid.

CHAPTER III

Nurturing Potential Talent
in a Diverse Population

A. HARRY PASSOW

In passing the Jacob K. Javits Gifted and Talented Students Education Act of 1988 (P.L. 100-297), Congress declared that youngsters with talent are found in all cultural groups, across all economic strata, and in all areas of human endeavor. The Act authorized the U.S. Department of Education to fund grants and provide leadership in the education of the gifted and talented. The legislation required that at least one half of the awards each year include projects aimed at serving gifted and talented students from impoverished backgrounds and that priority be given to projects that serve youngsters with limited English skills or who are disabled or are at-risk of being unrecognized and underserved.

P.L. 100-297 reaffirmed the truism that in every population on any given characteristic there is a range of potential, ability, and achievement, and that there are some individuals at the high end. It supports the notion that among the poor and minority populations, there are students with potential for superior or outstanding achievement who are in environments where this potential may not be nurtured or even recognized.

Along with the acknowledgment that talent potential exists in all segments of America's diverse population, there has been growing acceptance of the concept of the existence of a diversity of talents that can and must be identified and nurtured. The traditional view of giftedness consisting only of high intelligence as measured by a standardized test is no longer held as tenaciously as in the past.

These developments are accompanied by the reemergence of a number of issues that have persisted through the years in connection with efforts to identify and nurture talents of America's children and youth. Foremost among them is the perennial issue of equity *and*

A. Harry Passow is the Jacob H. Schiff Professor Emeritus of Education at Teachers College, Columbia University, New York City.

excellence, frequently expressed as equity *versus* excellence. In *A Nation at Risk*, the National Commission on Excellence in Education asserted that a strong commitment to excellence and educational reform need not mean a diminution in the commitment to high quality education for America's diverse student population: "The twin goals of equity and high quality schooling have profound and practical meaning for our economy and society, and we cannot permit one to yield to the other either in principle or practice."[1] Yet at the time that the Javits grants and other programs were stimulating efforts to attain greater equity by nurturing excellence among populations that have been seriously underrepresented in programs for the gifted, many such programs came under serious attack and were even eliminated because they were perceived as creating inequities.

A Slowly Evolving Concern

Education of the gifted has a long history, one that goes back at least to 1868 when the St. Louis Public Schools initiated frequent promotions as a means for caring for "rapid learners." By the turn of the century, dozens of school systems across the country had initiated program and curriculum modifications for academically able students. However, low-income and minority groups received little special attention in these efforts and a concern for students with high ability in those groups was slow in evolving.

For instance, when the National Society for the Study of Education published *The Education of Gifted Children* in 1924, its second yearbook in four years on the topic, an annotated bibliography of 453 entries contained not a single reference to minorities or other disadvantaged populations.[2]

The thousand-plus subjects in Terman's classic longitudinal study (begun in 1922 and still continuing), designed "to discover what physical, mental, and personality traits are characteristic of gifted children as a class, and what sort of adult the typical gifted child becomes," included very few from racial minorities or unskilled labor groups.[3] The 223-item bibliography in the 1951 publication of the American Association for Gifted Children, *The Gifted Child*, included three items that dealt with the intelligence of Negroes. The annotation for one entry, a 1948 article in *Scientific Monthly*, read as follows:

Points to studies showing that a considerable number of Negro children are found at the level of gifted children. The extreme deviates reach the upper limits attained by white children. Believes that race *per se* (as represented by the American Negro) is not a limiting factor in intelligence, but that the common assumption of inferiority of the Negro race and cultural limitations restricts motivation and achievement even among the brightest.[4]

Although there were very few articles dealing with racial or ethnic minorities and gifted education, beginning in the 1930s a number of studies probed the discrepancies in achievement among various socioeconomic classes. For example, in his 1948 Inglis Lecture, sociologist Allison Davis examined differences among social classes in the United States with respect to their impact on the basic socialization and academic achievement of the child. Davis posed two questions and answered them affirmatively:

1. Does the public school emphasize a range of mental problems and skills which is too narrow to develop most of the abilities necessary for attainment even in middle-class culture itself?

2. Does the public school select a range of mental problems and skills which is so narrow that the school fails to develop much of the mental potential of lower-class pupils?[5]

Beginning in the late 1930s, the Educational Policies Commission (EPC) issued publications reviewing significant educational issues and proposing policies. In 1944, the Commission published a volume titled *Education for All American Youth*, followed by *Education for All American Children* in 1948.[6] These reports pointed out the common needs of students as well as the differences among them and proposed "that a common core of experiences should be shared by *all* students in elementary and secondary schools and that these students should have differentiated opportunities to meet their varied needs."[7] Two years later, the EPC issued another policy paper that it described as an extension of the earlier volumes, in which it observed that "the educational needs of individuals who have superior intellectual capacity and of those who possess special talents in high degree differ in some important respects from the needs of other individuals."[8] The Commission was convinced that "the gifted members of the total school population constitute a minority which is too largely neglected."[9]

The EPC saw the changes in American society—"the closing of the frontier, the urbanization and mechanization of American life, the increased complexity of our economic life and our culture"—resulting in a greater need for higher education and specialization. The public schools, the EPC report noted, carried an especially heavy responsibility for nurturing social mobility:

The public schools can, and should, seek to diminish the force of such handicaps (i.e., limited financial resources) by giving all gifted children and youth—and particularly to those who are handicapped by disadvantageous family background—the kind of education, the guidance, and the incentive that they need in order to prepare themselves for roles of leadership in American life.[10]

The Commission lamented the waste of talent in American life that had occurred and was continuing to occur: "That a large amount of human talent possessed by individuals now living is lost through stultification and isolation can be convincingly demonstrated—although admittedly the precise dimensions of loss defy measurements."[11] It asserted that, in shaping policy to reduce waste of talent potential, it was important not only to know the causes—economic, social, psychological, and educational—but also where such waste most frequently occurs—in low-income groups, rural groups, and minorities. Pointing to discriminatory practices that minorities endure, the report observed:

Lacking both incentive and opportunity, the probabilities are very great that, however superior one's gifts may be, he will rarely live a life of high achievement. Follow-up studies of highly gifted young Negroes, for instance, reveal a shocking waste of talent—a waste that adds an incalculable amount to the price of prejudice in this country.[12]

The EPC's policy recommendations covered a range of ways of dealing with talent potential presently "lost to society through underdevelopment, underuse, or misuse," and attributable to economic barriers, "social attitudes that tend to lower both incentive and opportunity for gifted children of families with low economic status," mental illness and emotional adjustments, and the failure of schools "to identify, to challenge, to hold, or to educate adequately some of their gifted children."[13]

The Educational Policies Commission report was significant because it contemplated the changing conditions in post World War II society, examined the education of the gifted in the context of providing adequate and appropriate education for *all* children and youth and, in highlighting the waste of talent among low-income and minority students, challenged schools and colleges to become "more effective agencies for the conservation and development of human talent."[14]

These same themes were taken up by the Commission on Human Resources and Advanced Training, a group established by the Conference Board of Associated Research Councils in 1947. In its 1954 report titled *America's Resources of Specialized Talent*, the Commission asserted:

The democratic ideal is one of equal opportunity; within that ideal it is both individually advantageous and socially desirable for each person to make the best possible use of his talents. But equal opportunity does not mean equal accomplishment or identical use. . . . Along with moral and legal and political equality goes respect for proper use of excellence.[15]

On the basis of a number of comprehensive studies, the Commission on Human Resources concluded that the nation was wasting much of its intellectual talent by not providing appropriate education for its brightest students, "whether they come from the farm or city, from the slum section or the country-club area, regardless of color or religious or economic differences, but not regardless of ability."[16]

The Commission analyzed the potential supply of talent, not from a supply and demand basis, but rather in terms of how much talent is not being utilized and how much insight could be acquired about human potential that the nation was failing to acquire. The analysis of the potential supply focused on factors that affected performance on college entrance examinations since higher education was viewed as critical in talent development. With respect to talent waste among Negroes—the term in use at that time—the Commission concluded that:

. . . there is no evidence of a significant difference in ability between white and Negro children at early ages. As they grow older, white children tend to make higher scores on intelligence tests than do Negro children. But most of the evidence indicates that this difference can be explained by the differential schooling, opportunity, and social and cultural conditions which affect the two groups. A smaller percentage of Negro than of white children of the highest ability get the kinds of education, encouragement, and intellectual stimulation which permit them, as adults, to work at the level of their high potential. If America is wasting a portion of its intellectual potential in talented white youth, it is wasting an even larger percentage of the Negro potential.[17]

The Commission focused its recommendations on ways of increasing the college-going rate from all races and socioeconomic groups so that more will develop their talent potential, and on better utilization of educated specialists. The key to increasing America's resources for specialized talents was to increase college attendance of all student populations, especially those from low socioeconomic and minority groups.

At about the same time, Columbia University's Conservation of Human Resources Project issued a series of reports, including one by Eli Ginzberg et al. entitled *The Negro Potential* and another by Douglas Bray dealing with *Issues in the Study of Talent*. Ginzberg and his associates appraised Negro potential and characterized it as the nation's largest untapped talent pool.[18] The Bray report observed that researchers had moved away from the concept that superior performance was primarily a function of innate ability and toward the recognition "that innate potential does not always result in developed talent and that superior performance depends upon more than talent."[19] The principal conclusion reached from a review of research was that:

superior performance in any society is limited by the number of individuals with a high order of intelligence but that in our society the number of such individuals could be substantially increased through improving the opportunities for members of the lower socioeconomic classes to become interested in and to acquire a good education.[20]

It was the challenge of the Cold War with the Soviet Union—the need for trained, specialized manpower that was to be nurtured mainly through college and university programs—that defined talent needs and "superior performance." The drive was intensified to identify students with potential for college success and to provide opportunities for them to attend institutions of higher education.

A variety of programs were initiated to increase college attendance. For example, the National Merit Scholarship Program (NMSP) was created in 1955 "to champion the able student—whoever he might be, from whatever stratum of society, no matter what career or college he might aspire to, from large school or small, public or private, rich town or poor." The NMSP aimed at identifying and recognizing the most able secondary school students—defined as the top 2 percent on an academic ability scale—and encouraging and enabling them to attend the college of their choice. Only the NMSP "finalists" received financial support but simply being designated a semifinalist or receiving a letter of commendation was found to encourage and facilitate college attendance.

In its report at the end of the first decade, after having appointed some 11,000 Merit Scholars, the NMSC highlighted the talent loss through underdevelopment of intellectual potential, noting that:

Such underdevelopment is more and more pronounced going down the socioeconomic ladder, and reaches almost disaster proportions in culturally deprived groups subject to discrimination, the obvious example being the Negro American population. The student from lower socioeconomic circumstances is appreciably less likely to enlarge his native gifts during the primary and secondary school years. Accordingly, as a high school junior [the point at which the NMSC test is taken] he is unlikely to place in the uppermost 1 percent at all, whatever his potential may have been. His gifts have been dissipated, perhaps in acute measure and probably irretrievably, and both he and the nation will suffer from the consequences of the loss.[21]

To confront the problem, the NMSC initiated a separate, parallel competition that it called the National Achievement Scholarship Program (NASP) to provide scholarships for black students. In the first year (fall of 1964), the NMSC invited all of the nation's high schools to nominate their outstanding black students, providing no guidance regarding a definition of "outstanding." A total of 1,280 schools nominated 4,288 students from which a committee selected 629 finalists. A second committee then selected 224 NASP Scholars who were awarded four-year scholarships plus stipends.[22] For the third NASP competition two years later, the process was modified and black students were identified through two methods: (1) high schools were again invited to nominate talented black students and (2) high-scoring black students on the National Merit Scholarship Qualifying Test (NMSQT) were identified. Of 5,624 students, about 20 percent were identified by nomination only, another 20 percent by test only, and the remainder by both test and nomination.[23]

Over the years, National Merit Scholarship Corporation studies have provided important insights about the characteristics of program participants, their college attendance, and college success. By 1970, both black and nonblack able youth were attending college at a rate three times that of 1955. Dealing as it did with such small numbers, the National Merit program alone obviously did not account for this escalation in college attendance for able youth. However, that program illustrates the shift from concern to programmatic efforts to develop talent potential—talent defined broadly as the ability to succeed in college or university programs.

Sputnik, the War on Poverty, and Talent Development

Following the Soviet Union success with Sputnik in 1957, Congress passed the National Defense Education Act (NDEA) of 1958 which aimed at attaining excellence in mathematics and science through curriculum reform, materials development, and preservice and in-service teacher education. Although NDEA was not limited to gifted students, that population certainly profited from those upgrading efforts. However, as Tannenbaum put it:

[With few exceptions], the national talent hunt failed to penetrate the socially disadvantaged minorities whose records of school achievement were well below national norms and whose children with high potential were much harder to locate because their environments provided too little of the requisite encouragement and opportunity to fulfill whatever promise they may have shown under other circumstances.[24]

In the mid-1960s educators and the nation as a whole "discovered" poverty and the presence of "culturally different" children and youth in the schools, and the significant gap between the academic achievement levels of the advantaged and disadvantaged. President Johnson's Great Society program with its "War on Poverty" in the mid-1960s spawned a plethora of program efforts aimed at reversing the pattern of underachievement of minority and disadvantaged children. A major program stimulus was Title I of the Elementary and Secondary Education Act of 1965, aimed at assisting local school districts with economically disadvantaged populations.

The thousands of ESEA Title I and state-supported programs were focused primarily on enhancing the basic skills—reading, mathematics, writing—of the lowest achievers and not on the potentially more able or "gifted" among minority and economically disadvantaged. Relatively few programs were directed at identifying and developing talent potential among economically disadvantaged and minority groups. These included publicly and privately funded programs that provided for instructional, counseling, financial, mentoring, and other types of support. Some illustrations of those programs follow:

The College Discovery and Development Program, a partnership of the New York City Board of Education and the City University of New York, aimed "to prepare educationally and economically disadvantaged and underachieving students to meet the standards associated with college admission, to provide an enriched intensified high school experience, change attitudes concerning success, motivate students toward self-growth and development, raise the aspiration level, and stimulate the students toward individual achievement."[25]

Upward Bound was a federally funded program "designed to reach low-income high school students who have potential for successfully completing a postsecondary program but who, due to inadequate preparation or lack of motivation, are prevented from seeking higher education or from meeting conventional criteria for admission to college, university, or technical institute."[26]

A Better Chance, Inc. arranges for minority youngsters of outstanding ability and motivation to complete their secondary school education at one of the "better" independent or public schools. ABC coordinates the network for identifying gifted disadvantaged (minority) youth, placing them, and providing them with support.

Special searches and programs were initiated to find the especially able minority youth in the areas of mathematics and science. Each year hundreds of colleges, universities, laboratories, and industries provide special Saturday, after-school, and summer opportunities for minority youngsters who show promise in mathematics, science, or engineering. However, these programs reach only a small number of students and tap only a small portion of the pool of potential talent.

The 1950s and 1960s were marked by massive efforts to desegregate or to create racial balance in schools and to reverse the spiral of futility and underachievement among minorities and the economically disadvantaged. Such programs included a variety of attempts to increase the flow of talent to institutions of higher education by improving the quality of education at the pre-college stages.

The Beginnings of Sustained Efforts for the Gifted and Talented

In 1971, the U.S. Commissioner of Education, Sidney P. Marland, Jr., submitted a status report on education of gifted and talented children in response to a 1970 Congressional mandate expressed in Public Law 91-230, Section 806. The law directed the Commissioner to define "gifted and talented" for purposes of federal education programs and to ascertain the "extent to which special educational assistance programs are necessary or useful to meet the needs of gifted and talented children."[27]

The definition established by the Commissioner's advisory committee was a broad one: "Children capable of high performance include those with demonstrated achievement and/or potential ability in any of the following areas, singly or in combination: (1) general intellectual ability, (2) specific academic aptitude, (3) creative or productive thinking, (4) leadership ability, (5) visual and performing arts, and (6) psychomotor ability."[28] Thus, what became known as the "Marland

definition" or the "U.S. Office definition" broadened the concept of
giftedness and talent beyond the traditional parameters of high intelligence.

The Marland Report noted that "Differentiated education for the
gifted and talented is presently perceived as a very low priority at federal, state, and most local levels of government and educational
administration," and that "Existing services to the gifted and talented
do not reach large and significant subpopulations (e.g., minorities and
disadvantaged) and serve only a very small percentage of the gifted
and talented population generally."[29] The clear conclusion of the Marland Report was that the needs of the gifted and talented were not
being met well in the nation's schools and the needs of the gifted and
talented among minority populations were being met even less well.

The Marland Report observed: "Since the full range of human talents is represented in all the races of man and in all socioeconomic levels, it is unjust and unproductive to allow social or racial background
to affect the treatment of an individual."[30] A number of studies completed during the 1950s and 1960s found that the schools' failure to
seek giftedness and talents within minority populations had "restricted
the educational opportunities open to them."[31] The report cited a 1957
study, for example, that estimated that only one in ten of the eligible
black population attended college and the majority attended poorly
endowed black colleges. A 1963 study by the same group reported that
only 1 percent of the college population was black.[32]

The Marland Report proved to be a watershed for programming
efforts for gifted and talented children. The definition established by
the Commissioner's Advisory Panel included the statement that:
"These are children who require differentiated educational programs
and/or services beyond those normally provided by the regular school
program in order to realize their contribution to self and society."[33]
The report stimulated state and local activities on an unprecedented
level. By 1990, all fifty states had formulated policies in the form of
legislation, regulations, rules, or guidelines supporting education of
the gifted. Of the thirty-two states that had enacted legislation mandating services to the gifted—only two had enacted those mandates
prior to the Marland Report. Of the states that enacted discretionary
or permissive support for programs for the gifted, only three had
passed legislation prior to the 1970s. Clearly, federal policy stemming
from the report had positive effects on state and local policies for
identifying and nurturing talent potential.

State policies varied widely with respect to definitions, identification procedures, programming, differentiated curriculum and instruction, counseling and other support services, teacher education and certification, evaluation and accountability, and funding, but in different ways all fifty states acknowledged that gifted pupils can and should be identified, that they require differentiated educational experiences and opportunities, and that additional resources may be needed in order to develop talent potential into talented performance.

In the two decades since the Marland Report, a number of developments have had an impact on talent identification and nurturance efforts including: (1) the emergence of new concepts of the nature of giftedness and of multiple types of giftedness and (2) increased attention on what are called "underrepresented or underserved populations"—the economically disadvantaged, racial and/or ethnic minorities, and those with limited English proficiency.

A 1974 conference that focused on the educational problems of culturally different gifted children identified a number of barriers and problems that impeded the identification and development of the talent potential of these students. These barriers ranged from those in the child's contact with the school environment; to the general problems of an unresponsive educational system; to the "child's ecology and his cultural values, as well as the types of social pressures that influence him"; to decision makers whose policies affect the establishment of support for special programs.[34]

The conferees argued for a new definition of the term "gifted" that would not rely only on high performance on intelligence tests and formal academic achievement. Such reliance limits the range of abilities of students who are chosen for gifted programs, denies opportunities to those who are not academic achievers, and discourages students from developing their potential in nonacademic areas where their abilities and achievements are neither valued nor recognized. They criticized the use of the IQ test as the single index of intellectual success, viewing "the inability to accept cultural pluralism . . . [as] part of the problem of education's inability to accept any substantial measure of cultural pluralism."[35] The conferees called for learning environments that were more open and community oriented, responding to the "diverse skills and interests and kinesthetic modes of expression which many culturally different children have carefully nurtured."[36] With the traditional rigid learning environment and inflexible curriculum failing disadvantaged students, the report called for major changes in curriculum design that would take into account the cultural backgrounds of children; provide content that would advance the skills necessary for upward mobility and increased options; furnish opportunities for active participation in expressive dimensions rather than passive listening; open opportunities for higher education; and deliberately enhance student self-concepts.[37] They proposed that teacher education programs should make teachers specialists in certain areas, enhance understanding of cultural diversity, and augment teaching strategies and styles. The group urged fuller use of community resources "the boundaries of the school should be the boundaries of the community."[38]

A Nation at Risk, the widely circulated 1983 report of the National Commission on Excellence in Education, was one of the many documents that launched still another education reform movement.[39] Included in the charge to the National Commission was a directive to do all things "needed to define the problems of and the barriers to attaining greater levels of excellence in American education.[40] As Boyer observed in the report on the study he directed, American schools were being "severely buffeted by changes in the community, in family life, and in student attitudes."[41]

Although *A Nation at Risk* had described the crisis in American education most dramatically ("Our once unchallenged preeminence in commerce, industry, science, and technology is being overtaken by competitors throughout the world"), it and the plethora of other national, state, and local reports gave little or no attention to the identification and nurturing of high ability students whose special talents might reverse what the report described as "the rising tide of mediocrity."[42]

In the decade of the 1980s and into the 1990s, every aspect of education and schooling—including curriculum, educational standards, testing, teacher education, staff development, school management and decision making—came under review and revision in efforts to improve educational achievement. By the 1990s, national and "world-class" standards had become part of the nation's goals to be attained by the year 2000.

The attainment of "equity and excellence" became one of the main themes of the reform reports of the 1980s. But, as I have noted elsewhere, a narrow definition of excellence prevailed:

The term "excellence" became one of the shibboleths of the reform movement. Excellence came to mean "higher standards," which were defined as tougher academic requirements, reduction or elimination of electives (especially "soft subjects"), more mathematics and science, more homework, more tests, tighter discipline, and longer days and school years.[43]

As for equity, the reform reports of the 1980s tended to ignore any particular needs of the poor and minorities except for the universal condemnation by reformers of the practice of tracking and, by extension, all ability grouping. These widely used practices were criticized as limiting access to knowledge for disadvantaged children who were overrepresented in the lower tracks. Some reformers, such as Boyer, advocated a single track that provided general education for all, together with a pattern of electives that would keep options open for both further education and work.[44] Other reformers, such as Adler, viewed a multitrack system as "an abominable discrimination" aimed at different goals for different students. As for the gifted, Adler argued that the quality of the Paideia curriculum he advocated would make special provisions for the more able unnecessary.[45]

There were numerous programs aimed at increasing access to higher education for disadvantaged populations as a way of attaining both equity and excellence. The College Board's Educational EQuality Project (EQ) illustrates one such effort. Trying "to hear and respond to the imperatives of equity as well as those of excellence," EQ planners asserted: "Rather than treating everyone identically, equity often requires taking into account and acting on the fact that not all students enjoy the same advantages. . . . [The Project] made special efforts to address explicitly situations of prior disadvantage."[46] The EQ Project identified "equitable academic standards," defining "what *all* students need to know and be able to do to prepare for college," and, through the preparation of materials, the provision of staff development programs, and the support of school-college collaboratives, tried to increase the number and diversity of students prepared for success in college.[47] The College Board undertook an aggressive advocacy effort with teachers, students, parents and decision makers to encourage "understanding, acceptance, and action" regarding the academic standards. The Project specifically identified a target population of minority students attending urban schools who were likely to be overlooked and underprepared and gave special attention to ways of increasing their college attendance.

Another College Board program provides a second example. Since 1955, the College Board's Advanced Placement Program (APP), has enabled high school students to complete college-level courses with credit or placement or both being granted to students whose achievement on the examinations meets the colleges' standards. In recent years, the AP Program has made specific efforts to increase participation by minority students, believing that experiencing "the academic rigors of college . . . fosters self-motivation, confidence, responsibility, and self-reliance" and increases college-going.[48] Since 1986, participation by African-American students increased from 3 to 4 percent of the total; by Hispanic students, from 4 to 7 percent; and by American Indian and Eskimo students, from 0.3 to 0.4 percent. The increase for Asian-American students during this period was from 11 to 14 percent. Although there has been a growth in minority participation, the participation of inner-city students is still a matter of concern. The AP Program is not limited to intellectually gifted students; others can "succeed through application—a result, perhaps of the rigorous nature of AP courses and examinations and the enthusiasm and dedication of AP teachers."[49]

A 1987-88 study was undertaken for the U.S. Department of Education to analyze districtwide and schoolwide efforts to develop the academic skills and creative talents of highly able, economically disadvantaged students in mathematics and science in order to identify programs and strategies to "provide our most promising disadvantaged students with opportunities to develop their academic potential, especially in the areas that affect our nation's ability to compete internationally in a global economy."[50]

The findings indicated little effort to develop talent among disadvantaged children in schools where low expectations, boredom, and lack of support were common. Among the findings were these:

Minority students are underrepresented in programs designed to serve gifted and talented students. Although minorities make up 30 percent of public school enrollment, they represent less than 20 percent of the students selected for gifted and talented programs;

Whereas students from low-income backgrounds comprise 20 percent of the student population, they make up only 4 percent of those students who perform at the highest levels on standardized tests (those who score at the 95th percentile or above);

High school seniors from disadvantaged families (in which the mother did not complete high school) are less than half as likely to have participated in gifted and talented programs as more advantaged seniors; and

Disadvantaged students are far less likely to be enrolled in academic programs that can prepare them for college and are about half as likely to take coursework in advanced mathematics and science than more advanced students. Only 2 percent of high school seniors from poor families take calculus, whereas approximately 7 percent of those from more advantaged backgrounds do.[51]

The study found that able disadvantaged students require extra instruction in the way of both enriched and accelerated courses to develop their talents—activities "designed to bolster students' current knowledge of subject content, extend their capacities for learning, and enhance their life experiences."[52] The analysis of case studies from nine sites disclosed a number of effective approaches for serving highly able disadvantaged students. Similar strategies were used for identifying, selecting, instructing, and supporting these students. Programs held high expectations, provided enriched and accelerated curricula, and utilized community resources. The schools created supportive environments for learning in often inhospitable surroundings. Noting that the case studies reflected a small sample of the efforts underway to serve highly able disadvantaged students, the researchers hoped that the strategies would encourage other schools to intensify their endeavors on behalf of this underrepresented population.

The purpose of the Jacob K. Javits Gifted and Talented Students Education Act of 1988 (P.L. 100-297), mentioned at the beginning of this chapter, was to provide national leadership for efforts to identify and serve gifted and talented students. Between 1989 and 1993, seventy-five programs were supported by Javits grants, most of them focused on minority disadvantaged children or those with limited English backgrounds. The grants were for projects that identified gifted and talented students, developed challenging curricula, sponsored summer institutes for top students, expanded educational opportunities by collaborating with business and industry, provided preservice and in-service training for teachers, and provided technical assistance for dissemination of information regarding services available to the gifted and talented.

A 1992 survey by Coleman and Gallagher of state policies related to the identification of gifted students, found that states were beginning to recognize multiple types of giftedness—"intelligence (IQ), achievement, creativity, artistic talent, leadership, critical thinking, psychomotor skills, psychosocial, and understanding one's cultural heritage"—and that this recognition had important implications for identifying "gifted students from special populations who sometimes are overlooked due to narrow identification criteria and heavy reliance on IQ scores and performance measures."[53] Coleman and Gallagher report that forty-three states have policies that encourage schools to serve minority and disadvantaged students. "In thirty-nine states, different criteria can be used to identify students from special populations, seven states use some form of quota system for inclusion, and twelve states allow trial placement or preplacement experiences to assist with decisions.[54]

The Case for Developing America's Talents

In 1993, the Department of Education issued its first report on the gifted and talented since 1972. In his foreword, Secretary of Education Richard Riley observed that there is still a "quiet crisis" in how America educates its top students and noted: "Youngsters with gifts and talents that range from mathematical to musical are still not challenged to work to their full potential. Our neglect of these students makes it impossible for Americans to compete in a global economy demanding their skills."[55]

Spelling out the bases for the charge that "there is mounting evidence that gifted and talented students do not learn as much as they could and compare unfavorably with students in other countries," the report noted that economically disadvantaged students were significantly underserved.[56] In current gifted education programs, 9 percent of student participants are from the bottom quartile of family income compared to 47 percent from the top quartile.[57] The report noted that:

The talents of disadvantaged and minority children have been especially neglected. Almost one in four American children lives in poverty, representing an enormous pool of untapped talent. Yet most programs for these children focus on solving the problems they bring to school, rather than on challenging them to develop their strengths. It is sometimes assumed that children from unpromising backgrounds are not capable of outstanding accomplishment.[58]

Based on emerging views on the nature of intelligence and talent derived from neuroscience and cognitive psychology, the report proposed a new definition, one based on the Javits legislation:

Children and youth with outstanding talent perform or show the potential for performing at remarkably high levels of accomplishment when compared with others of their age, experience, or environment.

These children and youth exhibit high performance capability in intellectual, creative, and/or artistic areas, possess an unusual leadership capacity, or excel in specific academic fields. They require services or activities not ordinarily provided by the schools.

Outstanding talents are present in children and youth from all cultural groups, across all economic strata, and in all areas of human endeavor.[59]

The report recommended (1) establishing challenging curriculum standards, (2) establishing high-level learning opportunities, (3) ensuring access to early childhood education, (4) expanding opportunities for economically disadvantaged and minority children, (5) encouraging appropriate teacher training and technical assistance, and (6) matching world performance. It maintained that:

Special efforts are required to overcome the barriers to achievement that many economically disadvantaged and minority students face. Stronger preschool programs and a stronger regular curriculum for all students will aid in this effort. In addition, schools and communities must develop strategies to serve students from underrepresented groups.[60]

In its request for reauthorization of the Elementary and Secondary Education Act (Improving America's Schools Act of 1993), the Department of Education proposed major shifts in the direction of a number of programs. With respect to the Javits Act, the Department proposed that it be redirected to "demonstrate that programs and strategies for gifted and talented students can be used to help all students in a school to meet challenging state performance standards" while still giving priority "to demonstration projects in schools with high concentrations of poverty."[61] The proposal for reauthorization would:

Target grants to schoolwide efforts to provide challenging curricula and enriching instruction (often offered in gifted and talented programs) *to all students*; at least half of the grants will go to high-poverty schools. Efforts will focus on improving the curriculum and educational environment of schools and on setting high expectations for all students in core subject areas, including high expectations for students who excel. By the end of the third year of a grant, each project would have to expand gifted and talented programs to serve all students in a school.[62]

In the mid-90s, the following observations can be made regarding the identification and development of America's talent:

1. The past two decades have witnessed significant research regarding the nature of human abilities that has resulted in a Copernican

shift in the conceptions of giftedness and talent. As the Department of Education report pointed out:

Research has challenged the long-held view of intelligence as a fixed, narrow concept measurable by one test. It is now understood that intelligence is complex, takes many forms, and therefore requires that many criteria be used to measure it.[63]

Educators and other decision makers are now attempting to identify and nurture diverse talents using multiple criteria, procedures, and processes.

2. As schools have become more culturally, ethnically, racially, and socioeconomically diverse, it has been recognized that some populations—particularly economically disadvantaged and minority children—have not had their talent potential adequately identified nor developed. This recognition that youngsters are being underserved and not provided with adequate opportunities to turn their potential into talented performance has not yet led to the elimination of the barriers to achievement. What has occurred is a recognition that in talent development, culture matters very much, that context within which talent potential thrives is important, that gifted programs of the past are not effective with today's diverse populations and diverse talents, and that schools are just beginning to understand the need for strategies and programs that take the sociocultural context into account.

3. The programs and strategies used with the gifted and talented are increasingly being viewed as a means for raising the academic performance of all students. The Department of Education has argued that the type of instruction and curricula developed for and used in gifted and talented education raises the achievement of all students:

Several of the Javits projects use such approaches to assess students' academic strengths, provide them with enriched learning opportunities, and give special opportunities to students who excel. These projects are promising models for raising standards for all students while providing appropriate opportunities for students who excel.[64]

Educators of the gifted and talented have long been confronted with the question: Isn't this program or activity for the gifted good for all children? However they have responded to that question in the past, increasingly they will now face two tasks. One is to help raise the achievement of all students by providing challenging content and problem-solving techniques that were previously afforded to only a relatively small number of identified gifted students. The second task is to continue to provide appropriate opportunities for students who excel. Is the concept of differentiated curriculum and differentiated experiences still relevant and, if so, how is it implemented if gifted and talented programs are to serve all students in a school? The question educators grapple with is, Can schools provide a gifted education for every child and, if so, what does a gifted education mean?

4. As the reform movement has moved through its many metamorphoses during the past decade, a number of dilemmas have arisen. On the one hand there has been a sharp increase in programmatic efforts aimed at upgrading the quality of education and extending equality of access to educational opportunities, especially for those for whom such access has been limited in the past. The Javits projects and a number of other programs exemplify this thrust. On the other hand, there has been a sustained, intense press to eliminate all kinds of ability grouping and tracking on the grounds that such strategies contribute to inequity, especially for minority and low-income students. One consequence of this "detracking" movement has been to eliminate provisions for the gifted that use some form of grouping and substitute instead heterogeneous grouping and cooperative learning.

The paradox is that at a time when schools are beginning to open up opportunities for the identification and development of diverse talents in a diverse population, a detracking movement will constrict those opportunities. History has shown that achieving the twin goals of equity and excellence is not easy, but when the nation is beginning to make some progress toward their attainment, the nurturing of talent potential to talented performance may be impeded by doctrinaire positions on the controversies surrounding ability grouping.

NOTES

1. National Commission on Excellence in Education, *A Nation at Risk: The Imperative for Educational Reform* (Washington, DC: US. Government Printing Office, 1983), p. 13.

2. Guy M. Whipple, Editor, *The Education of the Gifted*, Twenty-third Yearbook of the National Society for the Study of Education, Part 1 (Bloomington, IL: Public School Publishing Company, 1924), pp. 389-443.

3. Lewis M. Terman and Melita H. Oden, "The Stanford Studies of the Gifted," in *The Gifted Child*, edited by Paul Witty (Boston: D. C. Heath, 1951), p. 21.

4. Elsie H. Martins, "Annotated Bibliography on Gifted Children," in *The Gifted Child*, edited by Paul Witty (Boston: D. C. Heath, 1951), p. 284.

5. Allison Davis, *Social Class Influences upon Learning* (Cambridge, MA: Harvard University Press, 1948), p. 89.

6. Educational Policies Commission, *Education for All American Youth* (Washington, DC: National Association and American Association of School Administrators, 1944); idem, *Education for All American Children* (Washington, DC: National Education Association and American Association of School Administrators, 1948).

7. Educational Policies Commission, *Education for the Gifted* (Washington, DC: National Education Association and American Association of School Administrators, 1950), p. iii.

8. Ibid.

9. Ibid.

10. Ibid., p. 5.

11. Ibid., p. 14.

12. Ibid., p. 33.

13. Ibid., p. 86.

14. Ibid.

15. Dael Wolfle, *America's Resources of Specialized Talent* (New York: Harper and Brothers, 1954), p. 6.

16. Ibid.

17. Ibid., p. 169.

18. Eli Ginzberg et al., *The Negro Potential* (New York: Columbia University Press, 1956).

19. Douglas W. Bray, *Issues in the Study of Talent* (New York: King's Crown Press, 1954), p. 51.

20. Ibid.

21. National Merit Scholarship Corporation, *The Merit Program: The First Decade* (Evanston, IL: National Merit Scholarship Corporation, 1965), pp. 2-3.

22. Roy J. Roberts and Robert C. Nichols, *Participants in the National Achievement Scholarship Program for Negroes* (Evanston, IL: National Merit Scholarship Corporation, 1966).

23. Warren S. Blumenfeld, *Selecting Talented Negro Students: Nominations vs. Test Performance* (Evanston, IL: National Merit Scholarship Corporation, 1969).

24. Abraham J. Tannenbaum, "Pre-Sputnik to Post-Watergate Concern about the Gifted," in *The Gifted and the Talented: Their Education and Development*, edited by A. Harry Passow, Seventy-eighth Yearbook of the National Society for the Study of Education, Part 1 (Chicago: University of Chicago Press, 1979), p. 14.

25. Office of Special Programs, City University of New York, *Discovering and Developing the College Potential of Disadvantaged High School Youth: A Longitudinal Study of the College Discovery and Development Program* (New York: City University of New York, 1978).

26. Graham J. Burkheimer et al., "A National Study of the Upward Bound Program: Analysis, Major Findings, and Implications" (Paper presented at the Annual Meeting of the American Educational Research Association, San Francisco, April 1976).

27. Sidney P. Marland, Jr., *Education of the Gifted and Talented*, vol. 1, *Report to the Congress of the United States by the U.S. Commissioner of Education*; vol. 2, *Background Papers Submitted to the U.S. Office of Education* (Washington, DC: U.S. Government Printing Office, 1971).

28. Ibid., vol. 1, p. ix.

29. Ibid., vol. 1, p. xi.

30. Ibid., vol. 1, pp. II, 9-10.

31. Ruth A. Martinson, "Research on the Gifted and Talented: Its Implications for Education," in Sidney P. Marland, Jr., *Education of the Gifted and the Talented*, vol. 2, *Background Papers* (Washington, DC: U.S. Government Printing Office, 1971), pp. 2-27.

32. Richard Plaut, *Searching and Salvaging Talent among Socially Disadvantaged Populations* (New York: National Scholarship Service Fund for Negro Students, 1963).

33. Marland, *Education of the Gifted and Talented*, vol. 1, p. ix.

34. James J. Gallagher and Lucretia Kinney, *Talent Delayed-Talent Denied: The Culturally Different Gifted Child* (Reston, VA: Foundation for Exceptional Children, 1974).

35. Ibid., p. 6.

36. Ibid., p. 7.

37. Ibid., p. 18.

38. Ibid., p. 26.

39. National Commission on Excellence in Education, *A Nation at Risk*.

40. Ibid., p. 40.

41. Ernest L. Boyer, *High School: A Report on Secondary Education in America* (New York: Harper and Row, 1983), p. xi.

42. National Commission on Excellence in Education, *A Nation at Risk*, p. 1.

43. A. Harry Passow, "Present and Future Directions in School Reform," in *Schooling for Tomorrow: Directing Reforms to Issues that Count*, edited by Thomas J. Sergiovanni and John H. Moore (Boston: Allyn and Bacon, 1989), p. 16.

44. Boyer, *High School*.

45. Mortimer Adler, *The Paideia Proposal: An Educational Manifesto* (New York: Macmillan, 1982), p. 41.

46. Office of Academic Affairs, The College Board, *Educational EQuality Project: Internal Self-Study 1980-1989* (New York: College Board, 1989), p. 13.

47. Ibid., p. 4.

48. Advanced Placement Program, *1992-93 AP Yearbook: Challenging Students to Reaching for Excellence* (New York: College Board, 1993), p. 10.

49. Ibid., p. 3.

50. Judith A. Alamprese and Wendy J. Erlanger, *No Gift Wasted: Effective Strategies for Educating Highly Able, Disadvantaged Students in Mathematics and Science*, vol. 1, *Findings*; vol. 2, *Case Studies* (Washington, DC: U.S. Department of Education, Office of Planning, Budget, and Evaluation, 1989), vol. 2, p. 1.

51. Amprese and Erlanger, *No Gift Wasted*, vol. 1, p. 5.

52. Ibid., p. viii.

53. Mary Ruth Coleman and James J. Gallagher, *Report on State Policies Related to the Identification of Gifted Students* (Chapel Hill, NC: Gifted Education Policy Studies Program, University of North Carolina, 1992), p. 21.

54. Ibid., p. 18.

55. U.S. Department of Education, *National Excellence: A Case for Developing America's Talent* (Washington, DC: U.S. Government Printing Office, 1993), p. iii.

56. Ibid., p. 6.

57. Ibid., p. 17.

58. Ibid., p. 5.

59. Ibid., p. 26.

60. Ibid., p. 28.

61. U.S. Department of Education, *Improving America's Schools Act of 1993: The Reauthorization of the Elementary and Secondary Education Act and Amendments to Other Acts* (Washington, DC: U.S. Department of Education, 1993), Title III-6.

62. Ibid., Title III-7.

63. U.S. Department of Education, *National Excellence*, p. 25.

64. U.S. Department of Education, *Improving America's School Act of 1993*, Title III-7.

Section Two
STRATEGIES FOR EDUCATION
CHANGING POPULATIONS IN
THE SCHOOLS

Introduction

Particularly since World War II, policies and programs developed for educating low-income, minority, immigrant, and linguistically different youth no longer presuppose that they are mentally defective or lack character. That was the way an earlier social Darwinian and moralistic culture regarded some groups in the society. Recognizing that an entire segment of the population was not being well-served by the schools, the federal government created programs to help very young disadvantaged children be more ready for schooling and to compensate older disadvantaged youth for any deficiencies in their educational development that put them in danger of progressive academic failure or limited their future employability.

Three such national strategies are critically examined in chapters in this section. In looking at early childhood education, most signally Head Start, Sharon Lynn Kagan argues strenuously that efforts to help young children develop well are currently "log-jammed in a categorical, fragmented system bereft of political muscle or social strategy." What is more, despite the spread and effectiveness of early childhood education, she finds unresolved policy "tensions" in the programs. Do providers offer what parents want? Should programs be developmental or content-oriented? Should programs serve families as well as children? How can the lack of equity, continuity, and consistency in the programs be overcome? How can an active constituency be mobilized? To what extent should funds be used for direct services and how much should be used to build an infrastructure in early childhood programs?

In a similar vein, Erwin Flaxman, Gary Burnett, and Carol Ascher conclude that despite the government's increasing success in better distributing funds to equalize resources for disadvantaged youth through Title I (later Chapter 1) of the Elementary and Secondary Education Act, the programs have fallen short of their promise. In monitoring and administering the programs the federal government has been preoccupied with devising allocation formulas and funding streams rather than with assuring that the programs provide a quality education. What is more, the programs themselves have "ghettoized" disadvantaged students by removing them from their regular classrooms for special remedial instruction, thus effectively contributing to their progressive educational disadvantage. The authors argue, however, that the promise of these programs may be met by lessons learned from the current school reform efforts, which make the whole school the locus of improvement rather than concentrating on remediation of educational deficiencies of some students. In this way the educational needs of disadvantaged students will be better met because they will not be differentiated from the needs of all other children. "Good instruction and other good educational practices [will be] good for all."

Frederick Doolittle reviews the policy research on second-chance programs for youth. These are governmental employment and training programs that operate outside the traditional kindergarten through twelfth grade setting and are designed for students who have dropped out of school or have not learned enough in schools to be employable. Doolittle's conclusions are sobering. Targeted youth do participate in various education, training, and work-experience program. More of them receive equivalency diplomas than would have been the case had they not participated in the programs. Yet their opportunities for later employment and their earnings are not greater than they would have achieved without participation. What is more, the programs have not proven to be cost effective for the individual taxpayer or the larger society. Doolittle believes, however, that research does not argue for discontinuing the programs, but rather for learning from their success with some groups of youth and for seeking more innovative approaches to the design of second-chance programs.

Erwin Flaxman, Carol Ascher, Sue E. Berryman, and Morton Inger remind us that most students, including those we think of as nontraditional, are overlooked by educational policymakers because of a preoccupation with the most severely disadvantaged and with the gifted and talented students. This "forgotten" student, who will not necessarily drop out nor automatically go on to a four-year college, is often relegated to the general track, to an outmoded vocational education, or is assigned to courses with watered-down academic content. For these students, as well as for all students, the authors argue for an education that integrates academic and technical skills in the curriculum and for a pedagogy that is based on sound principles of cognitive learning. This is a promising approach for eliminating tracking and providing sound learning that can lead to postsecondary education and prepare *all students* for gainful employment in a demanding and changing workplace.

Many argue that the successful education for poor, minority, and linguistically different students requires that the schools satisfy the political and social demands of their communities. Not to do so is tantamount to failing to provide an education for these students. This is a premise of three other chapters in this section.

In her review of curriculum controversies in multicultural education, Christine E. Sleeter maintains that multicultural education must be a process of reforming—and transforming—all the structures and processes of schooling so that the power of all sociocultural groups will be equal. She argues that merely making egalitarian changes in the content of the curriculum and using a variety of teaching techniques that are more sensitive to students' diverse learning styles are not sufficient. Multicultural education must also empower unempowered groups.

In their chapter, Robert Lowe and Harvey Kantor view the failure of plans to desegregate schools to redistribute educational opportunity as a sign that the nation has not responded to the most urgent demand of minority communities for the education of their children. If the equality of educational resources that school desegregation can bring were the norm, particularly in urban schools, we would not need compensatory education to help students overcome educational deficiencies and multicultural education to empower them.

Finally, Charles Glenn looks at the deliberate and legal establishment of separate schooling for minority students—in their best interests—throughout the world. He acknowledges the right of parents to make decisions about the content of the education that their children receive without forfeiting public funds, as long as there is proper government oversight to guarantee that the schools are educationally sound, do not violate constitutional principles or international human rights covenants, and satisfy the requirements of educational laws.

CHAPTER IV

Normalizing Preschool Education: The Illusive Imperative

SHARON L. KAGAN

Listening to today's rhetoric, one might conclude that the care and education of young children in general and poor young children in particular has soared to the apex of the American educational agenda. While there are good reasons to believe this, the reality is that services to America's youngest citizens remained logjammed in an inequitable, categorical, fragmented system bereft of the political muscle or social strategy needed to convert popular rhetoric to reality. In this chapter I will examine recent data to chronicle why changes in the social, demographic, and research context of the nation have made preschool education an imperative despite its political illusiveness. I will suggest that until specific tensions are addressed, significant advances in early care and education are likely to remain remote from reality. I will close by making recommendations for normalizing early childhood services, with the knowledge that only in making such services available for all children will the real needs of the nation's poorest children be met.

Young Children and Early Childhood Services: What the Data Say

So strong is the stated belief that preschool-aged children (ages three to five) should have access to services and so weak and idiosyncratic is the database supporting this view that, in the past several years, attempts to chronicle the nature of early care and education services to young children have mushroomed. Significant efforts to provide better data at the national level have emanated from the U.S. General Accounting Office, the National Education Goals Panel, the National Commission on Children, the Urban Institute, and the combined offices of the U.S. Departments of Education and Health and Human

Sharon L. Kagan is Senior Associate at the Bush Center in Child Development and Social Policy at Yale University.

Services.[1] Reports have also been commissioned by state houses and state legislatures throughout the nation. These data provide a new perspective on the demand, supply, and the match between supply and demand for early care and education.

CHANGING DEMAND

Not surprisingly, studies reveal that more children are in need of out-of-home care as their mothers frequent the work force. Of the nation's 22 million children under the age of six in 1990, 12 million lived in families in which either both parents or the single parent worked.[2] Between 1976 and 1990, the number of children in child care quadrupled.[3] By the spring of 1991, 80 percent of the nation's parents of preschool children reported that their youngsters were being cared for by nonparental figures, were attending early care and education programs, or had received some sort of nonparental care at one point.[4] Unlike past eras, child care is now needed for ever younger and younger children, with the numbers of infants and toddlers in out-of-home care soaring. Willer et al. found that 25 percent of mothers of infants were employed full time and 15 percent part time, putting a total of 40 percent of infants in need of supplemental care.[5]

While demand for early care and education is increasing across all populations of young children, the need for such services is particularly profound among poor children. Of the nation's children under the age of six, nearly one in four lived in poverty in 1991.[6] These children are likely to be members of minority groups. For example, the Hispanic Policy Development Project found that 40 percent of Hispanic children lived in poverty.[7] Young poor children are also likely to live in households headed by a single parent and in areas of concentrated poverty where violence is prevalent.[8] Furthermore, these children are less likely than their middle-class counterparts to see pediatricians, receive dental care and immunizations, and live in homes where their development is nurtured to its fullest.[9] As a result, poor children often enter school bearing social, emotional, physical, and cognitive burdens that impede their development and progress in the educational setting. Worse, the results of early school failure often convert into later school dropout, delinquency, and teen pregnancy.[10]

The dramatic consequences of poverty, coupled with the lack of preschool intervention, have become well known, particularly as the positive effects of early intervention have been publicized. Long-held concern about the harmful effects of child care and early intervention have all but been eradicated, with social scientists demonstrating that high quality care does not harm children and in fact may benefit youngsters across the income spectrum.[11] Study after study has indicated short-term benefits of early care and education, with many also pointing out positive long-term effects[12] and noting considerable cost savings due to decreased likelihood of welfare dependency or incarceration.[13]

While such studies often are based on research from high-quality settings (and as a result are not generalizable to all early childhood programs), the findings have been grasped as a social antidote to poverty. Policymakers are well aware of the social advantages that accrue to low-income children who participate in high-quality preschool programs and have become sensitive to the importance of early educational experiences for such youngsters. Welfare advocates realize that low-income mothers will be unable to escape welfare dependency unless safe, dependable care is available to them during their education, training, and employment. And finally, corporate America, cognizant of the problems of an unprepared work force, has recognized that education begins before formal schooling and has stressed the connection between high quality early experiences and preparation for the work force.[14]

The demand for care has become more sophisticated and specialized as it has increased among parents and across the research, corporate, and policy sectors. Parents have become far more interested in the nature and quality of care, causing such issues to be discussed more frequently and more seriously. For example, parent preferences for different types of programs have developed. Data reveal that most parents of preschool-aged children prefer early care and education services that are center-based as opposed to home-based. In 1991, 53 percent of parents with preschool children receiving care chose center-based programs, while a total of 31 percent chose nonrelative or relative home-based care.[15] African-American and white children were almost equally likely to attend center-based care, while Hispanic preschoolers were less represented in centers.[16] Parents of infants were also less likely to choose center-based care, with only 14 percent enrolling their infants in centers and 20 percent using family day care.[17]

In addition to developing preferences for types of care, parents have begun to specify what they expect from the services they select. Among parents using centers in 1990, 57 percent said provider/staff characteristics (warmth, training) were most important in their choices of centers; 18 percent maintained that the goals of the program were critical; 14 percent indicated that the characteristics of the child's group (size, pupil-teacher ratio) were key; and 11 percent cited characteristics of the program and setting as most important. Among parents using family day care, the numbers were similar, with 68 percent focusing on provider characteristics, 19 percent on the child's group, 8 percent on characteristics of program and setting, 2 percent on the goals of the program, and 3 percent on other factors.[18]

Such demand for and specificity about the quality of early care and education services has been strengthened by a greater emphasis now being placed on readiness for school. Many parents view high quality preschools as preparatory schools for kindergarten—an attitude that may help to account for statistics showing that one half of the children of nonworking mothers regularly use early care and education services.[19]

CHANGING SUPPLY

In addition to establishing clarity of the demand for child care and early education, new data have given us a more precise picture of the supply and funding of care. We now recognize that early care and education is supplied under a variety of auspices, with providers adhering to different rules, regulations, funding amounts and patterns. For example, of all the child care settings in America, 35 percent operate in the for-profit sector and 65 percent in the nonprofit sector. Of the nonprofits, 8 percent are sponsored by public schools, 8 percent by other agencies, 9 percent by Head Start, 15 percent by religious groups, and 25 percent are run independently. Overall in 1990, there were 80,000 regulated centers and 118,000 regulated family day care providers; in addition, there were an estimated 550,000 to 1.1 million nonregulated family day care homes.[20]

Most early care and education services are funded by parental fees, with 40 percent of centers and 17 percent of family day care providers receiving public assistance targeted at low-income children.[21] Subsidized care is also available through Head Start, Title IV of the Social Security Act, and the Child Care and Development Block Grant. Furthermore, the federal government supports early care and education through the Dependent Care Tax Credit, but as indicated by the 1988 tax year, the credit has not been used to its full extent: 22 percent of families earning less than $15,000 a year, 27 percent of families earning $15-$35,000 a year, and one third of families earning over $35,000 a year claimed the tax credit.[22] Taking such statistics into consideration, it has been estimated that early care and education is a five billion dollar industry, with the vast majority of the cost being borne by parents.

Supply of early care and education can be measured in terms of quantity of services, but a more complete picture requires that supply also be considered in terms of quality. For many years, it was thought that poor children in America were supplied with the lowest quality child care and that working class children and their more well-to-do counterparts had access to superior quality care. Recent studies refute these assumptions. Kagan and Newton found that children who were in government centers (predominantly low-income youngsters) actually received higher-quality care than their peers who were enrolled in private nonprofit or for-profit care.[23] The National Child Care Staffing Study found that nonprofit centers (presumably serving more low-income children) had better staff-to-children ratios, more developmentally appropriate activities, and more teaching staff in the classroom than did the for-profit centers.[24] Furthermore, in examining the quality of life in preschool programs targeted at disadvantaged children, Layzer, Goodson, and Moss found that the programs maintained "a level of quality that [could] be characterized as adequate."[25] However, within this study, Head Start programs were among the highest rated in terms of quality. Chapter 1 programs that serve low-income children were found to be of "acceptable" to "good" quality, with few demonstrating poor quality.[26]

THE MEETING OF SUPPLY AND DEMAND

In the beginning of 1990, 88 percent of the spaces in early care and education centers and 82 percent of the spaces in regulated family day care homes were filled. For regulated family day care, the statistics varied regionally with 77 percent of the spaces filled in urban centers, 84 percent filled in suburban areas, and 88 percent filled in rural areas.[27]

The above perspective provides a relatively bright picture, with supply apparently easily meeting demand. But when the cost of care and other financial factors are taken into consideration, the situation appears less encouraging. A U.S. General Accounting Office report in 1993 shows that preschool participation rates for poor children fall below 45 percent in all states. It indicates that about 49 percent of poor four-year-olds, compared with 57 percent of non-poor four-year-olds, participate in preschools,[28] exacerbating the inequities among children in our nation. Reflecting this situation, studies show that subsidized services are not meeting needs in the low-income population. In 1992, even with considerable expansion, Head Start served only 30 percent of all eligible children; underserved populations included children in families with employed mothers, children in the South, and white and Hispanic (as opposed to African-American) children.[29] Moreover, in 1988, only 27 percent of three- and four-year-old Hispanic children were enrolled in preschool programs of any kind.[30]

Poverty is one cause of restricted access to services, but there are others. Infants, sick children, children with handicapping conditions, and children in need of full-day care have more difficulty locating services than other youngsters. So while overall supply seems adequate to the present need, it does not account for populations with special needs nor does it meet child and family needs equitably.

Tensions around Early Childhood Services: What the Data Do Not Say

Though they present a much clearer portrait of the status of young children and represent a significant breakthrough in our collective knowledge about the nature of services young children and young poor children actually receive, the data are quite silent on a number of issues that critically inhibit the advancement of early care and education services. Eight major tensions underlie the statistical data reported above, and until and unless they are given careful attention, advances in the care and education of young children will be seriously hampered.

TENSION I: WHAT PARENTS WANT AND WHAT PROVIDERS PROVIDE

On the surface, it appears that most parents feel quite satisfied with the care their young children are receiving. When probed, however, parents across classes indicate that they had few opportunities for real choice among programs.[31] Choices are limited by the supply of care that is available, by the ability of parents to pay for that care, and/or by the logistical flexibility that parents have. In reality, parents select the "best" care from what is available to them and, perhaps to assuage their own guilt, often report satisfaction.

More revealing, however, are data showing that 53 percent of parents, if given the opportunity, would alter their child care choices.[32] Some would do so to upgrade quality; others would do so to eliminate the dissonance between what they expected and what caregivers delivered. Indeed, tension between caregivers and parents is so pronounced that programs have been developed to bring them together.[33] In part, such tensions are to be expected and are woven into the structural fabric of child care and early education. Yet when dealing with very young children, differences in parents' and providers' expectations and beliefs can have serious consequences. For example, in a recent analysis by the National Center for Education Statistics comparing parents' and teachers' beliefs regarding children's readiness for kindergarten, it was found that parents were more likely than teachers to rate behavioral and school-related tasks such as learning the alphabet, counting to 20 or more, and using pencils and paints as very important or essential for school readiness; few kindergarten teachers shared these beliefs.[34] Such differences between parental and teacher expectations are not only widespread, but profound.[35] Because parents structure learning experiences for their children according to their values rather than according to the expectations of teachers or schools, children often appear ill prepared for school and are kept out to their further educational detriment.[36] Without understanding parental values, teachers make inappropriate judgments about young children that can have far-reaching consequences.

While it is unrealistic to expect complete congruence between the values of parents and caregivers or teachers, the reality is that differences in belief systems—particularly when culturally rooted—are often ignored and are seldom systematically discussed. At the personal level differences swell, while at the institutional level few mechanisms are established to redress the tensions.

TENSION II: DEVELOPMENTAL VERSUS CURRICULAR APPROACHES
TO INSTRUCTION AND MEASUREMENT

As important as tensions between teachers and parents are, attention must also be directed toward the critical and often overlooked tensions among educators themselves. Two different camps—developmental and curricular—have developed and have clashed in the field. The National Education Goals Panel, reflecting the developmental orientation of most early childhood specialists, has enunciated a set of domains related to the readiness of young children, including: (1) physical well being and motor development; (2) social and emotional development; (3) approaches toward learning; (4) literacy and language development; and (5) cognition and general knowledge.[37] After extensive

review by professionals from many disciplines,[38] these dimensions have
been widely accepted in the early childhood field. Indeed, the Technical Planning Group for Goal 1 of the National Education Goals has
gone forward to amplify these dimensions, clarifying their content, dis-
cussing their utility in ascertaining the nation's progress toward the
first National Education Goal, and considering them as a guide for the
development of curriculum and instruction through the early grades.[39]

Simultaneously, in an effort to specify the content standards that
will guide instruction and assessment from kindergarten through
grade 12, major professional organizations are creating detailed standards for what children should know and be able to do in at least the
five areas specified in the third National Education Goal: English, history, geography, social studies and mathematics. In general, such
efforts begin from a premise of the importance of various academic
subjects. While they acknowledge the developmental trajectory of
young children, such efforts are often quite curricular in orientation,
making infrequent accommodations for young children's unique ways
of knowing and learning.

The dilemma arises when one attempts to fuse the developmental
orientation and its specifications with the curricular orientation and its
standards. Such fusion occurs to some extent in the preschool and primary years, but is most confounded in kindergarten, where inconsistencies between developmental and curricular approaches have existed
for years.[40] In the past, when kindergartens were truly considered play
gardens for youngsters, when kindergartens oriented children to formal schooling, and when there were few defined criteria for performance in kindergarten, tensions between developmental and curricular orientations were finessed by talented teachers. Today, however,
with increasing pressure for academic development from parents, as
noted above, and with the specification of learning standards for all
grades forthcoming, reaching some consensus on the philosophic base
of early learning will be necessary.

It is disconcerting, however, that reconciliation of pedagogical perspectives and philosophies—perhaps the major challenge currently
faced in the early childhood field—presently has no forum for dia-
logue. So divided are the field's systems (including training and cre-
dentialing) that while test makers maintain their curricular orientation, while early childhood specialists advocate a developmental
approach, and while teachers feel the dichotomy daily in their work,
little is underway to bridge the schism.

TENSION III: SERVICES TO CHILDREN VERSUS SERVICES TO FAMILIES

Those who have been trained in early care and education recognize the importance of families in fostering healthy child development. And, indeed, throughout the history of the early childhood field, numerous family-focused efforts have been manifest such as parent co-ops and the engagement of families in Head Start. Although efforts to engage families vary in their scope, intensity, and efficacy,[41] family orientation is deemed valuable and is now manifest throughout general education.[42] Recently, rejuvenated commitment to families has found expression in the proposed reauthorization of the Elementary and Secondary Education Act and through the burgeoning family support movement.[43]

Early educators should be elated with such an expanded focus on families. Yet, in reality, the worsening state of American families, coupled with new recognition of their importance, places a heavy burden on the early childhood field. Today, early educators, along with policymakers, debate whether emphasis should be placed on serving children or on serving parents. Ideally, programs should do both and many do, with an entire new breed of two-generation service programs being developed. These efforts provide parents with parenting education and support and also offer general education development programs and preemployment training as a means to self-sufficiency.[44] Some are freestanding and some are attached to early care and education settings.

As important as these efforts are, they raise clear tensions for those working in child-oriented programs. With limited resources, a staff trained to work primarily with children, and with other agencies in communities already serving adults, practitioners in child-oriented programs question their appropriate role as well as their capacity to deliver high-quality programs to adults. Staff feel especially unprepared for the challenges involved in working closely with substance-abusing parents or low-achieving adults. In programs where demands are especially heavy and resources tight, the press to serve parents in new and more intense ways is a burden that weighs heavily on practitioners and derails them from their primary job. Practitioners end up feeling as if they are robbing Peter (the children) to serve Paul (the parents). In short, while the well-intentioned layering on of services to families seems appropriate for a field long dedicated to parents and children alike, such a movement, unless accompanied by specialized training and increased resources, may represent the straw that breaks the camel's back.

Those involved in early care and education recognize its functional imperfections. Emanating from a history that accorded hegemony to the home and privacy and primacy to the family, early care and education services have been handmaidens to national social crises. The Great Depression called forth the first federal commitment to child care, which was dismantled when the crisis ended. World War II called forth the second (the Lanham Act) and this effort was also disbanded when the crisis ended.[45] Until Head Start, which was created to meet the third crisis (the War on Poverty), there was no permanent federal commitment to early care and education.

Such episodic support, coupled with a legislative structure that encourages the development of categorical programs, has led to an early childhood nonsystem so scattered that agreement cannot even be reached on the number of federal programs that exist. Illustrating this situation, the National Research Council noted that one source identified twenty-two child care programs while the U.S. Department of Labor identified thirty-one programs in eleven federal agencies.[46] Each of these programs comes with its unique federal regulations, funding sources, and funding patterns, with few incentives to collaborate.[47]

While heuristically interesting, such categorical approaches create havoc in the field, causing practitioners across various auspices to compete for children, staff, and space.[48] Parents, never sure of their options or of real differences in programs, are often forced to piece together services so their children will receive full care. The result is that children are juggled from program to program, rarely experiencing programmatic or philosophic continuity. This patchwork, makeshift system is detrimental to families, children, and providers alike. Historically problematic, such systemic inconsistencies and the competition they engender are multiplied as the field expands, bereft of any comprehensive plan or strategy. Rather than integrating the pieces, national policy has simply added more parts to a puzzle that had no coherence or equity to begin with.

TENSION V: INTEGRATED VERSUS SOCIALLY SANCTIONED SEGREGATED PRESCHOOLS

In part due to limited national funding and the categorical and fragmented nature of early care and education, poor children, who arguably need and benefit from services most, have the least access to them, placing them in double jeopardy when compared to their middle- and upper-class agemates who do receive services. Moreover, because of categorically driven, means-tested entry criteria, poor children are often segregated into programs with other low-income children, thus simultaneously defying the law of the land that mandates integration for children in education and depriving them of the benefits of mixed educational settings. In spite of long-standing concerns about segregation, the hard reality is that due to a categorical approach to funding and limited national support, the nation's services for young children are still segregated, with little evidence of alteration.

Increasingly diverse, the current population of preschoolers presents special challenges for preschool educators. On the one hand, early childhood classrooms, perhaps more than other educational settings, are designed to be exciting and enriching environments where learning opportunities are highly individualized. Such environments would appear to be natural, if not optimal, settings for work with diverse populations. On the other hand, preschool teachers are rarely trained for the demands that diversity requires. For example, some preschool programs earmarked for speakers of languages other than English are conceptualized as compensatory or characterized by deficit philosophies. As a result, teachers may be subtly socialized to hold low expectations for children. Without specialized training regarding the importance of the home language,[49] the processes and tempo for second language acquisition,[50] and the role of culture in social adaptation,[51] teachers are left without the skills and knowledge they need to work effectively with language diverse populations.

The challenge of diversity, however, does not simply present itself in teaching, but also in the assessment of children and in policy formulation. In these areas, we have been willing to assume that what works best for some low-income children will automatically work best for many children despite the fact that they come from divergent backgrounds and present different needs. For example, the intervention necessary for a low-income, urban African-American child in New York City may differ from that needed by a Native American child on a Southwestern reservation. The assumption that generalizations can be made across populations affects not simply what and how teachers teach, but how children are assessed, how data are conceived and reported, and how policy based on such data is crafted.[52] Access to differing educational opportunities is often determined by assessments that use majority-culture norms or that ignore cultural competence. As a result, a cognitively normal but physically disabled or a limited-English-speaking child may be confined to special classes. By basing assessments of intellectual competence on genetic or developmental variables and disregarding cultural or contextual variations,[53] we have misunderstood and simplified constructs of diversity.

TENSION VII: A FOCUS ON DIRECT SERVICES OR ON INFRASTRUCTURE

Not surprisingly, the nation's early care and education system, pre-occupied with sustaining its basic services, has not focused on the development of an infrastructure to support those services. Throughout the 1980s, the policy emphasis on supporting and expanding direct services to children and families was strong, creating an atmosphere in which advocating for anything else seemed close to heresy, akin to taking food from the mouths of starving children. In some quarters of the field, this attitude persists.

Recently, however, a growing segment has recognized that by themselves direct services to children will continue to be jeopardized if supports do not exist to shore up the system; if there are no training mechanisms to assure the quality of those coming into the field; if there is no capacity to give the field a voice alongside others advocating for different causes; and if there is no data collection to chronicle the status of services. Though not the primary goal of early care and education, it has become apparent that for the field to advance, it needs to develop a vision extending beyond direct services. Indeed, an early care and education infrastructure is needed, replete with specific functions that such a system must carry out. Chronicled by the *Quality 2000* Initiative, these functions include: (1) fostering cross-system collaboration; (2) enhancing consumer and public involvement; (3) assuring quality control; (4) maintaining adequate levels of financing; and (5) fostering the development of the work force.[54] Still somewhat fresh, these ideas are generating controversy regarding the appropriate use of limited expenditures. Until such tension is resolved, the field will find it difficult to move forward cohesively.

TENSION VIII: LACK OF A MOBILIZED CONSTITUENCY

Given the divisiveness that exists in the field, it is not surprising that a common early care and education constituency has not been developed. To the contrary, when legislation is being considered the field presents such a divided front that legislators are overwhelmed by the different requests and positions proffered. The existence of large for-profit and nonprofit sectors, which often profess antithetical legislative goals, is one source of tension in the field. A second source is the tendency for program providers to advocate the expansion of their own programs over others or over the development of systemic infrastructure. A third reason for the field's fractured constituency is that parents have not been routinely or effectively mobilized to play an advocacy role, with Head Start being the one key exception from which the field could learn. Indeed, parents who use early care and education services for a brief time during their lives may demonstrate intense commitment to their child's center during the enrollment period, but rarely advocate beyond their programs or sustain their commitments to young children as their own children age. Unlike being disabled or gifted—persistent conditions around which parent constituencies have been effectively mobilized—being young and in child care is temporary so that parents' attentions naturally turn elsewhere with time. Adding to the dilemma, until the recent birth of Parent Action, there has been no organized force to coalesce parents across different program types.

Inundated with worries about program funding and operations, practitioners rarely have the time or energy to focus on building a constituency. Funds are lacking for the development of the kind of strategy that could educate the public and develop such a constituency. Training opportunities focusing on this goal are limited. The reality is that workers in early care and education have been inner-directed for decades, ferreting through various definitions of quality, determining effective ratios, and developing curriculum strategies. To meet the changing needs of families and children, more outer-directed, consumer- and constituent-based efforts must be conceptualized and undertaken.

Addressing the Tensions: Considering Action Steps

The nation's recognition of the importance of early care and education is exemplified by verbal commitments and action steps being taken by governors and other policymakers, as well as by the corporate and voluntary sectors. To be sure, such efforts are helpful to and appreciated by the early care and education community. However, when measured against the proliferating needs and tensions articulated earlier in this chapter, present commitments are hardly robust. One might say that current efforts represent important first steps. On the other hand, one might say that they are but a "fig leaf" covering the real issues; that in providing a highly visible protective shield, they obfuscate true needs and problems. Recognizing that there may be a facade of commitment and preventing it from being mistaken for action constitute the first steps in addressing the tensions.

The second action step is to acknowledge that decades of piecemeal policy have yielded a system laden with inequities for children. But it is no longer sufficient simply to bemoan the conflicts occasioned by the categorical nature of young children's programming. Such conflicts—along with their consequences for children, families, and providers—must be documented with concrete examples. What effects, for example, have befallen children because Chapter 1 is not fully coordinated with Head Start? What ills occur because funding or eligibility is not coordinated across categories? The early childhood field needs to discern the real nature of the problems that exist and to define them with greater precision. Rather than encouraging the proliferation of additional categorical programs for some children, we must seriously examine the viability of normalizing early childhood education so that it is available for all children. Given our national history, it is very likely that until early childhood education is recognized as an educational imperative for all youngsters, as was kindergarten, poor and special needs children will be excluded from its benefits.

The third step is to get beneath the problems and examine the assumptions that undergird them. In some cases, ideological assumptions—the danger of out-of-home care, for example—that may have guided policy and practice can be dispelled by data. In other cases, new technology may eclipse conventional ways of thinking about development and learning. In still other cases, the nature of the legislative and regulatory processes may be less rigid and more porous than previously thought. In short, it is not simply demographics that have changed; our entire mode of operation needs to be examined for changes in technology, in the data collected, and in the political situation that are presently more conducive to supporting young children.

The fourth step is to bring fresh perspectives and knowledge to bear on the issues at hand. Lessons from allied fields, including health and higher education, need to be applied to early care and education. An examination of the relationship between the profit and nonprofit sectors needs to be undertaken as does an analysis of new strategies for the preparation and compensation of the work force. Alternatives to regulation should be explored so that incentives for positive action rather than sanctions against negative action or inaction prevail. Moreover, such fresh perspectives must be framed by the realities of government: the deficit, the related press to restructure (downscale) government bureaucracy, and the current preoccupation with other domestic priorities such as health care.

The fifth step is to systematically mobilize new constituencies, making their commitment to the care and education of young children durable. Not easy to accomplish, garnering such commitments will be realized only when the constituent groups recognize personal benefits in supporting early care and education. For example, when American businesses realized that high quality early care and education would better prepare their future work force, many of them invested dollars and human resources to enhance early care and education services. Beyond a top-down strategy, the mobilization of constituents must include a more systematic bottom-up approach. Parents and teachers—those closest to children—must be encouraged to understand that while commitment to an individual child or to an individual group of children—a class—is critical, it is not sufficient. Individual children are products of their sociocultural contexts and these contexts—whether marked by violence or by fragmented, inequitable services—need attention as well. In short, the personal commitments of the 1980s must be converted into societal commitment in the 1990s.

The sixth step in addressing the problems in early care and education is to use new knowledge in concert with new constituencies to build a social strategy in behalf of young children. Such a strategy must be built upon a vision of what child care and early education should be well into the twenty-first century. It must be accompanied by a long-term scheme that will eventuate in comprehensive child development and early education legislation designed to integrate programs, enhance access and equity, and assure quality and continuity for children and families. Short-term strategies developed to meet the larger goal will need to specify legislative and executive undertakings and delineate roles for action, assigning lead responsibility to an empowered early care and education community.

In sum, this discussion suggests that changes in the nation's demography, coupled with changes in our knowledge about the efficacy of early care and education, have generated the need to convert what has been a piecemeal, episodic approach to the construction of early childhood social policy into a new normative system for children in America. Such a system, implied by the word *normative*, must be so universal and so regularized (without being compulsory) that participation in it will be as natural and unstigmatized for all populations as is participation in our education system. The early care and education system must be understood as part of the essential infrastructure of a democratic nation, not as a transient or luxurious benefit to some children only. In short, early care and education must no longer be illusive; it must be normalized for all and actualized as the imperative it is.

NOTES

1. U.S. General Accounting Office, *Poor Preschool-aged Children: Numbers Increase But Most Not in School*, Briefing Report to the Chairman, Subcommittee on Children, Family, Drugs, and Alcoholism, Committee on Labor and Human Resources, U.S. Senate (Washington, DC: U.S. General Accounting Office, 1993); National Education Goals Panel, *Reconsidering Children's Early Development and Learning: Toward Shared Beliefs and Vocabulary* (Washington, DC: National Education Goals Panel, 1993); National Commission on Children, *Beyond Rhetoric: A New American Agenda for Children and Families* (Washington, DC: National Commission on Children, 1991); Sandra L. Hofferth, "Who Enrolls in Head Start? A Demographic Analysis of Head Start Eligible Children" (unpublished manuscript, the Urban Institute, Washington, DC, 1993); Barbara Willer, Sandra Hofferth, Ellen Kisker, Patricia Divine-Hawkins, Elizabeth Farquahar, and Frederick Glantz, *The Demand and Supply of Child Care in 1990: Joint Findings from the National Child Care Survey 1990 and a Profile of Child Care Settings* (Washington, DC: National Association for the Education of Young Children, 1991).

2. Center for the Study of Social Policy, *The Challenge of Change: What the 1990 Census Tells Us about Children* (Washington, DC: Center for the Study of Social Policy, 1992).

3. Willer et al., *The Demand and Supply of Child Care in 1990*.

4. National Center for Education Statistics, *National Household Education Survey: Profile of Preschool Children's Child Care and Early Education Program Participation*, NCES 93-133 (Washington, DC: Office of Educational Research and Improvement, U.S. Department of Education, 1993).·

5. Willer et al., *The Demand and Supply of Child Care in 1990*.

6. Children's Defense Fund, *The State of America's Children* (Washington, DC: Children's Defense Fund, 1992).

7. Hispanic Policy Development Project, *Closing the Gap for U.S. Hispanic Youth* (Washington, DC: Hispanic Policy Development Project, 1988).

8. National Center for Children in Poverty, *Five Million Children: A Statistical Profile of Our Youngest Citizens* (New York: Columbia University Press, 1990).

9. James Garbarino, "The Meaning of Poverty to Children," *American Behavioral Scientist* 35 (1992): 258-274; Sheila Rosenbaum, "The Health Consequences of Poverty," *American Behavioral Scientist* 35 (1992): 275-289; Richard Gelles, "Poverty and Violence toward Children," *American Behavioral Scientist* 35 (1992): 258-274.

10. Lisbeth Schorr and Daniel Schorr, *Within Our Reach: Breaking the Cycle of Disadvantage* (New York: Doubleday, 1988).

11. Allison Clarke-Stewart, *Daycare*, rev. ed. (Cambridge, MA: Harvard University Press, 1993); Donna King and Carol E. MacKinnon, "Making Difficult Choices Easier: A Review of Research on Day Care and Children's Development," *Family Relations* 37 (1988): 392-398.

100   CONCEPTUALIZING PRESCHOOL EDUCATION

12. Irving Lazar and Richard Darlington, "Lasting Effects of Early Education: A Report from the Consortium for Longitudinal Studies," *Monographs of the Society for Research in Child Development* 47, nos. 2-3 (1982), Serial No. 195.

13. John R. Berrueta-Clement, Lawrence J. Schweinhart, S. Steven Barnett, Ann S. Epstein, and David P. Weikart, *Changed Lives: The Effects of the Perry Preschool Program on Youths through Age 19* (Ypsilanti, MI: High/Scope Press, 1984).

14. Committee for Economic Development, *Why Child Care Matters: Preparing Young Children for a More Productive America* (New York: Committee for Economic Development, 1993).

15. National Center for Education Statistics, *National Household Education Survey: Profile of Preschool Children's Child Care and Early Education Program Participation.*

16. Ibid.

17. Willer et al., *Demand and Supply of Child Care in 1990.*

18. Ibid.

19. National Center for Education Statistics, *National Household Education Survey: Profile of Preschool Children's Child Care and Early Education Program Participation.*

20. Willer et al., *Demand and Supply of Child Care in 1990.*

21. Ibid.

22. Ibid.

23. Sharon Lynn Kagan and Jamie Newton, "For-profit and Nonprofit Child Care: Similarities and Differences," *Young Children* 45 (1989): 4-10.

24. Marcie Whitebrook, Carollee Howes, and Deborah Phillips, *Who Cares? Child Care Teachers and the Quality of Care in America* (Oakland, CA: Child Care Employee Project, 1989).

25. Jean B. Layzer, Barbara D. Goodson, and Marc L. Moss, *Life in Preschool: An Observational Study of Early Childhood Programs* (Cambridge, MA: Abt Associates, 1993), p. 101.

26. Patricia Seppanen, Ken Godin, Jeffrey Metzger, Martha Bronson, and Donald Cichon, *Chapter 1 Funded Early Childhood Programs* (Dover, NH: Development Assistance Corporation, 1993).

27. Willer et al., *The Demand and Supply of Child Care in 1990.*

28. U.S. General Accounting Office, *Poor Preschool-aged Children.*

29. Hofferth, "Who Enrolls in Head Start?"

30. Hispanic Policy Development Council, *Closing the Gap for U.S. Hispanic Youth.*

31. Ellen Galinsky, Unpublished Presentation at the Ninth Annual Symposium of the A.L. Mailman Foundation, Rye, NY, 1992.

32. Ibid.

33. Christiann Dean, *Parent-Caregiver Partnerships* (Ithaca, NY: Cornell University Cooperative Extension, 1992).

34. National Center for Education Statistics, *Readiness for Kindergarten: Parent and Teacher Beliefs*, NCES 93-257 (Washington, DC: Office of Educational Research and Improvement, U.S. Department of Education, 1993), p. 2.

35. Deborah Stipek, Linda Rosenblatt, and Laurine DiRicco, "Making Parents Your Allies," *Young Children* 49 (1994): 4-9.

36. Mary L. Smith and Lorrie A. Shepard, "What Doesn't Work: Explaining Policies of Retention in the Early Grades," *Phi Delta Kappan* 69 (1987): 123-128.

37. National Education Goals Panel, *The Goal 1 Technical Planning Subgroup Report on School Readiness* (Washington, DC: National Education Goals Panel, 1992).

38. Cynthia Prince, *Reactions to the Goal 1 Technical Planning Subgroup Report on School Readiness: Report to the National Education Goals Panel,* Technical Report 92-03 (Washington, DC: National Education Goals Panel, 1992).

39. National Education Goals Panel, *Reconsidering Children's Early Development and Learning.*

40. David Elkind, *The Hurried Child* (Reading, MA: Addison-Wesley, 1981); Lilian Katz, *More Talks with Teachers* (Urbana, IL: ERIC Clearinghouse on Elementary and Early Childhood Education, 1984).

41. Barbara Bowman, "Home and School: The Unresolved Relationship," in *Putting Families First: America's Family Support Movement and the Challenge of Change,* edited by Sharon Lynn Kagan and Bernice Weissbourd (San Francisco, CA: Jossey-Bass, 1994); Sharon Lynn Kagan, "Home-School Linkages: History's Legacies and the Family Support Movement," in *America's Family Support Programs,* edited by Sharon Lynn Kagan, Douglas Powell, Bernice Weissbourd, and Edward Zigler (New Haven, CT: Yale University Press, 1987); Douglas Powell, *Families and Early Childhood Programs* (Washington, DC: National Association for the Education of Young Children, 1989).

42. Joyce Epstein, "Parent Involvement: What Research Says to Administrators," *Education and Urban Society* 19 (1987): 119-136; Norma Fruchter, Anne Galletta, and J. Lynne White, *New Directions in Parent Involvement* (Washington, DC: Academy for Educational Development, 1992).

43. Sharon Lynn Kagan and Bernice Weissbourd, eds., *Putting Families First: America's Family Support Movement and the Challenge of Change* (San Francisco, CA: Jossey-Bass, 1994).

44. Sheila Smith, Susan Blank, and Raymond Collins, *Pathways to Self-Sufficiency for Two Generations: Designing Welfare to Work Programs that Benefit Children and Strengthen Families* (New York: Foundation for Child Development, 1992).

45. Emily Cahan, *Past Caring* (New York: National Center for Children in Poverty, Columbia University, 1989).

46. National Research Council, *Who Cares for America's Children?* (Washington, DC: National Academy Press, 1990).

47. Sharon Lynn Kagan, *United We Stand: Collaboration for Child Care and Early Education Services* (New York: Teachers College Press, 1991): Jule M. Sugarman, *Building Early Childhood Systems: A Resource Handbook* (Washington, DC: Child Welfare League of America, 1991).

48. Irene F. Goodman and Joanne P. Brady, *The Challenge of Coordination* (Newton, MA: Education Development Center, 1988).

49. Lily Wong-Fillmore, "When Learning a Second Language Means Losing the First," *Early Childhood Research Quarterly* 6, no. 3 (1991): 323-346.

50. Kenji Hakuta, *Mirror of Language: The Debate of Bilingualism* (New York: Basic Books, 1986).

51. Eugene Garcia, *Early Childhood Bilingualism* (Albuquerque, NM: University of New Mexico, 1983).

52. Luis Laosa, "The Cultural Context of Construct Validity and the Ethics of Generalizability," *Early Childhood Research Quarterly* 6, no. 3 (1991): 313-322.

53. National Education Goals Panel, *Reconsidering Children's Early Development and Learning.*

54. Sharon Lynn Kagan and the Quality 2000 Essential Functions Task Force, *The Essential Functions of the Early Care and Education System: Rationale and Definitions* (New Haven, CT: Bush Center on Child Development and Social Policy, 1993).

CHAPTER V

The Unfulfilled Mission of Federal Compensatory Education Programs

ERWIN FLAXMAN, GARY BURNETT, AND CAROL ASCHER

Since the War on Poverty, launched in 1965, compensatory education has been the means for providing for the education of disadvantaged students. But now, thirty years later, in an indictment of federal compensatory education programs under Title I and Chapter 1 for failing to increase the academic skills of disadvantaged children, Jendryka fires this sardonic salvo: "If Chapter 1 were a business, it would be in Chapter 11."[1] He asserts that, having spent $135 billion (in real 1992-93 dollars), the nation has "little to show for it" in helping disadvantaged children make and hold on to the academic gains they need for success in school. But it is not only the students who have failed, he charges. The designers have also failed to come up with compensatory education programs that work, and now they also are bankrupt of ideas.

This is a far cry from the promise of compensatory education in the 1960s and 1970s when Title I of the Elementary and Secondary Education Act of 1965 first provided federal funds for compensatory education to educate low achieving students in poverty throughout the nation. Title I was the centerpiece of a panoply of federal programs—Head Start, Upward Bound, Job Corps, Neighborhood Youth Corps, Manpower Development and Training, and Teacher Corps, to name a few—designed to improve the education and social opportunities of disadvantaged children and youth in the United States. A bankruptcy of ideas was the last fear in anyone's mind then.

Federally Supported Compensatory Education

THE PURPOSE OF TITLE I AND CHAPTER 1

The purpose of the federally supported compensatory education programs is deceptively simple. From its beginnings as Title I the programs

Erwin Flaxman is Director of the ERIC Clearinghouse on Urban Education at Teachers College, Columbia University. Gary Burnett is Research Associate at the Clearinghouse and Carol Ascher is Senior Research Associate there.

were funded "to provide financial assistance to local education agencies servicing areas with concentrations of children from low-income families to expand and improve their education programs by various means . . . which contribute particularly to meeting the special needs of educationally deprived students" (Public Law 89-10). The Educational Consolidation and Improvement Act of 1981, which tried to radically rethink the federal role in compensatory education, did not substantially change any functions of the program designated in the original legislation, nor were those functions altered much in the Hawkins-Stafford Amendments to the reauthorization of the law in 1988.

Title I and Chapter 1* were predicated on a strong link between the economic status of students attending a school and their academic achievement, and thus funds should be allocated according to the poverty of that school, not according to the low achievement status of its students. It had been found that the longer a child grows up in a family experiencing poverty, the greater the likelihood that he or she will fall behind grade level.[2] What is more, such students attend schools with high concentrations of other poor students, a condition that multiplies the deleterious impact of poverty on a child's academic achievement.[3] Much of the Government's monitoring, and the accountability of the state and local educational agencies in implementing the program, then, has been to determine whether the money has flowed to schools that the legislation has designated as most needy. How the programs would function was left to the discretion of the local educational agencies, which were initially given the opportunity "to expand and improve their educational programs by *various means.*"

FUNDING AND ACCOUNTABILITY

Both Title I and Chapter 1 divide program responsibilities among the federal government, state education agencies (SEAs) and local school districts (LEAs). The federal government allocates funds to states, as well as establishes, interprets, and enforces requirements governing the use of federal dollars. States then distribute funds to

---

*A word about nomenclature will be helpful at the outset of this discussion. From the passage of the Elementary and Secondary Education Act (ESEA) of 1965, federal compensatory education programs were known familiarly as "Title I Programs." After the passage of the Education Consolidation and Improvement Act (ECIA) of 1981, they became known as "Chapter 1 Programs." When we speak of the programs generally in this chapter, we refer to them as "Title I and Chapter 1 programs" or "federal compensatory education programs" or simply "compensatory education programs." When we refer to their individual and historical policies or practices, we write "Title I" or "Chapter 1," as appropriate.

school districts, approve local applications, monitor local projects for compliance, provide technical assistance, and run their special state programs. School districts then are responsible for designing and carrying out the Chapter 1 programs. School districts have wide latitude to decide on grade levels, subject areas, kinds of services, teaching methods, classroom settings, and types of staff. However, because of funding and accountability requirements, there has been relatively little variation or experimentation in Chapter 1 programming at the local level.

The elaborate funding mechanisms of Title I and Chapter 1 were intended to equalize opportunities. Despite some successes, however, these mechanisms may actually have created new educational inequalities. These inequalities stem from two weaknesses. First, the current system of funding "serves as a disincentive to raising the performance of participants," since once test scores show improvements, funds are reallocated to students and schools with lower scores.[4] Second, money is both spread too widely and allocated to too few high-poverty and too many affluent counties, districts and schools. Currently, Chapter 1 funds go to almost all counties, to 93 percent of all school districts, and to 71 percent of all public elementary schools.[5]

Currently, the rate of and the concentration of poverty among children in the United States are growing, and the financial difficulties of public schools in urban districts with great tax burdens and other districts with low property taxes have increased. The proportion of Chapter 1 schools that are high-poverty schools doubled between 1985-1986 and 1991-1992.[6] Moreover, there are significant differences between high- and low-poverty schools: student absenteeism and mobility and teacher mobility are more serious problems in high-poverty than low-poverty schools.[7] Thus, although low-income children have greater educational needs than more affluent children, they attend schools with substantially fewer resources, despite the law which requires that Chapter 1 and non-Chapter 1 schools within the same district receive comparable resources before Chapter 1 funds are added. However, even when Chapter 1 money is used to fund personnel at the same level as in high-revenue districts, it may not be available to provide other services that are vital to students' improvement in high-poverty, low-revenue districts. This is not only because the districts' own resources are overburdened, but because low-revenue districts appear to receive lower funding from states for other programs such as compensatory education, special education, and programs for limited-English-proficient students.[8] The mechanism that most local school districts use to meet the changing Title I and Chapter 1 accountability requirements is the norm-referenced test. Students' test scores determine everything from program eligibility to evaluation of program outcomes. In addition, Congress and the U.S. Department of Education use accumulated standardized test data to justify continued appropriations and authorizations, to weigh major policy changes in the program, to target states and districts for federal monitoring and audits, and to carry out Congressionally mandated studies of the program.[9] For states and local school districts receiving funding, the tests have been used to target funds and assure fiscal compliance.[10] It is ironic that, since funding is cut to those schools that make achievement gains, the reliance on test scores has worked against schools with strong programs.[11]

The heavy reliance on norm-referenced tests in Chapter 1 has been subject to a number of criticisms over the years. They may serve as indicators of participants' educational progress in the basic subjects, but they reveal little about other program goals (such as redistributing resources to poor areas, mitigating the social effects of childhood poverty, building children's self-esteem, keeping children in school), and about the impact of Chapter 1 supportive services. They underestimate the program-related growth that children experience, and in the academic areas they measure achievement in skills that were never intended to be taught and ignore skills that students learn as a result of participation over the long-term.[12] What is more, because of changes in student populations, because of incentives encouraging certain students to take (or not take) tests, and because of the lack of consistency between tests and instructional programs, the quality of a Chapter 1 program cannot be measured by comparing test-score fluctuations from one year to another or by comparing schools or classrooms on test scores.[13] Finally, as is universally acknowledged, norm-referenced multiple-choice tests are an impediment to good teaching and high student achievement because teachers drill students on a narrow range of information covered by the tests instead of engaging them in interpretation and problem solving.

Models for Implementing Title I and Chapter 1 Programs

ORGANIZATIONAL MODELS

Although the goal of Title I/Chapter 1 is fairly clear and straightforward, programs established under this legislation have become increasingly intricate and often confusing. Traditionally, schools have used four basic models to demonstrate that funds are used only to benefit Chapter 1 students. In the following pages we briefly describe these models.

Pullout programs. Long the primary model for Chapter 1 implementation and delivery, pullout programs remove Chapter 1 students from the regular classroom for short periods during the day for intensive supplemental instruction. They were originally designed to provide a specialized environment for Chapter 1 students by separating them from mainstream classrooms and placing them in smaller groups where they would receive more closely focused and individualized instruction.[14] They were also founded upon the philosophy that children—whether disadvantaged or not—had to learn the "basics" before moving on to higher-level skills and a more challenging curriculum based on problem solving.[15] It was argued that pullout programs were an ideal way to address directly the needs of compensatory education students, allowing them to master the basics while freeing them from the distractions of heterogeneous classes. In addition, through the use of pullouts, schools could more easily give Chapter 1 students the benefits of receiving instruction from specialists, rather than requiring regular classroom teachers, who often were not trained to deal with the special needs of these students, to take on the additional burden of teaching the Chapter 1 curriculum while teaching the regular curriculum. Not only did pullouts meet the administrative requirements of a Chapter 1 program but, when managed well, they could assure more on-task time for both students and teachers.

Pullout programs, however, have not, for the most part, had a salutary effect.[16] Indeed, as many critics have pointed out, their impact has all too often been the opposite, causing Chapter 1 students to lose instructional time simply because they must move from their normal classroom to another site. While they may gain time for remedial work in mathematics and reading, they do so at the expense of work in social studies, science, physical education, as well as in nonremedial mathematics and language arts.[17] Furthermore, by separating Chapter 1 instruction from regular instruction—that is, by compartmentalizing it—pullouts can fragment the education of Chapter 1 students. At least as significantly, they can isolate Chapter 1 students from their peers, treating them as a separable, homogeneous group, thus effectively functioning as a mode of educational segregation. And because Chapter 1 teachers must do their jobs in a separate room, pullouts can work to undermine communication between them and mainstream faculty.[18] Finally, and most seriously, pullouts can place serious limits on what Chapter 1 students can learn. Instead of providing the benefits of specialized and individualized supplementary instruction, they can lead to lowered expectations for the achievement levels of the students they are intended to benefit. Too often limited to repetitious drilling of the "basics," they do little to teach the students how to think or to solve problems. As recently as the 1990-91 school year, pullout programs were still offered by a full 82 percent of school districts.[19] They persist largely because of tradition and entropy.[20]

There is evidence that this continued reliance on pullouts may be in the process of changing, however. Major nationwide assessments of Chapter 1 in 1987 and 1993 have called for a major reduction in the number of pullout programs. In addition, the 1988 Hawkins-Stafford Amendments to Chapter 1, with some success, encouraged schools to favor other models. Even schools that still use pullout programs no longer use them in isolation, but tend to merge them with other models, a trend which has been especially pronounced in high-poverty schools.[21]

Replacement programs. Replacement programs, often called "extended pullouts," are still relatively uncommon. Replacement programs remove students from their regular classrooms for more than 25 percent of their instructional time and replace all or part of their regular instruction with a program designed to meet the students' special educational needs.[22] In other words, where standard pullouts are intended to augment regular instruction in a particular subject, replacement programs *take the place of* such regular instruction. In so doing, they are designed to address some of the shortcomings of standard pullouts by cutting the time lost in moving from place to place and mitigating some of the resulting fragmentation. In addition, only one teacher is responsible for a given subject area, thus eliminating some of the problems caused by a lack of communication between teachers.[23] Still, like standard pullouts, replacement programs isolate Chapter 1 students, in effect segregating them from other students in their schools. And while they are not explicitly designed as tracking mechanisms, they do make it clear that Chapter 1 students occupy a track of their own. Thus, like pullout programs, replacement programs may have the unintended effect of lowering expectations for achievement by Chapter 1 students.[24]

108 AN UNFULFILLED MISSION

Add-on programs. Add-on programs (also known as extended-time programs) are intended to provide more instructional time to students than pull-outs can, through such mechanisms as extended-day kindergarten classes, before- or after-school programs, home-based programs, Saturday programs, and extended-year or summer-school programs. The principle governing add-on programs is that extra time spent on-task can have a positive impact on the achievement of disadvantaged students, although such benefits require that increased instructional time must be used effectively and must take advantage of practices that enhance students' learning, including challenging curricula, high expectations, and individualized instruction. Unfortunately, like any other implementation model, add-on programs are not immune from the damaging effects of watered-down curriculum and lowered expectations. In addition, they require a commitment of time beyond what is required by programs that take place during the regular school day and year, and thus can face serious attendance problems. They also place a burden on parents, who must often find ways of transporting their children to and from school. Finally, they can mean considerable extra expense for schools since they are offered outside of regular school hours.[25]

In-class programs. In-class Chapter 1 programs, in obvious ways, provide the mirror image of pullout programs. That is, in-class programs provide instruction as part of the regular classroom routine, thus reducing the fragmentation of Chapter 1 education. In general, they avoid some of the logistical complications caused by replacement and add-on models, and thus have become more popular over the last few years.[26]

It is uncertain, however, whether the in-class model, as typically implemented, offers distinct advantages over the pullout model. While in-class programs do not move Chapter 1 students into a separate classroom, many do move them into isolated groups within the classroom.[27] In addition, these students, even in the primary classroom, are taught by special teachers—and often by aides—rather than by the room's main teacher.[28] Thus in-class programs often function effectively as pullout programs even though they require no change in setting. They also present other potential problems: a reduction in the variety of materials available to the Chapter 1 instructor, the lack of needed joint planning time for the classroom and Chapter 1 teachers, additional scheduling conflicts, and the disturbances caused by two distinct groups receiving instruction simultaneously in a single classroom.[29]

There seems to be no obvious reason for schools to prefer in-class models over pullout programs. Indeed, as Kennedy and colleagues suggest in their major evaluation of Chapter 1, neither the pullout nor the in-class model is inherently superior to the other; rather, each can be effective—or ineffective—in different settings.[30] In addition, as Rowan and Guthrie conclude, the implementation of a particular organizational model—whether pullout, replacement, add-on, or in-class—is not the most important question, even though it has received so much attention.[31] Rather, other concerns should take precedence: a concern with the needs of students in a particular context, the amount of direct contact between student and teacher, and the nature of the curriculum. Educational issues are much more important than pure delivery issues for the success of Chapter 1.

Schoolwide projects. Schoolwide projects have been designed with the hope that they can address some of these issues more adequately than other models. Under the Hawkins-Stafford School Improvement Amendments of 1988, schools with an enrollment of at least 75 percent low-income students may use their Chapter 1 funds to create schoolwide projects for the improvement of educational programs throughout the entire school rather than for implementing separate remedial programs. Such projects have been permitted since 1978; they were, however, rarely implemented prior to 1988, when the Hawkins-Stafford School Improvement Amendments eliminated a requirement that districts match federal grants with funds of their own.[32] Since then, there has been widespread enthusiasm for schoolwide projects. Some 2,000 schools nationwide now have such projects, which have been touted as an ideal method for providing underachieving students with extra help, and even as a means of removing the "disadvantaged" label from the poorest Chapter 1 schools.[33]

The intent of schoolwide projects, then, is to build good schools, not just good programs. Designed to benefit entire schools while also improving the education of Chapter 1 students, schoolwide projects can increase the flexibility of Chapter 1 implementation beyond what is possible through other methods, in part because they can incorporate aspects of all the other forms of Chapter 1 implementations. Nearly 85 percent of the principals in schools with schoolwide projects have this perception. However, schoolwide projects vary widely across the country, and most schools have used them only to reduce class size and to strengthen a variety of already existing programs.[34]

Critics of schoolwide projects suggest that many of the perceived benefits reflect administrative convenience rather than a true concern with educational reform or improved outcomes.[35] They are also concerned that, because schoolwide projects make resources available to all students without distinction, the resources will be diverted from those who need them the most, thus subverting the intent of Chapter 1 legislation. While the programs can provide schools with significant flexibility in fulfilling the goals of Chapter 1, they have too often led to nothing more than cosmetic and administrative changes. To be more effective than other models, they will have to do much more. The quality of any Chapter 1 model can never be any higher than the quality of instruction provided within that model.

CURRICULUM AND INSTRUCTION MODELS

The story of curriculum and instruction in Chapter 1 programs is an easy one to tell because it has been limited to raising the basic skill levels in only two primary curricular areas: reading and mathematics. The basic mission of Title I—to meet the special educational needs of educationally deprived students—has been translated to mean providing supplementary instruction in the basics of reading and mathematics in pullout situations. The ultimate goal is to move disadvantaged students with educational deficits into the mainstream. From the beginning, assumptions about learning deficits clearly have had a formidable and lasting impact upon the design of curricula for disadvantaged children, although too often without sufficient consideration of the effects of such curricula. Although there has been steady movement away from the use of pullouts in recent years, for the most part remedial curricular models are still in place. Indeed, an observation made by Gordon in 1970 was reaffirmed in 1988 by Passow who wrote: "In contrast to the rather well-designed and detailed research into the characteristics of disadvantaged groups, the description and evaluation of educational programs and practices for these children have generally been superficial."[36] This is so because compensatory education programs have, almost across the board, emphasized instructional processes—delivery mechanisms—rather than curriculum.[37]

This tendency holds whether the classroom is devoted to mathematics or to reading. In mathematics, the emphasis is not on an understanding of the ways in which mathematics can apply to the world outside the classroom, but on "a static collection of concepts and skills to be mastered one by one,"[38] presented through a repetitious series of worksheets and multiple-choice exams. Where Chapter 1 reading classes stress decoding to the exclusion of comprehension, mathematics classes stress the retention of "right answers" rather than an understanding either of the ways in which those answers are derived, the ways in which they are related to one another, or the ways in which they might be applied.

Romberg argues that, taught in this way, mathematics becomes merely an abstract process to Chapter 1 students, rather than a tool for thinking about and gaining understanding of the world.[39] Calfee makes much the same point regarding Chapter 1 reading programs,[40] where the emphasis is not on comprehension and the application of reading skills to the world outside the classroom—on what Calfee calls literacy broadly defined—but rather on the most elementary forms of decoding. Instead of focusing on written language as a medium of communication, in the Chapter 1 classroom reading is taught as a series of discrete skills, such as sounding out words and letter recognition. Thus, what is taught in both Chapter 1 mathematics and reading is a set of discrete and watered-down low-level skills rather than the information structures and processes needed to make skills meaningful for the students in their lives outside of the classroom.[41]

One of the most significant impediments to changing this much-maligned curriculum is the continued reliance on standardized, norm-referenced tests to assess student progress in Chapter 1 programs.[42] The overemphasis on standardized tests in Chapter 1 programs has several untoward consequences. Because such tests almost always use a multiple-choice format, they are best designed to measure low-level skills rather than higher-order abilities. Because they of necessity cannot be modified in accordance with local curricular practices, they are of limited usefulness in measuring local educational goals. Because they cannot adequately measure higher-order abilities, they can serve to undermine the efforts made in innovative programs which may have good results that are not reflected in test scores. Conversely, because multiple-choice tests easily measure low-level skills, they encourage teaching only those skills which can translate into test gains.[43]

Of course, not all Chapter 1 programs teach only isolated and limited skills. Legters and Slavin point out that there are mathematics and reading programs which emphasize exploration and discovery rather than rote learning.[44] While these programs aim for an understanding

112   AN UNFULFILLED MISSION

of the basics, they do so in a contextualized way, not isolating those basics from the ways in which they can be applied outside the classroom. In addition, they emphasize an integrated approach in which mathematics and reading are taught across the disciplines. In mathematics, this new curriculum allows students to discover mathematical principles rather than merely memorizing them; it emphasizes problem solving and group work instead of the completion of work sheets by students isolated at their desks. In reading, it employs a "whole language" approach, minimizing the overreliance on phonics and workbooks and emphasizing the use of novels and the integration of reading and creative writing.

Unfortunately, the programs that Legters and Slavin describe, as they themselves acknowledge, have not yet affected a majority of Chapter 1 schools.[45] Further, current testing and accountability requirements are actively impeding their spread. The recent nationwide study of Chapter 1 implementation conducted by Millsap and her colleagues points out that the major focus of Chapter 1 mathematics and reading classes is neither to engage students with the content of the curricula nor to introduce them to higher-order thinking skills.[46] Rather, it remains—according to 84 percent of teachers in reading and language arts programs and 97 percent of teachers in mathematics programs—the reinforcement of basic concepts through repeated drill and practice.

MODELS OF PARENT PARTICIPATION IN CHAPTER 1

Educators and researchers universally agree that the support and active involvement of parents in their children's education is indispensable for educational achievement. However, securing parent participation in compensatory education and Chapter 1 has not been a simple matter. For one thing, all parents—not only those from poor or minority communities—can sometimes be "hard to reach."[47] In addition, the most common methods used by schools to support the interaction of parents and teachers—Parent Teacher Associations and teacher conferences—are often ineffective in reaching the parents of students in compensatory programs.[48] In addition, poor and minority parents may feel particularly unwanted or unwelcome in the schools, either because of their own lack of education, or because of an institutional resistance to their presence: a feeling among some administrators and educators that parents do little more than interfere in the educational process.[49] As a way of overcoming this institutional reticence and guaranteeing that all Chapter 1 parents may have the opportunity to become involved in their children's education, parent participation has thus been built into Title I and Chapter 1 legislation since the inception of the program in 1965.

To say that parent participation has always been built into Chapter 1, however, is not to say that the program has had either consistent or coherent policy support. Indeed, the character of parent participation in Chapter 1 has repeatedly been subject to redefinition and reinvention. In large part, such a continually shifting definition has been a function of the recurrent need for legislative approval of Chapter 1; however, the requirements in Chapter 1 for parent participation have perhaps been subject to even more extensive changes than other facets of the program.

McLaughlin and Shields outline two primary models for effective parent participation, each of which has been part of Chapter 1 from its earliest years: (1) the advisory model, in which parents serve on councils to help develop and administer Chapter 1 programs, and (2) the partnership model, in which parents do not take part in the decision-making process, but rather take an active role in the educational process itself, whether in the classroom or at home.[50] Of these, the first—parents participating as advisors in the decision-making process—has loomed large in the schools for much of the history of Chapter 1. This is primarily due to requirements prior to 1981 mandating parent advisory councils.[51] However, the very fact that such councils were mandated as part of Title I led to resistance from school administrators, who often felt that they impeded rather than aided the educational process.[52] Thus, these councils, which are intended to give parents a strong voice in the development of Chapter 1 policy, have not provided a consistently successful method for generating and sustaining parent participation.[53] However, the recent increase in the number of schools developing school-based management strategies may well bring about a new enthusiasm for parent participation in decision making.[54]

As a result of the perceived shortcomings in the advisory model, much of the emphasis has shifted to the partnership model. This model is now not only the predominant type of parent program in Chapter 1, but is generally thought to be more effective, both in encouraging the participation of parents, and in the educational benefits it can bring to students. Not surprisingly, since it is easy to implement and has the support of almost all teachers, many principals consider it to be the most effective parent activity in their Chapter 1 programs.[55] A full 75 percent of elementary schools make it possible for parents to volunteer as Chapter 1 classroom tutors and aides.[56] Some critics have argued, however, that because this practice increases the number of nonprofessional and untrained instructors in Chapter 1 programs, it can actually lead to the increased segregation of Chapter 1 students from their mainstream peers, who remain with professional teachers.[57]

There is now an increased emphasis on finding ways to enhance parents' at-home participation in their children's education; thus, by the 1991-92 school year, 55 percent of schools, had developed home-based activities aimed at supporting and augmenting the Chapter 1 classroom instruction.[58] Such home-based models can run the gamut from strategies to get parents to become involved in helping their children with homework, to full-fledged programs for training parents as in-home instructors and programs in which trained paraprofessionals visit the homes of Chapter 1 students.[59]

Teachers for Chapter 1 Programs

The legislative requirements of Title I and Chapter 1 have not only had an impact upon students, but have also helped to define the teachers who offer services to them. That is, because Chapter 1 has traditionally been defined as a distinct, supplementary program, added on to normal classroom instruction—and particularly because of its reliance upon pullouts—it has required a separate, specially trained group of instructors.

A number of studies have shown that there are few differences in the backgrounds of Chapter 1 and non-Chapter 1 teachers.[60] But one study, conducted as part of the 1993 national evaluation of Chapter 1, painted a rather different picture, suggesting that Chapter 1 teachers may in fact exhibit characteristics quite different from their non-Chapter 1 colleagues, at least in terms of educational background. According to this study, a full 62 percent of Chapter 1 teachers hold master's degrees or higher, compared to only 39 percent of regular classroom teachers.[61] In addition, principals tend to rate their Chapter 1 instructors more favorably than other teachers, a fact that perhaps reflects the extra training of the instructors.

In the Chapter 1 classroom, however, nearly all of the actual teaching of students is handled by aides, who constitute nearly half of Chapter 1 staff nationwide.[62] Not surprisingly, in the highest-poverty schools, where the need is often greatest, these aides (most of whom do not have a college education) take on an even greater share of the burden of teaching. In these schools, 56 percent of in-class instruction in mathematics is provided by aides; in low-poverty schools, this drops to 7 percent.[63] Clearly, such a heavy reliance on instructional aides as the primary instructors in high-poverty schools can tend to mitigate the effects of a more highly educated cadre of certified Chapter 1 teachers, particularly since many aides have been inadequately trained.[64]

Strong in-service training can remedy this problem, although Chapter 1 has long been weak in providing such training. In terms of overall numbers, there does appear to be an extensive effort to promote staff development in Chapter 1: nearly all teachers in the program—92 percent—participated in in-service training of some form or another in 1991. However, the actual time spent in training has been and continues to be very small. Of certified teachers, fewer than one third spend more than four days in training per year. Chapter 1 aides spend considerably less time in in-service training; in 1991, fewer than 10 percent received more than thirty-five hours of training time. In addition, this time, for both teachers and aides, is divided among a number of different subjects, with the result that very little time is spent on any given subject.[65]

The effectiveness of current in-service training programs is uncertain. While Millsap and her colleagues report that most teachers find that they help to improve instruction at least somewhat,[66] Chambers and his colleagues report that, in their survey, "teachers' assessments of the quality of [their] training were uniformly low."[67] Whichever is a more accurate reflection of the state of in-service training, both Millsap and Chambers agree that it is one of the weak links in the current operation of Chapter 1.

Chapter 1 Services to Other Students

LANGUAGE MINORITY STUDENTS

Students who come from homes in which the primary language is something other than English present a particular problem in Chapter 1. Many of these students could clearly benefit from the kinds of services offered by the program, and, indeed, as a group they are more likely than their English-speaking peers to fit most of the criteria for Chapter 1 eligibility.[68] However, as part of its "supplement, not supplant" provisions, Chapter 1 legislation does not allow the use of Chapter 1 funds to offer services to these students which are already required by other federal, state, or local laws.[69] In addition, the program's funds may not be used to offer Chapter 1 services to students whose "educational deprivation" is related to their limited English proficiency.

Students who are formally defined as Limited English Proficient (LEP) may fall through the cracks of Chapter 1, although 94 percent of elementary school principals report that their district policies do not necessarily exclude such students. Yet the extent to which such exclusion actually takes place is not clear.[70] For one thing, districts across the country vary widely in their standards for defining students as LEP; thus, a student who might be eligible for Chapter 1 in one district may be ineligible in another.[71] In addition, districts also vary widely in the way they link services for LEP students and Chapter 1 services: some districts offer services to students simultaneously, while others require that students achieve English proficiency before they are considered eligible for Chapter 1.[72] And, finally, many districts exempt LEP students from taking the kinds of standardized tests which they use to determine eligibility for Chapter 1, assuming that their educational problems are a function of their limited English proficiency. While this practice spares students the burden of taking tests which do not accurately or fairly measure their abilities, it can lead to the unfortunate side effect that districts may fail to identify these students for Chapter 1 at all.[73]

MIGRANT STUDENTS

Like language minority students, students who come from families of migratory workers offer special challenges to Chapter 1, and as early as 1966, one year following the passage of Title I, concerns about their education led to the creation of the federal Migrant Education Program (MEP).[74] This group of students, numbering approximately 597,000 in the 1990-91 school year, face a particularly difficult set of educational challenges. Not only are they highly transient, often averaging more than one move in each twelve-month period, but they must also deal with the language barriers and poverty faced by other Chapter 1 students.[75] Many of the nearly 30 percent of these students who were born in Mexico must move not only from school to school within the United States, but between countries.[76] Further, nearly one-fourth of all migrant students do not enroll in school until more than thirty days after the beginning of the school year.[77]

The impact of the MEP has been somewhat uncertain, particularly in regard to its relationship to other federal compensatory programs. There is evidence that the MEP often supplants these other programs, including regular Chapter 1;[78] indeed, in Florida—a state with a large population of migrant students—only 14 percent of students who are currently migratory receive aid from other programs, including Chapter 1.[79] Most significantly, a major recommendation for change in the MEP calls for increased flexibility in the implementation of the program to allow improved coordination with other federal programs.[80]

The Future of Federal Compensatory Education

As Darling-Hammond has written, despite its critics, Title I and Chapter 1 have benefitted the nation by (1) bringing attention to the educational needs of low-income, low-achieving students who before the War on Poverty were neglected by the educational system, (2) helping to equalize educational spending, (3) institutionalizing parent involvement in the schools, and (4) "probably help[ing] to narrow the gap in basic skills achievement between majority and minority students."[81] Yet federal compensatory education programs have not done enough, and no one is satisfied with the mechanisms for distribution and accountability, the organization and instructional practices, or the outcomes.

Title I and Chapter 1 were never intended to "ghettoize" low-income students by removing them from the regular classroom and the regular curriculum; they only expressly provided funds to local educational agencies serving areas with concentrations of children from low-income families to *supplement* the educational services they receive in the regular classroom. In practice, however, the programs are a major part of a "second system" of categorical special programs for students who need special instructional support. This system is a patchwork of programs, funding streams, eligibility requirements, and identification and monitoring efforts over which educators feel little instructional ownership.[82] Arguably, Chapter 1 is not an instructional program at all now because it is not designed to deliver the most effective instruction but rather to adhere to the current funding streams. The procedures and rules for bringing these programs into being do not help teachers, administrators, and parents to design the programs they believe can be most successful in the culture of their schools. Unlike the past, many observers now maintain that the object of federal compensatory education policy in the future should be to improve the competence of the schools that serve predominantly low-income children.[83] Allocation formulas should provide more funds to schools, districts, and counties with greater concentrations of poor students

who need remedial help. Not only should the formulas provide funds
to be used just for remediating students. They should also include incentives, supports, and rewards for schoolwide projects that improve
the school in ways that we already know have had limited success.[84]
The promise of whole-school reform, as advanced most prominently
by Henry Levin, Robert Slavin, James Comer, and Theodore Sizer, is
that it makes no distinction between the educational needs of poor
children and those of all children. Good educational practices are seen
as good for all.

Federal funds are also needed to provide more learning time for
low-income, low-achieving students, who have spent too little time on
academic tasks. For too long the local implementation of the "supple-
menting" requirements of the legislation have led schools to pull students out of their regular classrooms for remedial instruction in one
form or another. This has resulted in less time for instruction and a
diluted curriculum. Students in these classes learn by rote using worksheets to perform low-level cognitive tasks unrelated to the skills they
need to learn to get out of a remedial track into the regular class and
into the upper tracks so that they can learn the higher level cognitive
tasks necessary to advance in school, enter postsecondary education,
and become employable beyond entry-level jobs. As Darling-Hammond quite rightly asserted after she reviewed studies of the effect of
instruction on achievement, it is the quality of instruction, not race,
ethnicity, nor socioeconomic status—all status rather than functional
characteristics of students—which accounts for their success as learners.

Even in a coming cybernetic age, education remains a social engagement between persons, a teacher and a learner. Federal money
must therefore be available also for staff development for both teachers and administrators. Teacher preparation in the use of effective
teaching strategies is instrumental in the teaching of higher-order
learning in subjects like mathematics, science, and early reading, and
in responding to students' particular learning needs and styles. What
is more, with this kind of professional development teachers do not
need to resort to remedial measures to educate their poor, low-achieving students for they have a broader and different repertoire of skills
and strategies.[85]

Finally, the success of federal compensatory education programs
must be evaluated differently. As discussed earlier, most local school
districts use standardized test scores to determine how to meet changing Title I and Chapter 1 accountability requirements. In turn, the

government uses accumulated standardized test data to justify continued appropriations and authorizations, to weigh major policy changes
in the program, to target states and districts for federal monitoring
and audits, and to carry out Congressionally mandated studies of the
program.[86] For states and local school districts receiving the funding
the tests have been used to target funds and assure fiscal compliance.[87]
But even more, the use of standardized tests has been particularly dis-
astrous for evaluating the outcomes of the Chapter 1 programs because it trivializes other indicators of success, like the number of students at grade level, retention rates of students in high schools who
were in the programs in elementary school, and the changes in the
number of students over time in any school or district who are considered special.[88]

In all of our policy formulations and in the organization and
design of instruction in federal compensatory education programs, we
should keep before us the historical purpose of Title I and Chapter
1—to improve schooling so that programs like compensatory education will not be needed by subsequent generations of students.

NOTES

1. Brian Jendryka, "Failing Grade for Federal Aid: Is It Time to Close the Book on Chapter 1?" *Policy Review* 66 (Fall, 1993): 77.

2. Mary M. Kennedy, Richard K. Jung, and Martin E. Orland, *Poverty, Achievement, and the Distribution of Compensatory Education Services: An Interim Report of the National Assessment of Chapter 1* (Washington, DC: Office of Educational Research and Improvement, U.S. Department of Education, 1985).

3. U.S. Department of Education, *Prospects: The Congressionally Mandated Study of Educational Growth and Opportunity: The Interim Report* (Washington, DC: U.S. Department of Education, 1993).

4. U.S. Department of Education, *Statement of the Independent Review Panel of the National Assessment of Chapter 1* (Washington, DC: U.S. Department of Education, 1993), p. 7.

5. Jay Moskowitz, Stephanie Stullich, and Bing Deng, *Targeting, Formula, and Resource Allocation Issues: Focusing Federal Funds Where the Needs Are Greatest*, A Supplemental Volume to the National Assessment of the Chapter 1 Program (Washington, DC: U.S. Department of Education, 1993).

6. Mary Ann Millsap, Marc Moss, and Beth Gamse, *The Chapter 1 Implementation Study: Final Report, Chapter 1 in Public Schools* (Washington, DC: U.S. Department of Education, Office of Policy and Planning, 1993).

7. Jay G. Chambers et al., *Translating Dollars into Services: Chapter 1 Resources in the Context of State and Local Resources for Education, Final Report* (Palo Alto, CA: American Institutes for Research, 1993); Millsap, Moss, and Gamse, *The Chapter 1 Implementation Study: Final Report.*

8. Chambers et al., *Translating Dollars into Services.*

9. Nancy Kober, *The Role and Impact of Chapter 1, ESEA, Evaluation and Assessment Practices* (Washington, DC: U.S. Congress, Office of Technology Assessment, June 1991).

10. Allan Odden, "How Fiscal Accountability and Program Quality Can Be Insured for Chapter 1," in *Policy Options for the Future of Compensatory Education: Conference Papers*, edited by Denis P. Doyle, Joan S. Michie, and Barbara I. Williams (Washington, DC: Research and Evaluation Associates, 1987).

11. Iris C. Rotberg and James J. Harvey, *Federal Policy Options for Improving the Education of Low-Income Students*, Vol. 1, *Findings and Recommendations* (Santa Monica, CA: RAND Institute of Education and Training, 1993).

12. Kober, *The Role and Impact of Chapter 1, ESEA, Evaluation and Assessment Practices.*

13. Rotberg and Harvey, *Federal Policy Options for Improving the Education of Low-Income Students*; U.S. General Accounting Office, *Chapter 1 Accountability: Greater Focus on Program Goals Needed* (Washington, DC: U.S. General Accounting Office, March, 1993).

14. Launor F. Carter, "The Sustaining Effects Study of Compensatory and Elementary Education," *Educational Researcher* 13, no. 7 (1984): 4-13; Frederick King and Andrew Sommer, *Chapter 1: Does the Model Matter?* (Portland, OR: Northwest Regional Educational Laboratory, 1990).

15. Commission on Chapter 1, *Making Schools Work for Children In Poverty: A New Framework Prepared by the Commission on Chapter 1* (Washington, DC: Commission on Chapter 1, 1992).

16. King and Sommer, *Chapter 1: Does the Model Matter?*

17. Ibid.

18. Carter, "The Sustaining Effects Study of Compensatory and Elementary Education"; King and Sommer, *Chapter 1: Does the Model Matter?*

19. Mary Ann Millsap et al., *The Chapter 1 Implementation Study: Interim Report* (Washington, DC: U.S. Department of Education, Office of Policy and Planning, 1992).

20. Beatrice F. Birman et al., *The Current Operation of the Chapter 1 Program*, Final Report from the National Assessment of Chapter 1 (Washington, DC: U.S. Department of Education, Office of Educational Research and Improvement, 1987).

21. Millsap, Moss, and Gamse, *The Chapter 1 Implementation Study: Final Report.*

22. U.S. Department of Education, Office of Elementary and Secondary Education, *Chapter 1 Flexibility: A Guide to Opportunities in Local Projects* (Washington, DC: U.S. Department of Education, Office of Elementary and Secondary Education, 1992).

23. Frederick King, *Alternatives to the Pullout Model* (Portland, OR: Northwest Regional Educational Laboratory, 1990).

24. Ibid.

25. Ibid.

26. Millsap, Moss, and Gamse, *The Chapter 1 Implementation Study: Final Report*; Millsap et al., *The Chapter 1 Implementation Study: Interim Report.*

27. Sharon A. Harpring, "Inclass Alternatives to Traditional Chapter 1 Pullout Programs" (Paper presented at the Annual Meeting of the American Educational Research Association, Chicago, 1985).

28. "Low Achievers Can Catch Up: Chapter 1 Expects More of Schools," *Harvard Education Letter* 7, no. 1 (1991): 1-4.

29. Francis X. Archambault, "Instructional Setting: Key Issue or Bogus Concern?" in *Designs for Compensatory Education: Conference Proceedings and Papers*, edited by Barbara I. Williams, Peggy A. Richmond, and Beverly J. Mason (Washington, DC: Research and Evaluation Associates, 1986).

30. Mary M. Kennedy et al., *The Effectiveness of Chapter 1 Services: Second Interim Report from the National Assessment of Chapter 1* (Washington, DC: U.S. Department of Education, Office of Educational Research and Improvement, 1986).

31. Brian Rowan and Larry F. Guthrie, *The Quality of Chapter 1 Instruction: Results from a Study of 24 Schools* (San Francisco: Far West Laboratory for Educational Research and Development, 1990).

32. U.S. Department of Education, Office of Policy and Planning, *Reinventing Chapter 1: The Current Chapter 1 Program and New Directions*, Final Report of the National Assessment of the Chapter 1 Program (Washington, DC: U.S. Department of Education, Office of Policy and Planning, 1993); Millsap et al., *The Chapter 1 Implementation Study: Interim Report*.

33. Mark Gittleman, *Chapter 1 Program Improvement and Innovation across the States: An Overview and State Profiles* (Washington, DC: Council of Chief State School Officers, 1992).

34. U.S. Department of Education, *Reinventing Chapter 1*.

35. Ibid.

36. A. Harry Passow, *Curriculum and Instruction in Chapter 1: A Look Back and a Look Ahead* (New York: Institute for Urban and Minority Education, ERIC Clearinghouse on Urban Education, Teachers College, Columbia University, 1988), pp. 14-15. Edmund W. Gordon's statement is in his "Introduction" to an issue of *Review of Educational Research* (40, no. 1 [1970]), p. 8, that is devoted entirely to the topic of "Education for Socially Disadvantaged Children."

37. Walter Doyle, "Vision and Reality: A Reaction to Issues in Curriculum and Instruction for Compensatory Education," in *Designs for Compensatory Education: Conference Proceedings and Papers*, edited by Barbara I. Williams, Peggy A. Richmond, and Beverly J. Mason (Washington, DC: Research and Evaluation Associates, 1986).

38. Thomas A. Romberg, "Mathematics for Compensatory School Programs," in *Designs for Compensatory Education: Conference Proceedings and Papers*, edited by Barbara I. Williams, Peggy A. Richmond, and Beverly J. Mason (Washington, DC: Research and Evaluation Associates, 1986), p. 11.

39. Ibid.

40. Robert Calfee, "Curriculum and Instruction: Reading," in *Designs for Compensatory Education: Conference Proceedings and Papers*, edited by Barbara I. Williams, Peggy A. Richmond, and Beverly J. Mason (Washington, DC: Research and Evaluation Associates, 1986).

41. Doyle, "Vision and Reality."

42. Advisory Committee on Testing in Chapter 1, *Reinforcing the Promise, Reforming the Paradigm*, Report of the Advisory Committee on Testing in Chapter 1 (Washington, DC: U.S. Department of Education, 1993).

43. Ibid.

44. Nettie Legters and Robert E. Slavin, *Elementary Students at Risk: A Status Report* (Baltimore, MD: Center for Research on Effective Schooling for Disadvantaged Students, 1992).

45. Ibid.

46. Millsap, Moss, and Gamse, *The Chapter 1 Implementation Study: Final Report*.

47. Diane A. D'Angelo and C. Ralph Adler, "Chapter 1: A Catalyst for Improving Parent Involvement," *Phi Delta Kappan* 72, no. 5 (1991): 350-354.

48. Milbrey W. McLaughlin and Patrick M. Shields, "Involving Parents in the Schools: Lessons for Policy," in *Designs for Compensatory Education: Conference Proceedings and Papers*, edited by Barbara I. Williams, Peggy A. Richmond, and Beverly J. Mason (Washington, DC: Research and Evaluation Associates, 1986); E. Deborah Jay and Patrick M. Shields, *Parent Involvement in Local Chapter 1 Programs* (Menlo Park, CA: SRI International, 1987).

49. Wayne C. Riddle, *Education for Disadvantaged Children: Major Themes in the 1988 Reauthorization of Chapter 1*, CRS Report for Congress (Washington, DC: Library of Congress, Congressional Research Service, 1989).

50. McLaughlin and Shields, "Involving Parents in the Schools."

51. Ibid.

52. Riddle, *Education for Disadvantaged Children*.

53. McLaughlin and Shields, "Involving Parents in the Schools."

54. Carrie B. Chimerine, Karen L. M. Panton, and Alexander W. W. Russo, *The Other 91 Percent: Strategies to Improve the Quality of Out-of-School Experiences of Chapter 1 Students*, Supplement to the National Assessment of Chapter 1 (Washington, DC: U.S. Department of Education, Office of Policy and Planning, 1993).

55. Millsap, Moss, and Gamse, *The Chapter 1 Implementation Study: Interim Report*.

56. Ibid.

57. Adriana de Kantor, Alan Ginsburg, and Ann M. Milne, "Parent Involvement Strategies: New Emphasis on Traditional Parent Roles," in *Designs for Compensatory Education: Conference Proceedings and Papers*, edited by Barbara I. Williams, Peggy A. Richmond, and Beverly J. Mason (Washington, DC: Research and Evaluation Associates, 1986); Jay and Shields, *Parent Involvement in Local Chapter 1 Programs*.

58. Millsap, Moss, and Gamse, *The Chapter 1 Implementation Study: Interim Report*.

59. Chimerine, Panton, and Russo, *The Other 91 Percent*.

60. U.S. Department of Education, Office of Policy and Planning, *Reinventing Chapter 1*; Chambers et al., *Translating Dollars into Services*.

61. Millsap, Moss, and Gamse, *The Chapter 1 Implementation Study: Interim Report*.

62. U.S. Department of Education, *Reinventing Chapter 1*.

63. Millsap et al., *The Chapter 1 Implementation Study: Interim Report*.

64. Northwest Regional Educational Laboratory, *Paraprofessional Training Manual* (Portland, OR: Northwest Regional Educational Laboratory).

65. Millsap et al., *The Chapter 1 Implementation Study: Interim Report*.

66. Millsap, Moss, and Gamse, *The Chapter 1 Implementation Study: Final Report*.

67. Chambers et al., *Translating Dollars into Services*, p. 62.

68. E. William Strang and Elaine Carlson, *Providing Chapter 1 Services to Limited English Proficient Students, Final Report* (Washington, DC: U.S. Department of Education, Office of Policy and Planning, 1991).

69. Ibid.

70. Millsap, Moss, and Gamse, *The Chapter 1 Implementation Study: Final Report*.

71. Strang and Carlson, *Providing Chapter 1 Services to Limited English Proficient Students*.

72. Ibid.

73. U.S. Department of Education, *Reinventing Chapter 1*.

74. Ibid.

75. Ibid. See also, Lamarr Cox et al., *Descriptive Study of the Chapter 1 Migrant Education Program* (Washington, DC: U.S. Department of Education, Office of Policy and Planning, 1992).

76. National Commission on Migrant Education, *Invisible Children: A Portrait of Migrant Education in the United States* (Washington, DC: National Commission on Migrant Education, 1992).

77. Cox et al., *Descriptive Study of the Chapter 1 Migrant Education Program*.

78. U.S. Department of Education, *Reinventing Chapter 1*.

79. National Commission on Migrant Education, *Invisible Children*.

80. Ibid.

81. Linda Darling-Hammond, "Commentary," in *Federal Options for Improving the Education of Low-Income Students*, vol. 2, edited by Iris S. Rotberg (Santa Monica, CA: RAND, 1993), p. 26.

82. Richard L. Allington, "Commentary," in *Federal Options for Improving the Education of Low-Income Students*, vol. 2, edited by Iris C. Rotberg (Santa Monica, CA: RAND, 1993).

83. Thomas B. Timar, "Commentary," in *Federal Options for Improving the Education of Low-Income Students*, vol. 2, edited by Iris C. Rotberg (Santa Monica, CA: RAND, 1993).

84. U.S. Department of Education, *Statement of the Independent Review Panel of the National Assessment of Chapter 1*, p. 7.

85. Linda Darling-Hammond, *Federal Policy Options for Chapter 1: An Equity Agenda for School Restructuring* (New York: National Center for Restructuring Education, Schools, and Teaching, Teachers College, Columbia University, 1993).

86. Kober, *The Role and Impact of Chapter 1, ESEA, Evaluation and Assessment Practices*.

87. Odden, "How Fiscal Accountability and Program Quality Can Be Insured for Chapter 1."

88. Jere E. Brophy, "Commentary," in *Federal Options for Improving the Education of Low-Income Students*, vol. 2, edited by Iris C. Rotberg (Santa Monica, CA: RAND, 1993).

CHAPTER VI

Second-Chance Programs for Youth

FREDERICK DOOLITTLE

In the modern economy, the employment prospects of young people who drop out of high school are bleak. In 1992, fewer than half of all United States residents between the ages of sixteen and twenty-four who were not in school and did not have a high school diploma or a general equivalency diploma (GED) worked during the year; among African-Americans only about one-fourth worked. These employment problems are not new; since World War II, those without a high school diploma have faced increasing employment pressures as the economic base of the country has shifted from manufacturing and agriculture toward services.

Starting in the 1960s, federal, state, and local governments, and community groups have operated programs outside the traditional kindergarten through twelfth grade setting to provide school dropouts with a "second chance" to succeed in the labor market. Although these programs operate outside of traditional schools, they do provide an important alternative for those students who, for whatever reason, opt out of the schools. To put it simply, second-chance programs take on some of the work of the schools, providing educational experience for students who otherwise find themselves on the outside of the nation's educational system. Thus, although they are in a sense outside of the scope of this volume, they do provide, in another sense, examples of needed changes in the provision of educational services to at-risk youth; they provide services that are beyond the capacity of the nation's already overwhelmed schools.

Social scientists have conducted a number of evaluations of the implementation and effectiveness of second-chance programs. While much of this research has not provided solid answers to crucial policy questions, due to methodological or data problems, or because many

---

Frederick Doolittle is an economist and is Assistant Director of Research at the Manpower Demonstration Research Corporation in New York City.

program approaches have not yet been rigorously studied,[1] there are now enough reliable findings to develop general observations about the impact of second-chance programs.

In this chapter I review key studies of second-chance education, training, and employment programs for economically disadvantaged youth who lack a high school diploma or a general equivalency diploma (GED). The central question in most of this research is whether these programs improve the later employment prospects of the young people they serve, though attention is also given to whether the programs achieve intermediate outcomes such as attainment of a GED or high school diploma. Following a review of the research record, several policy implications of these findings are discussed.

The conclusion of the chapter is sobering: while the programs often show encouraging "in-program" results (for example, youth do participate in education, training, and/or work experience and more receive a GED), they have neither—with one notable exception—led to a substantial increase in the youths' later employment and earnings above the level that would have occurred without the program, nor proven cost effective from the perspective of taxpayers or society as a whole. Nevertheless, within this overall story there are more encouraging findings for some subgroups of young people and some types of programs. Given the severity of the problems faced by young dropouts, this research record highlights the need for continued efforts to prevent young people from leaving school prematurely and for broader tests of innovative second-chance approaches. I argue in this chapter that, as part of our efforts to change schools and education, we must find a strategy for building on the existing research findings and operational experience to improve the lives of young economically disadvantaged dropouts. Second-chance programs provide one possible strategy.

Research on Second-Chance Programs

Research on the effectiveness of second-chance programs examines whether postprogram benefits to participants and society exceed the costs involved in providing the program. The costs of these programs are incurred both by program participants, in the form of a lowered income during the program period, and by the society as a whole, in the form of tax dollars and subsidies. Similarly, both program participants and the society as a whole can reap benefits from a successful program. Most research to date has focused on quantifiable benefits and costs such as increased earnings, reduced criminal behavior, decline in the number receiving welfare, and the direct costs of the services provided.

In most jurisdictions in the United States, children up to a specified age (often sixteen) are required to participate in educational activities; in addition, few children work because of child labor laws or lack of interest or skills. However, young dropouts beyond the age of compulsory school attendance—the target group for many second-chance programs—face a number of alternatives. Participation in second-chance programs has typically been voluntary, though recent amendments to the federal Aid to Families with Dependent Children (AFDC) program now require some young parents who are school dropouts to participate in education programs. Many dropouts, especially those who are not parents, are seeking jobs, though weak skills often limit their success. In addition, there are great differences in employment experience among subgroups of school dropouts. Typically, youths apply for a program when they have lost a job or have decided to make an effort to enter the labor force.

These features of young dropouts' lives have three key implications for research on second-chance programs. There is not space in this chapter to review these implications in detail; however, they can be summarized as follows:

First, because the employment rate and average earnings of those in the "control group" (those who are not receiving the services under study, to whom program participants are compared) gradually rise over time, the employment and earnings benchmarks that programs must "beat" to be considered effective also typically increase, even in the relatively short run.

Second, because participation in most second-chance programs is voluntary, and because those in the groups to which program participants are compared may participate in other programs, it is difficult to isolate the impact of second-chance programs in comparison to the alternative of no service. Rather, in recent years government agencies funding second-chance programs have made the pragmatic decision to emphasize research approaches designed to produce comparable program and comparison groups and accurate estimates of the benefits of an increase in services.

Third, there can be often large, and often inconsistent, differences in program impacts on earnings among subgroups of young dropouts defined by demographic characteristics or prior work experience. This, again, makes it difficult to summarize program impacts simply.

Some of these difficulties can be seen in the experience of the National Job Training Partnership Act (JTPA) Study. This project sought to estimate the impact of three service strategies (classroom training, on-the-job training [OJT], and a residual category of all other services) for the youths that local JTPA staff recommended as appropriate for each. Not surprisingly, the youths recommended for the three approaches differed in background characteristics such as prior work experience and education.[2] For example, those recommended for on-the-job training were typically more job ready than those recommended for classroom training. Thus, the selection process complicated any direct comparison of the impacts of service strategies, since the groups differed in two ways: first, members of the groups were given access to different types of services; and, second, they had different initial characteristics.

Despite such complications, however, as more research findings accumulate, patterns in the program impacts observed across types of services may be clearer.

Lessons from Research on Second-Chance Programs for Youth

The program impact findings reviewed in this section are not encouraging; few programs have shown significant and enduring effects. With the exception of the Job Corps, the small number of rigorously studied second-chance education, training, and employment programs for youth have not been effective in increasing employment and earnings in the postprogram follow-up period. There is, however, some evidence that program impacts are somewhat more positive for young women than for men, and that certain types of sites appear to have stronger impacts than others.[3]

The remainder of this chapter summarizes key findings for a range of service approaches, starting with programs focusing on linking youths to jobs, followed by programs designed to increase basic or occupational skills through education or training or both. Some service approaches are not listed (for example, basic skills instruction as a stand-alone service), either because they are infrequently offered or because their impacts have not been carefully studied.[4]

JOB PLACEMENT ASSISTANCE

Job placement or job search assistance programs are designed to speed the rate at which young people find jobs or to provide access to better jobs than they would find on their own. These programs

128   SECOND-CHANCE PROGRAMS FOR YOUTH

typically offer encouragement in the job search effort to boost motivation, inform young people about employer expectations and the traits they value, help them to prepare a résumé, provide practice in contacting potential employers and interviewing, and offer assistance in finding job leads. During the late 1970s and early 1980s, this type of program grew in popularity, as the large federal employment programs of earlier years (under the Comprehensive Employment and Training Act [CETA]) declined in funding, and placements in unsubsidized private employment were increasingly emphasized. This type of program was especially common during the mid-1980s following passage of the Job Training Partnership Act (JTPA); partly as a result of this, JTPA acquired a reputation for providing short-term, low-cost services to those with relatively good prospects for employment. However, recent amendments to JTPA, which are intended to focus program enrollment on more disadvantaged individuals and to encourage more intensive services, authorize the provision of job search and job placement assistance only in combination with other more intensive, skill-building services.

The shift away from job placement assistance as a stand-alone service appears to be supported by research. Several studies have found initial increases in employment rates and earnings for this type of program, although the effects start to decline by the end of the first year of follow-up and disappear by the second year. Most of the initial increases in earnings appear to occur because more youth were working, rather than because they were finding better jobs than they otherwise would have found.

Recent interim findings from the National JTPA Study illustrate the dangers of identifying relatively job ready youth and providing them with job search assistance as a stand-alone service. In the JTPA Study, staff in the sixteen participating sites first recommended a service or services for applicants and then random assignment was done, allowing a comparison of the experiences of the youth in the program with those of the group recommended only for job search assistance. Not surprisingly, staff selected relatively job ready youths for this service plan, as illustrated by a comparison of the average earnings for these versus other youths: among the comparison group, male out-of-school youths recommended only for job search assistance had average earnings of $15,534 over eighteen months, as compared to an average for other male youths of $10,649. For this relatively job-ready subgroup, program impacts on earnings were actually negative: males in the program group who had been recommended only for job search assistance had average earnings for the eighteen months that were more than $5,000 lower than their comparison group counterparts. These findings must be interpreted with caution because of the small sample of youths recommended only for job search assistance and (for the purposes of this chapter) because about 40 percent of the male youths in the JTPA sample already had a high school diploma or GED. However, they suggest that there are real dangers in identifying job-ready youths and providing only job search assistance through a means-tested government program.

WORK EXPERIENCE

Over the last three decades, the federal government has provided funds to state and local governments for temporary, subsidized employment of out-of-school youths. During the CETA years prior to the passage of JTPA, public service employment was an important service; throughout that period, summer youth employment programs received substantial federal funding and were seen as a way of lessening the chances of urban unrest when jobs are scarce. During the mid-to-late 1970s, the federal government funded the Supported Work Demonstration, which tested the effects of offering intensive work experience, gradually increasing work responsibilities, close supervision of work performance, and peer support to several seriously disadvantaged groups, including young dropouts.

Research findings on the effects of work experience as a standalone service for young dropouts have generally been discouraging. In the Supported Work Demonstration, the clearest test of a strong work experience program for seriously disadvantaged youths, in-program effects on employment, hours worked, and earnings were strong at the one-year point but quickly declined following the end of subsidized employment and were gone after eighteen months. Another demonstration operating at roughly the same time, the Youth Incentive Entitlement Pilot Project (YIEPP), offered a separate test of the effect of paid work experience as an inducement for young dropouts to return to school. In YIEPP, low-income youths in selected cities who had not yet completed high school were guaranteed a part-time minimum wage job during the school year and a full-time job during the summer if they attended school and made satisfactory progress. The offer was open both to current students and to dropouts who agreed to return to high school or to an approved alternative program. Again, the program had an in-program effect on employment and earnings, but did not affect the rate of school completion by dropouts who returned to school. Unfortunately, longer-term follow-up has been very limited, making it difficult to draw conclusions about longer-term employment effects.

This pattern of research findings contributed to a move to combine work experience with other services. The core federal summer jobs youth program under JTPA for students and school dropouts now combines work experience with basic education. Further, new versions of work experience (discussed in more detail later in this chapter), including youth conservation corps, urban volunteer corps, and YouthBuild involve work experience with an explicit community service focus combined with basic education and other services. These build on the example of the Ventures in Community Improvement (VICI) program of the 1970s, under which out-of-school youths gained work experience in construction trades working on public or low-income housing in their community under the supervision of union journeymen. Although there was no educational component to the program, participants were encouraged to complete a GED preparation course and pass the examination.[5]

This experience and new research on learning theory have led to a recent rethinking of the potential of work experience in second-chance programs. Some researchers and program operators now emphasize the role that work experience can play in motivating the learning of basic and occupational skills and in reenforcing what is learned in the classroom through application in the work setting.[6] This topic is discussed in the final section of this chapter.

OTHER RELATIVELY SHORT-TERM SERVICES

Under Title II of JTPA, the federal government provides grants on a formula basis to states, which in turn pass them on to local service delivery areas (SDAs). These JTPA funds can be used to provide a long list of services to adults and in-school and out-of-school youths who meet income guidelines and/or face other special barriers to employment.[7] Notably absent from the list of permitted JTPA activities are public service employment and the payment of stipends to participants, two important features of CETA, the predecessor to JTPA. Youth programs include year-round programs providing individualized service plans based on applicant interests and service needs, as well as summer jobs programs emphasizing work experience and basic education. Nationally, out-of-school youths have typically made up about half of all young people served under Title II year-round programs, with school dropouts accounting for slightly less than half of these youths.

During the early years of the program, performance standards for SDAs emphasized such short-term outcomes as the employment rate on "terminating" from the program, the "positive termination" rate for youth (which included employment and other favorable outcomes), the wage at placement, and the cost per placement. Such standards, however, created incentives for local programs to provide relatively low-intensity services and to be cautious in enrolling participants who faced severe barriers to employment.

As a result, the Department of Labor modified the JTPA performance standards over time to include other outcomes, eliminate cost standards, and extend the follow-up period. Amendments to the federal statute in 1992 reenforced this shift in program emphasis, requiring more intensive program services as well as the targeting of program outreach to those with multiple barriers to employment.

In 1986, the Department of Labor began a study of the impacts of JTPA services in sixteen local programs; out-of-school youth were included in this research. These sixteen sites are not a statistically representative sample of all local programs; however, their programs appear to be similar in many ways to the averages for all programs nationally. As mentioned earlier, this research sought to estimate the impacts of three service strategies (classroom training, on-the-job training [OJT], and other services) for individuals recommended for each by local staff; findings based on thirty months of follow-up have been released.

In practice, the three service strategies did end up having different service emphases, though the results were not quite as expected. About 75 percent of program group youths recommended for classroom training were later enrolled in JTPA,[8] and most received either basic education or occupational training. Among program group youths recommended for OJT, the JTPA enrollment rate was only 60 percent; only about half of these participated in OJT, reflecting the continuing difficulty of arranging OJT placements for youths. In fact, a similar percentage received job search assistance with the goal of a placement in a regular, unsubsidized job; as a result, the service strategy was renamed OJT/job search. The "other services" category emphasized basic education and miscellaneous services, including job readiness training and career exploration.

Adding to the difficulties of assessing the impact of JTPA, a substantial percentage of the control group received services through other sources. As a result, differences in the rate of receipt of basic education between the program and control group were small, and it was not possible to measure differences in the receipt of job search assistance or several miscellaneous services. The service difference between the program and control group should, therefore, be seen as significant but modest for many types of services, and the impacts reported here (which measure the changes in earnings caused by this difference in service) should be interpreted accordingly.

The most striking finding at thirty months of follow-up was a lack of significant earnings impacts. For all three service strategies, program impacts on earnings were insignificant for females and for the majority of males who entered the program without a prior arrest. However, for the one-fourth of males who entered the program with a prior arrest, there was some evidence that the program may have actually led to a reduction in earnings through thirty months of follow-up.[9]

The findings for females illustrate impacts at the service strategy level. Females recommended for classroom training experienced a slight decline in earnings over the first six months of follow-up and their later gains in earnings were not large enough to produce significant earnings impacts over the entire thirty months. Females recommended for the OJT/job search service strategy experienced a moderate initial gain in earnings, which was not sustained over time. Females recommended for the other services strategy experienced negligible changes in earnings throughout the entire thirty months.

EDUCATION PLUS OCCUPATIONAL TRAINING

Some programs have been explicitly designed to provide a more intensive, multicomponent service mix to address the various problems facing economically disadvantaged youths. These programs are based on the theory that employment and training programs must move beyond the narrowly defined labor market problems to address other issues in youths' lives that lessen their chances for success. The Job Corps, the oldest and best known of these programs, combines basic education, occupational training, job placement assistance, health care, and numerous support services in a residential setting where room and board are provided. The program also provides a lump-sum payment for those who complete the program. Participants

are out-of-school youths, many of whom have low basic skills and little work experience. Participants on average are active for about six
months, although many continue in services for much longer. Funding
for the program has been relatively stable, in part because favorable
evaluation findings have been used to fend off budget cuts.

An influential study completed in the early 1980s found that the
Job Corps produced statistically significant impacts lasting throughout
four years of postprogram follow-up on educational attainment (primarily receipt of a GED), time spent employed, earnings, receipt of
public assistance or unemployment compensation benefits, health, and
criminal activity.[10] Earnings impacts for the full sample were $567 a
year (in 1977 dollars), or a 28 percent increase over the four-year postprogram period. Employment and earnings impacts were similar for
males and for females without children, while impacts for females with
children were weaker and unstable over time. The findings suggest
that those who completed the program benefitted the most and early
dropouts benefitted little or not at all.[11] Impacts on criminal activity
were especially strong during the in-program period, as would be
expected in a residential program. The study also found that program
benefits exceeded costs from the perspectives both of society as a
whole and of program participants, though nonparticipants (i.e., taxpayers) did incur a small net cost reflecting an income transfer to participants from the rest of society.

These encouraging findings for the residential Job Corps program
led to calls for a test of a less expensive nonresidential program offering many of the same components.[12] The JOBSTART Demonstration,
which operated from 1985 to 1988 in thirteen sites, was a response.[13]
JOBSTART provided 17- to 21-year old, low-skilled school dropouts
with basic education, occupational training, and job placement assistance. It involved less extensive support services, and was operated as a
nonresidential program within the regular JTPA Title II program.
Youth in the program group participated an average of 400 hours in
JOBSTART services over six months; about 33 percent participated
for more than 500 hours. Thus, it represented a more intensive contrast to the prevailing JTPA practices of the 1980s.

Early findings from the JOBSTART Demonstration were as
encouraging as the Job Corps findings. The programs found ways to
operate within the JTPA structure and recruit the target population.
In addition, many of the young people invested substantial time and
effort in the program (amounting to a doubling of the participation

rates in education or training and average hours of the control group). Further, JOBSTART produced significant increases in the proportion of youths who received a GED; 42 percent of the program group had a high school diploma or GED at the four-year point, as compared to 29 percent of the control group.

In the later years of follow-up, however, the gains in employment and earnings (and declines in welfare receipt and criminal activity) for the full sample of youths were insufficient to produce significant earnings gains for participants or to compensate society as a whole for the resources devoted to program services. For example, for all youths in the sample, JOBSTART led to a $499 decline in earnings in the first year of follow-up (primarily an in-program period), followed by a very small decline in the second year, and increases of somewhat over $400 during each of the third and fourth years, for a negligible four-year impact on earnings.

There were bright spots, however, for some subgroups and at some types of sites, though many of the findings are not statistically significant under conventional tests, in part because of small samples. Earnings impacts were positive—nearly $2,500 over the four-year period—for males with an arrest prior to entering the program and slightly negative for males without a prior arrest, a reversal from the pattern in the JTPA study. Youths who had previously dropped out of school because of educational difficulties or other school-related reasons (as opposed to a desire to find work or because of pregnancy) experienced positive earnings impacts of $726 in year three and nearly $600 in year four. Further, welfare receipt decreased among young women who were not caring for children of their own when they entered the program, with drops both in the percentage of young women receiving aid and in the amount of aid received. In addition, as in the Job Corps study, there is evidence suggesting that those who participated the longest benefitted the most.

Finally, impacts at one JOBSTART site—the Center for Employment Training (CET) in San Jose—were large (over $6500 for the four years) and statistically significant despite the site's relatively small sample. This finding, coupled with similar strong results in another recent study (the Minority Female Single Parent Demonstration), is growing evidence of the effectiveness of the CET program.[14] Unfortunately, it is difficult to isolate the reason for CET's strong impacts, because the program is unusual in several respects: it provided a relatively concentrated dose of JOBSTART services (i.e., a short length of participation but near-average hours of activity), little up-front screening of applicants, integration of education and training, close ties to the employer community, a longstanding good reputation in the community, strong job placement efforts, a clear organizational mission, and experienced and stable staff.

What Should Be Tried Next for Disadvantaged Out-of-School Youths?

It might appear that the most likely conclusion from the completed evaluations is that almost nothing has enduring positive effects for disadvantaged youths. However, while the message from the recent research is far from optimistic, this conclusion is clearly overly pessimistic. The problem in JOBSTART, for example, concerned the extent of initial earnings losses for some sub-groups and the magnitude of later positive earning impacts, not the lack of any payoff. Further, recent changes in JTPA and other programs have created an environment more hospitable to the operation of more intensive, multicomponent programs.[15]

The remainder of this chapter presents ideas based on research findings and operational experience about how to build on past experience and take advantage of this more hospitable environment to improve program impacts. The discussion is divided into three parts: (1) suggestions on targeting program recruitment; (2) options for shortening and lessening the initial earnings losses during the participation period; and (3) ways of increasing the earnings payoff in later years.

TARGETING PROGRAM OUTREACH

Variations in program impacts among subgroups of youth are common; it is, thus, important to design outreach strategies to include those most likely to be helped by a given program. This suggests that outreach strategies must vary with program services. For example, there is evidence that a relatively intensive program like JOBSTART will have its best effect if youths with relatively serious employment barriers are recruited to participate. However, less intensive programs may have a different pattern of subgroup impacts; for example, the findings of the National JTPA Study suggest that, for relatively short-term services like those offered in the late 1980s, earnings impacts tend to be better for those who are more job ready.

In designing outreach strategies for more intensive programs, it is important to recognize that if *all* participants face serious barriers to employment, there will be fewer role models and success stories among the participants to help motivate youths and provide satisfaction for staff. Thus, even though these programs should include a substantial percentage of participants with serious barriers to employment, program managers should more closely monitor the achievement of intermediate and long-term milestones by participants and the morale and motivation of the young people and staff.

In general, the pattern of subgroup impacts found in JOBSTART suggests the following outreach strategies for similar programs:

- **Young women.** The findings for young women suggest that both mothers caring for their children and other women should be served. For those who are not mothers, community outreach is important; most of these women are not receiving public assistance, so referrals from other social service agencies may be less frequent than for young mothers.

- **Males with a prior arrest.** Programs can establish links to the justice system to aid recruiting, and might even start participation in the program before the end of incarceration or while young people are on probation. Further, participation might be made a condition for early release for those in prison, or the program could operate as an alternative to incarceration for first-time offenders.

- **Young people who dropped out for school-related reasons.** Recruiting young dropouts into an employment program such as JOBSTART may be easiest if the target is youths actively seeking a job or training, but the subgroup findings imply that programs should seek ways to identify young people who dropped out for school-related reasons. It may be possible to cooperate with local school counselors and teachers to find ways to inform young people who leave school for such reasons about the alternative to the traditional educational system provided by programs such as JOBSTART.

OPTIONS FOR COMBATING THE INITIAL EARNINGS LOSSES FOR PARTICIPANTS

For some young people, especially males, participation in an intensive program results in substantial costs in terms of foregone earnings. This can undermine efforts to keep them in the program long enough to improve their skills substantially or can overwhelm earnings gains in the years following program participation. Unfortunately, efforts to counteract initial earnings losses by providing in-program income can increase program costs and, unless there are substantial later earnings gains, can reduce the chance that the program will be cost-effective for funders or society. Thus, they must be coupled with efforts to improve later earnings impacts, as discussed below. The options for avoiding initial earnings losses are not necessarily consistent with one another, but could be appropriate in different circumstances depending on funding and operational constraints.

Linking education and training with paid work experience. If structured properly and offered as part of a program of education and training, paid work experience has the potential to improve later program impacts in addition to its obvious value in providing income during program participation. This argument hinges on several hypotheses. First, the young people's experiences on the job can become part of the program, serving to make the education and training more relevant and to reinforce their learning of skills through application in a real-world setting. Further, work experience can help the young people to be socialized into the adult world of work in a gradual, nonthreatening way and can bring them into contact with adult role models in a work setting. There is also growing evidence that young people value opportunities to make a contribution to their community; such service can change the way they see themselves and relate to others, and the way others see them. Finally, since many young people become involved in programs because they are seeking a job, paid work experience could help them to stay in the program longer, gaining more academic and occupational skills. The new JTPA amendments and regulations make paid work experience somewhat easier to provide.[16]

In considering work experience and related options, however, it is important to understand the responsibilities that providing service entails for program operators. Developing a large number of placements may be time consuming, especially when the clients are young people with low educational attainment and limited work histories. In addition, it is necessary to monitor both the nature of the work and the participant's job performance to ensure that the employment experience is worthwhile and contributes to program goals. Finally, in a slow-growing economy, wages may have to be partly or even fully subsidized, raising the costs of the service.

Restructuring the duration and sequence of program services. This option for lessening the costs of program participation can be accomplished through either of two quite different means: (1) concentrating intense participation in a short time period, or (2) allowing for extended and less intense participation in order to allow youths to work while in the program. The choice of approach would depend on the type of young people served.

The suggestion of concentrating program participation in a short period should be distinguished from a call for short-term, low-intensity programs; rather, the approach is more similar to a full-immersion program. However, there are trade-offs here as well. An intense and relatively short immersion in education and training requires that youths participate more hours per day; youths who lack the interest or ability to focus for extended periods at the point when they enter the program, who have other responsibilities (such as child care), or who need to work to cover their living expenses may not be able to participate.

Combining work and program participation over an extended period could be appropriate for relatively employable youths who want or need to work at least part-time. Services would have to be structured to allow participation to vary over time as the mix of education, training, and work shifts. In effect, the approach involves recognizing the intermittent nature of many youths' participation in programs and setting up program services to facilitate less intense but extended participation.[17]

OPTIONS FOR INCREASING LONG-TERM PAYOFFS

In this section I discuss three options for raising earnings impacts in the postprogram period: (1) linking program services more closely to the job market; (2) placing more emphasis on broadly defined life skills and youth development needs; and (3) continuing program services after the initial job placement.

Strengthening the link between education and training and the job market. Program guidelines should call for training in occupations in demand in the local job market. However, this is often difficult to do. CET/San Jose, the JOBSTART site with the strongest earnings impacts, was the most effective in involving employers in developing the program's occupational emphasis and curriculum. Training areas were chosen carefully, based on analysis of local labor market needs. The site was also unusual in the extent to which educational services were integrated and shaped by occupational training needs.

Job placement assistance is also important, although it also can be difficult to arrange for young dropouts. In several of the JOBSTART sites, for example, the participants were served by job placement staff who were also working with more job-ready clients. As a result, the understandably busy placement staff tended to work more with the non-JOBSTART clients, who tended to be easier to place. This experience highlights the importance of having staff members, whether job placement staff or occupational trainers, who accept that helping less job-ready clients find employment is a central part of their job.

There can also be job placement problems for youths who do not complete the program, since in most programs job placement services are focused on program graduates. It could be counterproductive to provide extensive job placement assistance to those in the early stages of program participation, since it might induce them to take a low-wage job when, with more participation, they could find a better job. However, it is important to have a "safety net" of placement assistance for those who stop participating before completing the program.

Finally, past program experience illustrates the necessity of having job placement staff with good connections to employers and the ability to find training-related jobs with long-term prospects that are better than what the youths could find on their own. Job placement cannot be an afterthought, with responsibilities assigned to staff who lack the appropriate skills. The demands on job placement staff are as challenging as those facing education and training staff.

Addressing the developmental needs of youths. Many young people who participate in employment and training programs have lived in relative poverty and isolation from the world of work for much of their lives. One of the greatest challenges these youths face is to overcome the emotional deprivation and psychological distress that result from the many housing, financial, personal safety, and other problems they confront each day.[18] Too many lack even a knowledgeable and trusted older person to help them cope with these problems and move through the normal stages of adolescent development.

Programs can help youths address these issues and teach them the interpersonal skills necessary for life at work and at home. Such skills include the ability to communicate with different types of people clearly, to work productively in a group, to make plans and carry them out, and to handle effectively the unexpected events that inevitably crop up in daily life. One approach to helping young people learn these interpersonal skills is to emphasize youth leadership development by giving participants serious responsibilities within the program. In the most innovative cases, such as YouthBuild programs, young people work together in groups, set the rules for the group, plan its activities, and carry out the plans. In addition, YouthBuild provides an intense work experience activity (renovating housing in the local community) that gives young people the opportunity to learn how to handle work-related problems in productive ways, demonstrate leadership, and feel the satisfaction and self-esteem that come from helping others. Proponents of this approach believe that this process will help young people develop the skills to address the many personal and situational problems they face both within and outside the workplace.

Continuing services after the initial job placement. Many young people in second-chance programs find a job but lose it or leave it fairly soon thereafter. Many programs, especially those funded under JTPA, "terminate" a person at the time of initial job placement in order to claim a positive outcome for performance standards. Once terminated, a person cannot receive further services without reestablishing income eligibility.

This practice seems ill-conceived for two reasons. First, new problems and stresses emerge for many program participants after they are placed in a job and start working. For example, young women with children discover that child care arrangements are less reliable than expected; individuals receiving public assistance learn how tightly they must budget their resources when they start working and their welfare check is cut; or conflicts with fellow workers or supervisors may arise. At the very time when such new and serious difficulties appear, support services are withdrawn.

Secondly, this practice does not reflect the fact that few economically disadvantaged young people are able to make a major leap in economic status through a first job. More typically, the initial job is not particularly good, but it allows the youth to learn new skills on the job and build a record as a reliable worker, which can lead to a better job.

Some programs have sought to maintain a connection with clients and provide counseling and other assistance as they encounter difficulties in their first job or as they are ready to enter further training or find a new job. These programs hold out an open-ended offer of assistance in making the many transitions needed for participants to achieve self-sufficiency. They recognize that youth development is not a quick or straightforward process; young people try different options, move in and out of training and work, and encounter new problems with each new situation. The challenge is to help them build on each experience toward self-sufficiency.

While none of these suggestions comes with a guarantee, together they provide a strategy for building on the existing research findings and operational experience to improve the lives of young economically disadvantaged dropouts.

NOTES

1. See Charles Betsey, Robinson Hollister, Jr., and Mary R. Papageorgiou, eds., *Youth Employment and Training Programs: The YEDPA Years* (Washington, DC: National Academy Press, 1985) for a review of the literature to that point. For a more recent review, see U.S. Department of Labor, Employment and Training Administration, *Dilemmas in Youth Employment Programming: Findings from the Youth Research and Technical Assistance Project*, Research and Evaluation Report Series 92-C, Vol. 1 (Washington, DC: U.S. Department of Labor, 1992), pp. 15-67.

2. These initial characteristics carried through into differences in the subsequent earnings of the control groups for each service strategy. See Howard S. Bloom, Larry Orr, George Cave, Stephen Bell, and Fred Doolittle, *The National JTPA Study: Interim Impacts at 18 Months* (Bethesda, MD: Abt Associates, 1993) and Howard S. Bloom, Larry L. Orr, George Cave, Stephen H. Bell, Fred Doolitle, and Winston Lin, *The National JTPA Study, Overview: Impacts, Benefits, and Costs of Title II-A* (Bethesda, MD: Abt Associates, 1994).

3. Several ongoing studies of programs for young women will soon release longer-term impact findings and this could change the overall picture somewhat. Among these studies are the Teen Parent Demonstration organized by the U.S. Department of Health and Human Services, the New Chance Demonstration organized by the Manpower Demonstration Research Corporation, and the Learning, Earning, and Parenting (LEAP) Program operated by the State of Ohio. Each has issued reports on program implementation and early impacts.

4. Other examples are occupational skills training or on-the-job training (OJT) as sole services. The National JTPA Study, reviewed in this section, does provide some insights on the effectiveness of these services but the youths in the sample recommended for these activities by local JTPA staff actually participated in a variety of services including these activities.

5. VICI was evaluated in a study which found short-term employment effects, but methodological problems in the research made the results questionable. For a discussion, see Betsey et al., *Youth Employment and Training Programs.*

6. For examples of this argument, see Sue Berryman and Thomas Bailey, *The Double Helix of Education and the Economy* (New York: Institute on Education and the Economy, Teachers College, Columbia University, 1992), and Thomas J. Smith and Michelle Alberti Gambone, *The Effectiveness of Federally Funded Employment and Training Strategies for Youth* (Washington, DC: U.S. Department of Labor, Employment and Training Administration, 1992). For a related argument, see Thomas Sticht, *Cast Off Youth: Policy and Training Methods from the Military Experience* (Westport, CT: Praeger, 1987).

7. To be eligible for JTPA services, an applicant's household income in the previous six months must be below the poverty guideline for the appropriate family size or 70 percent of the lower living standard set by the Department of Labor.

8. Prior to mid-1993, enrollment in JTPA was often delayed until the actual start of a service like classroom training or OJT. SDAs would often follow this practice, rather than enroll every eligible person who applied, because they did not have enough funds to serve everyone who was eligible and those enrolled were included in the performance standard system. Thus, enrollment in JTPA often meant that the person received some significant JTPA service.

9. The earnings losses are present in data from a follow-up survey but not in administrative records on earnings reported by employers to the Unemployment Insurance system.

10. During the in-program period, Corpsmembers made a short-term sacrifice of employment and earnings to participate in Jobs Corps activities. See Charles Mallar, Stuart Kerachsky, Craig Thornton, and David Long, *Evaluation of the Economic Impact of*

142   SECOND-CHANCE PROGRAMS FOR YOUTH

the Job Corps Program, Third Follow-up Report (Princeton, NJ: Mathematica Policy Research, 1982). See also the review in Betsey et al., *Youth Employment and Training Programs.*

11. This type of analysis is difficult because it is hard to identify the comparison group counterparts of program group members who complete the program, drop out early, or participate an intermediate amount. Thus the study authors treat findings on this issue as only suggestive.

12. See Betsey et al., *Youth Employment and Training Programs.*

13. For a discussion of the history of JOBSTART see George Cave, Hans Bos, Fred Doolittle, and Cyril Toussaint, *Final Report on the JOBSTART Demonstration* (New York: Manpower Demonstration Research Corporation, 1993).

14. See John Burghardt, Anu Rangarajan, Anne Gordon, and Ellen Kisker, *Evaluation of the Minority Female Single Parent Demonstration, Vol. 1, Summary Report* (New York: Rockefeller Foundation, 1992).

15. A further discussion of the suggestions in this section is contained in Cave et al., *Final Report on the JOBSTART Demonstration*, chapter 8.

16. Work experience in the public or nonprofit sector is permitted for youths only when it is accompanied by "other services designed to increase the basic education and/or occupational skills of the participant," as would be the case in programs such as JOBSTART. Further, other income-providing activities such as cooperative education placements or "limited internships" may be arranged in private, for-profit firms. On-the-job training, which is now more restricted for youths under JTPA, is also an option.

17. The challenges for program operators using this approach are substantial. It requires flexibility to allow for part-time participation, which could involve scheduling some activities at night and permitting open entry and exit in activities or individualized curricula. It also requires staying in touch with inactive participants so they know that the program will welcome them back when their work schedule permits them to participate again. These requirements all increase the management burden on program staff. There is also the possibility that involvement in the program would never become intense enough to make any real difference in the youths' skills or attitudes. Further, in part-time programs it is more difficult to develop the type of peer support and program cohesiveness that can develop in more intensive programs.

18. These issues are reviewed in depth in Smith and Gambone, *The Effectiveness of Federally Funded Employment and Training Strategies for Youth*, and other papers in the same volume.

CHAPTER VII

Preparation for Work:
The "Forgotten" Student

ERWIN FLAXMAN, CAROL ASCHER, SUE E. BERRYMAN,
AND MORTON INGER

Many young people complete high school equipped neither for the training required to enter jobs requiring middle-level skills nor, for the most part, to do college work. For the non-college-bound students who will go on to work, many of whom are low-income minority students, the situation is worse because the nation has no coherent strategy for developing their competence for work. We now know, moreover, that students not bound for college, who have traditionally been prepared for work in vocational classes, need to develop the same cognitive skills as college-bound students because both further academic education and success in a changing workplace at all job levels require similar abilities. This means that American education needs to be restructured to integrate vocational or work skills and academic course work for all students.

This is not a new recommendation; the movement for career education in the schools in the 1970s was an attempt to bring occupational concerns into all classrooms, where teachers would be able to demonstrate how their disciplines were relevant to the world of work.[1] Career education, however, like many previous strategies for reforming education for all students, was relegated to the margins. But for non-college-bound students, often the "forgotten" learners, career education was an improvement in their education, particularly for work. Economic and social pressures are now forcing us to reconsider how to build an educationally powerful system that can prepare middle-level students to take middle-level jobs in the labor force. The

Erwin Flaxman is Director of the ERIC Clearinghouse on Urban Education, which is located at Teachers College, Columbia University. Carol Ascher is Senior Research Associate at the Clearinghouse. Sue E. Berryman is Education Specialist with the World Bank in Washington, DC. Morton Inger is Research Associate at the Institute on Education and the Economy at Teachers College, Columbia University.

nation is in its infancy in thinking about and starting to build this system, and we already face a bewildering array of options and models. The purpose of this chapter is to review what has been learned about the various approaches to educating the "forgotten" learner and to recommend implementation strategies for building a strong school-to-work program that will open opportunities for these students.

The Renewed Interest in Preparation for Work

The realization that we have to build a system to prepare students for work emerged relatively suddenly in the 1980s. Several factors coalesced: changes in wage patterns, especially for those without a college education; the employment and unemployment trends for those with varying levels of education; trends in the relative growth rates of occupations using different average levels of education; research evidence on the implications of economic restructuring for the kinds of skills needed in the workforce; an understanding of how public education and training resources are now organized and allocated; and theories emerging from cognitive science research about how people learn most effectively and naturally.[2]

ECONOMIC FACTORS

Throughout the 1980s, less-educated workers were increasingly less likely to be employed, and when they worked increasing numbers of them earned less than better-educated workers. It is now very difficult for male high school graduates to earn a middle-class wage.[3] The wage and employment difficulties of the less educated reflect a deep shift in demand for workers in the American economy. As American industries convert from mass to flexible production, the need for low-skilled employees is reduced, and the need for better educated, highly skilled workers increases. The skill requirements of our economy have changed in two ways. First, occupations that need highly skilled workers are growing faster than those that rely on workers with lower skills. Second, the skills in many occupations have been restructured: a job may go by the same name, but the skills needed for that job have changed.[4]

To compete in the new economy, businesses need to integrate traditionally separate functions (for example, design, engineering, marketing), flatten their organizational structures, and decentralize responsibilities. This new approach gives lower-level employees more responsibility and discretion, and incorporates into their jobs many supervisory, planning, and quality-control functions previously reserved for higher-level employees. In short, skill is more valuable and the lack of skill more of a liability than before.

THE ALLOCATION OF EDUCATIONAL RESOURCES

In most schools, the curriculum and learning resources are not equitably distributed to prepare students for these changes in the economy. Most comprehensive high schools have no curricular structure for preparing students for middle-skill jobs; in fact, the world of work is nearly absent from the curriculum.[5] Curricula are organized around college-level preparation, out-of-date vocational education, and basic skills remediation in the form of general education courses. These priorities are mirrored in counseling, where counselors view career and occupational guidance as secondary to academic counseling some students for college or preventing others from failing courses and dropping out because of severe behavioral and academic problems.[6] Students who are neither high academic achievers nor severe problems are simply overlooked.

One might expect the vocational component of a comprehensive high school to be a logical partner in "building the middle," that is, in providing a suitable education for these forgotten students. However, vocational education has become nearly invisible in these schools. Academic graduation requirements have reduced vocational enrollments, and the vocational courses that remain do not reflect a deliberate educational strategy but the confluence of several ad hoc factors: attempts to retain "traditional" vocational courses such as sewing or auto shop, the relative seniority of individual vocational teachers, and the ability of the school or district to raise funds for vocational courses. What remains is a tattered and incoherent set of offerings—with only the most tenuous connection to the world of work—serving primarily as places to absorb students designated as "remedial" or "at risk."

EMERGING THEORIES OF LEARNING

Current research in cognitive science makes the case for eliminating the distinction between abstract and functional learning. Under such conditions the processes which we believe occur only internally become externalized: instruction becomes problem-centered, not didactic, and the role of the teacher changes from dispenser of knowledge to facilitator, coach, and guide. Students cease to be empty vessels receiving knowledge and become active participants who take responsibility for their own learning. The greater volatility of modern work increases the importance of two types of skills that this theory of learning allows. One is higher-order thinking, including problem defining, problem solving, and knowing how to learn. The other is understanding and being able to apply the principles that help a person respond intelligently to unexpected events.[7]

Dewey's notion of "education through occupations" has been revitalized by this recent research, which has called into question aspects of both academic and vocational learning as traditionally practiced. It shows that most students learn best when knowledge is made concrete, is related to a clear goal, and is contextualized. Thus, academic instruction is often regarded as too abstract and ungrounded for optimal learning, and vocational instruction is seen as suffering from an emphasis on narrow occupational skills and technical methods at the expense of meaning. That is, while most academic instruction would benefit from "situated learning" and an organizing principle for information, ideals, and intellectual growth, vocational instruction would be enhanced by a grounding in the knowledge, intellectual skills, and moral habits that make a good worker and citizen, and in "the culture of practice" demanded by students' future occupations.[8]

Organizational Approaches to Work-Based Education

Federal legislation with incentives to reform education to help students become better prepared for work, national efforts to restructure schools to improve their quality, and a tradition of organizational and curricular initiatives in vocational education have created a number of approaches in what can be considered a nascent system for work-related education in the United States.

THE INTEGRATION OF ACADEMIC AND VOCATIONAL EDUCATION

The integration of academic and vocational education is a curricular and instructional approach that transforms vocational education as we now know it. It eliminates the distinction between abstract (academic) and functional (vocational) education by constructing course work and course sequences in which all students achieve both academic and technical competencies and generic skills. Curricular integration reforms vocational education with its job-specific instruction by bringing out the intellectual, social, and ethical content of a range of occupations. At the same time, it transforms academic education, making the teaching of traditional academic subjects more active, more immediately meaningful, and more connected with out-of-school experience. The idea of curricular integration is not new, but we now take more seriously that neither vocational nor academic education as currently practiced provides students with the problem-solving and interactive learning skills required by further education, the economy, and social life.[9]

Such integration affects not just the curriculum; it also changes pedagogy. In classrooms where instruction is integrated, the teacher uses far fewer didactic methods of instruction and structures and supports learning much more frequently by acting as a coach, advisor, or resource for the student, becoming involved or withdrawing from the student's work as needed. In a fully operational integrated program, the teachers also work with each other in a number of ways: in curriculum planning, in developing materials, and in coordinating instruction. Programs to integrate academic and vocational education also change the organization of schooling: courses, course sequences, course clusters in academic and vocational programs, and even whole schools such as magnet schools. Integrated programs also involve the business community, which provides employment that ideally is related to course work. Importantly, it is the requirements of business and the competencies needed for the students' future occupations that drive the development of curriculum, pedagogy, and organizational structures in integrated programs.[10]

Integration is viewed as a solution to a number of specific educational, social, and economic problems. School reformers consider curriculum integration as a way of making academic learning more available and meaningful to all students, especially those who lack basic academic and higher-order thinking skills. Cognitive scientists support the concept of integration because it is based on recent findings that most people learn abstract or theoretical concepts most easily under contextualized or applied conditions. Both vocational educators and the critics of vocational education see integration as a way of improving the academic content of vocational courses and better preparing students for a workplace with greater and rapidly changing demands. Federal legislators view integrated education as a means of helping students develop the technological skills needed to function in a competitive world economy. Employers support integration because it can provide students with problem-solving skills needed to function in the high performance workplace. Social critics see integration as a strategy for distributing educational resources more equitably so that all youth have a better chance for an economic future.[11]

Integrated programs are promising ways of ending the stratification of schools that provides a rich educational program for middle-class students preparing them for higher education and high skills jobs and offers lower-income students only basic skills or remedial instruction. In integrated programs low-income students are not tracked; in a richer curriculum they are taught to actively solve problems rather than to memorize or complete drills. Like their more advantaged peers, they are guided in their educational planning rather than just counseled in moments of crisis.[12]

Tech Prep. Tech Prep is an organizational more than a curricular reform aimed at preparing students for high tech careers where the requirement for entry is graduation from a community college. Tech Prep engages students in four-year (2+2) or six-year (4+2) programs in which they can learn the competencies (knowledge, skills, and values) required for such careers. The completion of the Tech Prep program leads to an associate degree or a two-year certificate from a community college.[13]

As a structural and organizational reform, through articulation agreements, Tech Prep aligns academic and vocational course work into a common core at the secondary school and community college levels. Course work is logically sequenced not only to prepare students to meet the requirements of further education and training but also to qualify for jobs requiring technical skills. As a curriculum reform, it applies the principles and strategies of curricular integration: the content of the course work consists of applied academics, courses that incorporate applications and experienced-based knowledge into academic matter, and vocational courses that are broadened and deepened by intellectual content.[14]

Collaboration with the business community is also a critical part of Tech Prep. It ensures that the curriculum is in line with the demands of the workplace, and it makes work-experience opportunities more possible for students at all stages of the program. However, although Tech Prep is commonly viewed as the technical education alternative to the college preparatory program, its graduates can be prepared to enter four-year colleges as well as community colleges, technical institutes, and the workplace.

Articulation in Tech Prep programs—between high schools and postsecondary institutions and between high schools and the workplace—can have two significant benefits. First, it can coordinate different levels or systems of education to enable the learner to make a transition without delays, without a duplication of effort, or without a loss of credit. Second, it can arrange the curriculum so that students can choose more than one level of instruction, move to another without a gap or overlap in what they are learning, and enter the workplace to fill a job at their level of competence.[15]

There is a long history of articulated programs like Tech Prep in vocational education. Interest in them is now spreading for two reasons. First, there is a need to find an alternative to the general track in the comprehensive high school, particularly for the low-income minority students who populate general track classrooms and often graduate from high school (and community colleges) without employment skills. Second, regional businesses may threaten to leave the area if the schools cannot produce employable students to work in jobs requiring high-level skills. Tech Prep programs have the potential, currently unrealized, to develop learning environments that mimic the workplace and to create a logical sequence of courses which can prepare students for employment. A Tech Prep program can motivate students to stay in high school and complete their community college requirements because doing so can lead to gainful employment. Most significantly, because Tech Prep is the analog of "college prep," it can give students the same kind of educationally rich learning that college prep students traditionally receive, if the course content and the instruction change appropriately.[16]

Career Magnets and Career Academies. Career magnets are organized around an industry theme, such as aviation, agriculture, or fashion. Some operate as schools-within-schools and some are schoolwide. Ideally, academic subject matter is related to the career theme, and the vocational courses teach broad generic skills rather than limited job-specific skills. Students take a full academic course load (many of these schools prepare students for college) plus a larger number of career-related courses in what amounts to the equivalent of five years of high school course work completed in four years. Generally, the school's career orientation grounds school work in a practical, hands-on setting, and aligns the curriculum in a way impossible in the "shopping mall" model of the traditional high school.[17]

Career academies are always schools-within-schools rather than stand-alone schools. Unlike career magnets, which are open to all students, academies usually target students thought to be in danger of dropping out, but in both instances most students attend by choice rather than by assignment. Career academies are usually made up of a self-contained community of students, teachers, and counselors who remain together throughout the day and throughout the three- or four-year program by means of block scheduling. As with career magnets, attempts are made to integrate academic and vocational education.[18]

Career magnets and career academies try to maintain strong collaborative links with local business and industry. Employers from the field are directly involved in program planning, serve as informal staff (speakers, supervisors, mentors), and provide summer and school-year employment as part of the curriculum.

Because of their career focus, magnets and academies have the potential of providing for many disadvantaged students a rich education that is closely linked to the performance demands of the workplace which many of them will join after high school graduation. In many communities graduates of career magnets go on to college because they are academically prepared to do so.[19] Importantly, magnets and academies are designed to provide a better curriculum and better teaching to students traditionally denied access to these educational opportunities; career academies have already reduced dropout rates because their career focus is more engaging and motivating than the education available in the comprehensive school.[20]

Youth Apprenticeships. The American version of youth apprenticeships, which are modeled after the German dual apprenticeship system, has four essential components. First, the apprenticeship is designed to be an integral part of the basic education of a broad cross-section of youth; it is not for specific occupations or specific target groups. Second, apprenticeship programs are designed to teach broad employability skills and combine and integrate academic and vocational content. Third, a significant part of the basic education is to take place on the job, complemented by classroom instruction. Fourth, maintaining a youth apprenticeship program requires a system of credentials for students who successfully complete the program. These credentials certify achievement of specified levels of skills.[21]

This is very different from standard American apprenticeship programs, which are limited primarily to the building trades, serve few individuals, and focus on the not-so-young. Interest in apprenticeship as the basis for educational reform arose from the perception that European apprenticeship systems avoid many of the weaknesses of education in the United States and from a growing body of findings on the educational advantages of integrating school instruction with nonschool experiences at work.

There is the danger, however, that youth apprenticeships can become a dumping ground for less advantaged students not bound for college and will be educationally diluted. Another danger is that the opportunities for learning in the workplace will be economically and socially stratified; the more advantaged students will be given greater opportunities to become skilled workers, and the less advantaged will be given the less desirable apprenticeships.[22]

Cooperative Education. Co-op education is less formal, less standardized, and less well defined than many other curricular and organizational arrangements for work-related education. Students usually spend the morning in school classes recommended and approved by the school co-op coordinator, and the last half of their day working in a paid job for which they receive high school credits. The students do not usually have specially designed course work, and they attend traditional vocational and academic classes with students not in co-op education programs. They do, however, have a class which links their work experience to their school work or at least allows them to discuss their work experience. Co-op arrangements are worked out locally between individual employers and school staff and are subject to various state laws and local customs.[23]

In general, participation in a co-op program does not lead to skill mastery.[24] It does, however, expose students to work that may lead to a job after graduation, it provides wages to students while in high school, and it offers credits toward high school graduation. Unlike the promise of youth apprenticeship, the co-op program offers no guarantee that the youth will learn anything in the workplace which can lead to more advanced employment. What is more, because students in these programs have not succeeded in other school programs, they tend to be viewed as needing remediation, not as candidates for training for jobs requiring higher-level skills.

School-Based Enterprise. School-based enterprise is an activity that engages groups of students in providing services or producing goods for sale in establishments such as restaurants, print shops, auto repair shops, and retail stores. Extracurricular forms of school-based enterprise include school newspapers, yearbooks, plays, concerts, and debates. The objectives are to teach entrepreneurship, provide application of skills and knowledge taught in other courses, and enhance students' social and personal development.[25]

Barriers to Implementation

Researchers, practitioners, and policymakers have expressed a considerable number of concerns about the problems of implementing these programs or creating a national education training system.[26]

PROFESSIONAL AND STRUCTURAL OBSTACLES

Curriculum integration, Tech Prep, and youth apprenticeships especially face a number of structural and professional obstacles in meeting their instructional goal of an integrated academic and vocational curriculum. Disciplinary boundaries in most secondary schools remain strong, and teachers' fears of losing their identification with a discipline are important barriers to curriculum integration. Thus, the solution may be not to demolish disciplinary divisions and erase teachers' subject identities, but to strengthen them in a new way.[27] For example, an analysis of both vocational and academic classrooms in comprehensive high schools suggests that a wide range of subjects, including interior design, English, electronics, architectural drafting, and manufacturing, can all be taught in ways that will enable students to learn such generic skills as complex reasoning, cooperation, and useful work-related attitudes (the ability to take responsibility, to figure something out, and to make bold decisions), along with domain-specific skills and knowledge.[28] Limited experience with curriculum integration has also led some to believe that integration is easier in science, mathematics, and vocational and technical tasks than with social studies and the humanities, although this has been shown to be short-sighted.[29] However, the nature of the school subject is not the major obstacle to integration, but rather the resistance of teachers, the effects of university admissions requirements, and state regulations that prescribe prerequisites and course sequences.

A more important cause for concern in curriculum integration has been the low level of academic proficiency demanded by emerging curriculum materials, as well as the lack of rigorous evaluation of student outcomes. Unfortunately, regulations for using federal funds for curriculum integration provide only weak incentives for developing high-quality curriculum or assessing what is developed. Lacking technical and financial resources, many schools have opted to use federal money for modest changes like "applied academics," which conform to the law but show little evidence of success.[30]

Also, the historic division of the high school into classes for college-bound and non-college-bound students makes the promise of integration and Tech Prep to end tracking difficult to achieve. Integrated programs have the potential to end the stratification of schooling into a college-bound track for students who are strong academically, and general, remedial, vocational, and other tracks for academically weak students. Integrated programs replace the traditional tracks with new clusters or paths in which students of like occupational interests but of mixed academic abilities and previous academic attainments all learn together. Unfortunately, since most schools have long been accustomed to separating college-bound and non-college-bound students, they tend to direct integration and Tech Prep only to non-college-bound students, and these reforms are likely to fail unless *all* students are served by them.

Directing integration and Tech Prep to the non-college-bound student recreates the hierarchy that has plagued the traditional divisions between academic education and all other educational programs in the high school. It is this hierarchy that has turned vocational or general education teachers into second-class professionals, and their courses, which are often plagued by outdated and insufficient materials, are seen as dumping grounds for students who are less successful academically. Once students are tracked into a vocational or general track they are unlikely to be able to move out and thus to get enough academic course work for college entrance or for successful participation in the work world. This division also relegates the college-bound student to traditional academic classes, depriving them of career-focused, problem-centered, activity-based learning that is offered in the best vocational classes.[31]

What is more, many college-bound youth and their parents resist any reform that eliminates traditional college preparatory course work. Given the nature of academic requirements to enter college and college entrance examinations, this resistance may be well founded. Thus, the successful institutionalization of integration and Tech Prep into schools across the United States will also depend on a revised system of assessment for college entrance. In addition, many non-college-bound youth and their parents may resist Tech Prep and some aspects of curriculum integration because they fear that these reforms will limit opportunities for further education and training and are merely vocational education under a new name.[32]

WORKPLACE LEARNING

Workplace learning, increasingly viewed as a critical component of programs for improving students' transition from school to work, will succeed only if business and industry become full partners with the schools. Despite the considerable sums spent by corporations on remedial education and the fact that business might gain from participating in programs like integration and Tech Prep that include a workplace learning component, employers will not easily become involved in an elaborate system of work-based learning. First, with increasing amounts of work given to contract and temporary workers, corporations are unlikely to feel tied to the career of any worker, much less a future worker. Second, there are few financial or other incentives for employers in the United States to work with adolescents, who have a reputation as a particularly difficult age group, when, unlike Germany or Japan, there is no history or culture of employer participation in education in the United States. Third, in order to provide nationwide integration and Tech Prep programs with workplace components, an enormous number of companies would have to become involved in job training. According to one estimate, to train merely a quarter of those students who do not go on to college, one out of three companies would have to participate. Fourth, presumably few employers will be willing to be told by educators how they should structure their jobs to be more educational, how they themselves might be better supervisor/mentors, or which students they should employ. Finally, organized labor has resisted youth apprenticeships and other forms of job training, in part because they are seen as threatening to adult workers and as creating low-wage jobs at a time when all jobs for adults are scarce, and in part because unions are doubtful that much training will actually take place.[33]

For educators, two kinds of quality issues are raised by workplace learning. The first is how to describe and measure the quality of any job training. Students are very discriminating about what constitutes a good work experience, and only good experiences are of use in increasing students' skills or their persistence in school. The second is how to exercise quality control in the work situation, either through professional development for employers, or monitoring jobs. Educators have been reluctant to demand too much of employers and have never established standards for student employment, including what the cost will be to the employers if they are to become involved in the program.[34]

STANDARDS AND EVALUATION

For integration and Tech Prep to demonstrate success, new kinds of standards as well as new tools for evaluation must be developed.

Although there is a growing national consensus that the only way to improve schooling (regardless of the area of reform) is to create new standards and measures by which to drive and evaluate the change, most integration and Tech Prep programs do not have performance standards and appropriate means to measure performance. This is due to a lack of expertise in test development and of appropriate ready-made tests, to uncertainty about the goals of both integration and Tech Prep, and to the multiple aspects of both the programs and students' performance that might well be evaluated. In addition, outcome measures have been limited by their focus on short-term results. In order to create effective evaluations of students' gains in the programs, educators need to know how to implement authentic assessments, and more specifically, how to certify or reward students for career-based study.[35]

Authentic assessments include a variety of techniques based on real projects and problems. Occupational issues and examples provide one obvious source of such projects and problems, although not the only one. Since schools are only occasionally real workplaces, testing and measurement specialists are trying to develop ways of assessing students' work through simulations and scenarios.[36] Although involving vocational educators and business representatives in the development of assessments may help make them more "real," it may still be difficult to have truly realistic occupational issues incorporated into school-based assessments.

Because a high school diploma is no longer meaningful to employers, assessments must also indicate students' cumulative learning through school, particularly in the generic skills that are essential to successful performance in the workplace. However, the creation of certifications based on employment skills learned either at school or during the job involves several problems. One is timeliness: in a job world in which skills are continually shifting, the skills measured must be broad enough to make sense over time. This means that skills standards need to be continually revised, and schools must counteract their tendency to be ten or twelve years behind marketplace demands.[37]

PROFESSIONAL DEVELOPMENT

Although teachers must take on new roles to integrate academic and vocational education, they resist doing so because traditionally they are individualistic, occupation-specific, and skills-dominated in their work, and these reforms call for cooperation and collaboration.

Just as important is the fact that the professional development of teachers has traditionally been fragmented and intellectually shallow, based largely on a training paradigm of clearly defined practices, skill learning, and skill transfer. This paradigm and its delivery system in in-service education, the workshop, may work reasonably well to introduce those reforms that are "technical" or can be rendered as a "cookbook" of classroom practices. However, the present reforms do not lend themselves to such rote, step-by-step training. Instead, these reforms require that professionals grapple with broad principles involved in problem solving, and that they reflect such principles in their own practice, focusing on the "cultures of practice" that are demanded by different professional arenas.[38]

Teachers need to be given an adequate opportunity to learn skills like experimenting, consulting, and evaluating that are embedded in the routine organization of their work days. Thus, professional development must move from workshops to teacher collaboratives, team-based mini-grants, school-university partnerships, networks, and a variety of other supports for change. The teachers themselves must begin with their own cooperative efforts, breaking down departmental barriers and planning together. Collaborative efforts among teachers will also lead teachers to ask for participation from business, as well as for people and resources from the community. All this can be made easier when administrators promote team activities and understand and support the "risk taking" of teachers inside their classrooms.[39]

It is also important to recall that professional development for teaching an integrated curriculum does not occur in a vacuum. Rather, strains or supports from other allegiances and obligations can work against or shore up any professional development effort. For example, teachers by training and tradition are deeply rooted in their subject matter and departments. They may see integration as threatening their expertise, cutting into their domain, and watering down their subject with vocational (or academic) material.[40] In addition, many teachers and administrators are not convinced that major changes in curriculum and instruction are indicated, or they believe that these changes are needed only for at risk students. Teachers may also have little idea of what an integrated classroom should look like, and it will be hard for them to begin change without a vision of where they are going.

CHANGED GUIDANCE AND COUNSELING PRACTICES

Integration and Tech Prep change guidance and counseling practices in the schools through the curriculum, altered counselor roles, and greater involvement of other school staff and outsiders. Currently, most guidance and counseling services have been directed to college-bound students, assisting them in finding four-year colleges, or to troubled children and youth, helping them to avoid academic failure or to negotiate a personal or family crisis. These days, most students headed for work or a community college rarely see anyone from the guidance and counseling offices. Help with career planning is scarce in most schools, not only because there are few counselors present to offer it, but also because support for career development—and development generally—has not been a significant responsibility of the overburdened counselor, and few understand what is involved in work-related education or have been well-trained to provide this support for career development.[41]

Career development is not just a guidance function: it is a core educational outcome. Embedded in the curriculum, work-related education expands the responsibility for developing students' sense of careers. Thus it becomes part of the fabric of the whole school experience and the responsibility of many staff members. Just as all academic counseling and course work should prepare college-bound students to enter four-year colleges, integration and Tech Prep can reform high school guidance and counseling for students preparing to enter community colleges and the workplace. This expanded vision of counseling would obviously also help college-bound students. However, unlike precollege counseling, career development not only engages more professionals and other adults, but it diversifies the number of situations in which it can occur—in formal counseling events and informally through the basic curriculum as well as in special career-related curricula and in classroom exercises, through special mentoring programs, in school-based careers offices, and in the workplace. While counselors work with students in educational planning and career awareness and exploration, teachers take on new counseling roles; moreover, employers and other adults may take on guidance responsibilities as mentors in their informal contacts with youth.

POLICY FORMATION AND IMPLEMENTATION

Both integration and Tech Prep can be either facilitated or hindered by the policy and political environment in which they are implemented. That both have developed in a policy environment where federal regulations are purposely vague has created both opportunities and problems. While in the best case this regulatory vacuum has allowed for local initiative, in many instances schools and districts have taken the line of least effort, making only those changes that meet the letter of the law. Most obviously, federal money has often been used to initiate articulation agreements between high schools and community colleges without creating any curricular or structural reforms, to revise areas of high school curriculum without making related changes at the college level, or to purchase "off-the-shelf" curriculum materials of unknown value.[42]

At the federal level, integration and Tech Prep have been added to an already fragmentary system of vocational education programs, including the JOBS program, the Jobs Training and Placement Act, and the military. Some of these programs may be contradictory or overlapping, and there are likely gaps which might be filled if there were more coordination of programs. At the state level, in the absence of federal regulation and monitoring, there has been great variety in the implementation of program guidelines. While some states have invested their own resources, providing technical assistance to local districts, other states have left the administration of the reform entirely to the local level. A number of states are also experiencing problems as a result of conflicting educational policies. For example, while some state departments of education are adopting a work-based curriculum, they are still mandating hours of instruction in particular subjects, dictating rigid requirements for graduation, or demanding standardized tests, all of which are sure to prevent most school personnel from fully implementing the reform.[43]

Finally, the curricular and organizational changes intended by integration and Tech Prep challenge a number of deeply entrenched structures of secondary education. Most important is the division of schooling into subjects, which is supported by teacher licensing arrangements.[44] Other problems arise from a lack of local funds, which often limit the amount of released time available to teachers for planning, as well as from rigid union contracts that prohibit teachers from working with each other after class hours.[45]

A Final Word

The curricular and instructional arrangements for reforming schools so that all students will be prepared to participate in the world of work are especially important to low-income and minority youth because they equalize and redistribute educational resources for those who traditionally have been deprived of educational opportunities.

But as we have suggested, each of these reforms carries with it problems endemic to schooling at the present time, and each will require that schools change in very fundamental ways. For this change to occur, however, we need both political will and effort and appropriate policy instruments. The public and the federal, state, and local governments have to be willing to reconsider both the purposes of schooling and the range of students who must profit from it.

NOTES

1. See chapter 1 in this volume for discussion of the history of work-related education in the United States. See also, W. Norton Grubb et al., *The Cunning Hand, the Cultured Mind: Models for Integrating Vocational and Academic Education,* MDS-141 (Berkeley: National Center for Research in Vocational Education, University of California at Berkeley, 1991).

2. Sue E. Berryman and Thomas Bailey, *The Double Helix of Education and the Economy* (New York: Institute on Education and the Economy, Teachers College, Columbia University, 1992).

3. William T. Grant Foundation, Commission on Work, Family, and Citizenship, *The Forgotten Half: Non-College Youth in America* (Washington, DC: William T. Grant Foundation, January, 1988); idem, *The Forgotten Half: Pathways to Success for America's Youth and Young Families* (Washington, DC: William T. Grant Foundation, November, 1988); Frank Levy and Richard Murnane, "U.S. Earnings Levels and Earnings Inequality: A Review of Recent Trends and Proposed Explanations," *Journal of Economic Literature* 30, no. 3 (September 1992): 1333-1381.

4. Thomas Bailey, *Jobs of the Future and the Skills They Will Require: New Thinking on an Old Debate,* MDS-213, Reprint Series (Berkeley: National Center for Research in Vocational Education, University of California at Berkeley, 1990); Berryman and Bailey, *The Double Helix of Education and the Economy.*

5. Judith W. Little and Susan M. Threatt, *Work on the Margins: The Experience of Vocational Teachers in Comprehensive High Schools,* MDS-166 (Berkeley, National Center for Research in Vocational Education, University of California at Berkeley, June 1992).

6. Molly Selvin et al., *Who Gets What and Why: Curriculum Decision Making at Three Comprehensive High Schools,* MDS-028 (Berkeley: National Center for Research in Vocational Education, University of California at Berkeley, February 1990).

7. Sue E. Berryman, *Cognitive Science: Challenging Schools to Design Effective Learning Environments* (New York: Institute on Education and the Economy, Teachers College, Columbia University, September 1991).

8. Berryman and Bailey, *The Double Helix of Education and the Economy.*

9. Sue E. Berryman, Erwin Flaxman, and Morton Inger, *Building the Middle* (Berkeley: National Center for Research in Vocational Education, University of California at Berkeley, 1992).

10. Grubb et al., *The Cunning Hand, The Cultured Mind.*

11. Cathleen Stasz, "Integrating Academic and Vocational Education: A Synthesis Paper" (Paper prepared for a meeting of the Board of the National Center for Research on Vocational Education, January 1992).

12. Berryman, Flaxman, and Inger, *Building the Middle.*

13. Carolyn Dornsife, *Beyond Articulation: The Development of Tech Prep Programs,* MDS-311 (Berkeley: National Center for Research in Vocational Education, University of California at Berkeley, February 1992).

14. Gerald Hayward et al., "Synthesis Memo: Tech Prep Programs" (Paper prepared for a meeting of the Board of the National Center for Research in Vocational Education, January 1992).

15. Berryman, Flaxman, and Inger, *Building the Middle.*

16. Ibid.

17. Ibid.

18. David Stern, Marilyn January, and Charles Dayton, *Career Academies: Partnerships for Reconstructing American High Schools* (San Francisco: Jossey-Bass, 1992).

19. Berryman, Flaxman, and Inger, *Building the Middle.*

20. Stern, January, and Dayton, *Career Academies.*

21. Thomas Bailey and Donna Merritt, *School-to-Work Transition and Youth Apprenticeship in the United States* (New York: Manpower Demonstration Research Corporation, May 1992).

22. Ibid.

23. David Stern et al., "Work Experience for Students in High School and College," *Youth and Society* 21, no. 3 (March 1990): 355-389.

24. U.S. General Accounting Office, *Training Strategies*, GAO/HRD-90-88 (Washington, DC: U.S. General Accounting Office, 1990).

25. Berryman, Flaxman, and Inger, *Building the Middle.*

26. Carol Ascher and Erwin Flaxman, *A Time for Questions: The Future of Integration and Tech Prep*, A Report of a Three-Day Summit Sponsored by the Institute on Education and the Economy and the National Center for Research in Vocational Education, June 27-29, 1993, Washington, DC (New York: Institute on Education and the Economy, Teachers College, Columbia University, November 1993).

27. Judith Warren Little, *Two Worlds: Vocational and Academic Teachers in Comprehensive High Schools* (Berkeley: National Center for Research in Vocational Education, University of California at Berkeley, 1992).

28. Cathleen Stasz et al., *Classrooms that Work: Teaching Generic Skills in Academic and Vocational Settings* (Berkeley: National Center for Research in Vocational Education, University of California at Berkeley, 1993).

29. Cathleen Stasz, "Teaching Generic Skills," in *Education through Occupations*, edited by W. Norton Grubb (New York: Teachers College Press, forthcoming); Kenneth Koziol and W. Norton Grubb, "Paths Not Taken: Curriculum Integration and the Political and Moral Purposes of Schooling," in *Education through Occupations*, edited by W. Norton Grubb (New York: Teachers College Press, forthcoming).

30. Ascher and Flaxman, *A Time for Questions.*

31. Ibid.

32. Berryman, Flaxman, and Inger, *Building the Middle.*

33. Charles Benson, personal communication, July 31, 1993.

34. Ascher and Flaxman, *A Time for Questions.*

35. Ibid.

36. Clifford Hill and Eric Larsen, *Testing and Assessment in Secondary Education: A Critical Review of Emerging Practices*, MDS-237 (Berkeley: National Center for Research in Vocational Education, University of California at Berkeley, November 1992).

37. Ascher and Flaxman, *A Time for Questions.*

38. Berryman, Flaxman, and Inger, *Building the Middle.*

39. Judith W. Little, "Teachers as Colleagues," in *Educators' Handbook: A Research Perspective*, edited by Virginia Richardson-Koehler (New York: Longman, 1987).

40. Ibid.

41. Belinda McCharen, "Guidance and Counseling: An Essential Component for Successful Integration of Academic and Vocational Education," in *Education through Occupations*, edited by W. Norton Grubb (New York: Teachers College Press, forthcoming).

42. Ascher and Flaxman, *A Time for Questions*.

43. Ibid.

44. Little, "Teachers as Colleagues."

45. Susan Bodilly, Cathleen Stasz, and Kimberley Ramsey, *Policy Implications of Integrating Academic and Vocational Education: An Interim Report* (Berkeley: National Center for Research in Vocational Education, University of California at Berkeley, May 1992).

CHAPTER VIII

Curriculum Controversies in Multicultural Education

CHRISTINE E. SLEETER

The community in which I live is wrestling currently with multi-cultural education in a manner similar to that of many communities today. Most of the schools are predominantly white, although populations of color are growing rapidly and student bodies in many schools are becoming diverse. The community itself has historically been a volatile "melting pot" for European ethnic groups, and most residents use the template of the European ethnic immigrant experience to attempt to understand non-European groups, in the process denying alternative perspectives about race relations put forth by people of color. When called upon to provide information about multicultural education I encounter questions such as these: "Is it a new program?" "Does it work?" "Could you suggest some good international speakers or performers for a school's 'cultural' week?" "Isn't multicultural education unfair by asking teachers to bend over backward for 'those' children?" "Doesn't it retard rather than help the assimilation process?" "Isn't it just another form of 'political correctness'?"

In this chapter I briefly situate multicultural education in its historical context, and in the process I attempt to provide a broad conceptualization of what multicultural education means. I review criticisms of multicultural education that have permeated the media during the late 1980s and early 1990s, focusing on debates about curriculum, since these criticisms inform many educators' understanding of multicultural education. I then counter the criticisms with the research and theory undergirding multicultural education. I will argue (1) that multicultural education represents a challenge to historic forms of racial oppression in the United States more than a response to recent demographic

Christine E. Sleeter is a Professor in the Teacher Education Department, School of Education, University of Wisconsin—Parkside in Kenosha, Wisconsin.

changes; (2) that it attempts to shift power in educational decision making toward groups of color rather than being merely a program that one can "adopt"; and (3) that practices recommended by theorists of multicultural education rest on a growing base of research and theory.

What is Multicultural Education?
Where Did It Come From?

Multicultural education emerged seriously in the context of the Civil Rights movement of the 1960s. As African Americans, joined by other oppressed racial groups, demanded access to various institutions from which whites had historically excluded them, they formulated agendas for changing those institutions to support inclusiveness. In higher education, students demanded courses in ethnic studies as well as other programs and policies in support of diverse cultures. At the K-12 level, as schools began to experience desegregation, parents and educators criticized (1) the exclusion of people of color from curricula and from decision-making roles and (2) the low academic expectations white educators had for children of color, expectations which were buttressed by assumptions about cultural deprivation.[1]

As educators and community activists of color articulated their concerns about schooling, "multicultural education" became a term designating recommended changes. The prefix "multi" was adopted as an umbrella to include diverse groups of color. The term "multiethnic education" linked common concerns of diverse racial and ethnic minority groups; "multicultural education" expanded the umbrella to include gender, disability, and other forms of diversity.[2]

An Intergroup Education movement, which had been active during the 1940s and 1950s, is regarded by some educators as a precursor to multicultural education. Banks, however, locates the roots of multicultural education in the Civil Rights movement and the development of Black Studies, distinguishing these from Intergroup Education in this way:

Intergroup educators, most of whom are liberal white academics who worked in mainstream American institutions, placed more emphasis on a shared American identity than did black scholars, who were more concerned about creating accurate images of African Americans, empowering African Americans, and building African-American institutions.[3]

Multicultural education at its inception attempted mainly to synthesize the work of African-American, Latino, Native American, and Asian American scholars and activists.

Since the early 1970s, a great deal of material has been produced that articulates and develops changes that should be made in schools to support the strengths and aspirations of diverse groups. For example, in the ERIC listings of journal publications between January 1982 and June 1992, the descriptor "multicultural education" retrieves 911 entries; this does not include books, nor all resources catalogued under related descriptors such as "bilingual education" or "Asian Americans and education."

Clearly, the field of multicultural education is not new. Educators new to the field often derive their understanding of the term "multicultural education" from their notions about the term "culture" with the prefix "multi." They too often disregard (or assume a lack of) scholarship that has been developed in the field over the past twenty-five years. Many white educators also assume that multicultural education is related mainly to new immigrants, and they dissociate it from a critique of historical patterns of racism in schooling and society. For example, white teachers sometimes tell me that they already know "all about" African Americans and Hispanics, resent a stress on "them," and want some information about Hindu or Japanese culture. Part of the problem is that most teachers lack substantive knowledge of a nonwhite American group. In the absence of such knowledge, most teachers greatly underestimate what there is to know. In addition, any individual who has not lived in a racial minority community (as is the case with most whites and some educators of color) is less likely to view such communities in terms of strengths and resources than are the community members themselves.

So what is multicultural education? It is a process of school reform that is based on reciprocal dialog among diverse sociocultural groups and on genuine power sharing among groups. Historically, school structures, processes, and research have been framed largely by white middle- to upper-class educators and policymakers. The literature in multicultural education, although contributed to by a wide variety of people, has mainly represented attempts by educators of color to articulate the kinds of changes schools should make to reverse oppression based on race, language, ethnicity, and gender. Banks argues that multicultural education should entail a process of school reform that requires transformation of the school as a whole: "[To] transform the school to bring about educational equality, all the major components of the school must be substantially changed. A focus on any one variable in the school, such as the formalized curriculum, will not implement multicultural education."[4] Major components include relations with the community, teaching and learning styles, assessment programs, instructional materials, school policies, and the school staff. Grant terms this reform an "education that is multicultural" rather than multicultural education, since what is required is not the addition of a program, but the transformation of an institution.[5]

Institutional reforms discussed in the literature on multicultural education are supported by ethnographic research that documents various forms of inequality in schooling. Whether or not schools contribute to the reproduction of unequal relationships is an issue educators debate; multicultural education as a field takes the position that in many ways most schools do reproduce inequality, but could operate differently. Oakes's research, for example, critiques tracking, including its institutionalization of racial and social class disparities in access to education.[6] Rist documents processes by which African-American children were rendered "invisible" in a white desegregated school.[7] Grant and Sleeter portray various forms of racial, social class, and gender inequality found in many facets of a junior high school.[8] Phillips documents the breakdown in teaching that occurs when teachers' and students' styles of communication clash.[9]

Multicultural reforms are also supported by a wealth of anthropological and social-psychological research on cultural and language patterns that discredits notions about the superiority or deficiency of various cultures.[10] In addition, research in ethnic and women's studies has retrieved a tremendous amount of knowledge about diverse groups. This research has been synthesized into new perspectives and theoretical frameworks that provide a wealth of material for transforming curricula.[11]

In the literature on multicultural education, one can find discussions that vary in complexity and depth. Some of Gay's discussions of multicultural teaching practice are quite comprehensive,[12] while others are fairly short and prescriptive.[13] One can also find formulations, which range widely in focus, of exactly what changes might be made in schools.

Five Approaches to Multicultural Education

Grant and Sleeter distinguish five different approaches to multicultural education, each of which details a somewhat different set of recommended changes.[14] The main purpose of the first approach, "teaching the exceptional and culturally different," is to help students achieve well within schools largely as they are by building bridges between students' backgrounds and the schools in order to make the curriculum more "user friendly." Bridges may consist of instructional strategies that build on students' learning styles, culturally relevant materials, or use of students' native language to teach standard English. A second approach, "human relations," attempts to build positive affective relationships among members of diverse racial and cultural groups and/or between males and females in order to strengthen each student's self-concept and to increase interpersonal harmony. This is generally done through lessons about stereotyping and individual differences and similarities, conflict-reduction programs, and use of cooperative learning. "Single-group studies" is an umbrella term for a third approach, which consists of programs or courses of study that focus on particular groups, such as ethnic studies, labor studies, or women's studies. This approach seeks to raise consciousness about a group by teaching its history and culture, as well as how that group has interacted with the dominant society. The "multicultural" approach promotes cultural pluralism by reconstructing the entire education process. Disciplinary content, for example, is reorganized around the perspectives and knowledge bases of diverse American racial and ethnic groups, both sexes, and diverse social classes. This approach questions the use of tracking and ability grouping, advocating heterogeneous grouping as much as possible, with high academic expectations for all students. Finally, education that is "multicultural and social reconstructionist" teaches students to analyze inequality and oppression in society and helps them develop skills for social action. This approach organizes curriculum around contemporary issues of social justice, using disciplinary knowledge to examine those issues and create ways of effecting change.

Multicultural education, however, though often formulated as "how-to's" in an effort to illustrate changes schools could make, cannot be reduced to any one list of "correct" practices. In the context of the Civil Rights struggle, multicultural education was initially part of a larger quest by oppressed racial groups for decision-making power and control over the education of their own children. Writings articulated agendas of concerns and recommendations for practice, but they emerged as part of a larger quest for self-determination. In the context of the 1990s, however, most educators, especially those who are white, tend not to associate multicultural education with social movements and power sharing. Rather, white educators often appropriate its language and some of its practices in order to "solve" racial issues without dismantling white dominance.[15] From the perspective of those who connect multicultural education with empowerment and self-determination, common school practices such as food fairs and celebrations of racial and ethnic heroes miss the point.

For example, I often observe white teachers talking among themselves about what they believe are appropriate materials or teaching strategies to use with a culturally diverse class. They may seek input from a consultant and/or a colleague of color, but the decision-making power about schooling stays with the classroom teacher, the building principal, and the administrative hierarchy. Virtually excluded from decision-making power are the students, their parents, and their community, particularly if the community is poor and/or of color. In the case of one school, I recall teachers adding lessons about individual differences and Native American culture but continuing to dodge the question of how much academic achievement they could actually expect of students. In conversations with African-American and Latino community members, I was told (and was not surprised to hear) that academic achievement was their main concern. By defining themselves as the "experts" and the literature on multicultural education as a collection of ideas to use selectively, many educators undermine the basic impulse for dialog, power sharing, and self-determination that gave rise to multicultural education in the first place.

Thus, what began in a movement for self-determination in practice very often is reduced to additions to "business as usual" that do not actually change schooling or shift decision-making power toward oppressed groups. Multicultural education fundamentally means dialog and power sharing and the need for dialog and power sharing is as great now as it was three decades ago. While organized social movements may not be as visible in the 1990s as they were in the 1960s, the issues and basic conditions of life for Americans of color as well as for poor whites have not changed much since then. The small gains in income, employment, and status won by people of color as well as by women in the early 1970s have eroded.[16] Megacorporations have exported jobs from the United States. As Chomsky and others have argued, they have pitted white male workers, who are accustomed to having access to decent jobs, against Americans of color and women who are viewed as taking jobs unfairly through affirmative action, and against Third World people who are depicted as uncivilized.[17] Of course, schools alone cannot solve these problems, but schools embody and reflect them. Historically, multicultural education developed as a movement grounded in organized action aimed at social justice and educational equality for everyone; today the need for such organized action is as great as it has been for decades.

New Multicultural Curricula

Over the past three decades, multicultural education has produced some tangible fruit, the most visible of which is curriculum. As a reform movement, multicultural education cannot be reduced to curriculum. However, since curricular materials have emerged as the focus of heated national debate, I will concentrate on them.

Much "multiculturalized" curriculum actually ignores the main themes in scholarship and the experiences of oppressed groups. This happens when curriculum developers begin with existing curriculum as the base and then simply add on references to nondominant groups. These references may take the form of stories, biographical information, historic events, or pictures. To the observer whose conceptual viewpoint is congruent with that of white mainstream America, such a curriculum may seem multicultural. But to the observer whose viewpoint is rooted in a different conceptual space (such as someone with an Indian worldview), the curriculum looks "white" although with additions of color.[18]

There is, however, an expanding array of curricular materials that draw substantively on scholarship by oppressed groups. For example, a few secondary-level textbooks for African-American history[19] and African-American literature[20] make use of African-American scholarship. There are also a few anthologies with substantial offerings that are multicultural[21] as well as curriculum guides for teachers that illustrate how to help children learn to grapple with issues of social justice.[22]

But as one moves into the realm of textbooks to be adopted for courses required of all students, one encounters a hotly political terrain. It is the degree to which debates surrounding multicultural education have entered this terrain that has prompted popular publications such as *Time*, *U.S. News and World Report*, and *The New York Times* to feature articles about multicultural education. Cornbleth and Waugh have noted that "not unexpectedly, two of the places where the America debate [debate about what it means to be 'American'] has

emerged most boisterously are New York and California, the states
with the largest numbers of immigrants and the widest variety of people."[23] I review briefly here some curriculum development efforts in
three states—California, New York, and Oregon—that have been fea-
tured prominently in the national debates.[24]

During the mid-1980s, the state Superintendent of Public Instruction in California directed the state to revise various subject area
frameworks. A committee approved by the State Board of Education
drafted the California *History/Social Science Framework* that guided the
adoption of a textbook series.[25] The *Framework* takes what Cornbleth
and Waugh describe as a "modest" approach to multiculturalism, situating California's diverse population within the immigrant mold.[26] An
anchoring idea of the *Framework* is that the United States is a nation
of immigrants: everyone who is not an immigrant is a descendant of
immigrants, and Native Americans are depicted as the first immigrants. As such, all Americans share a common national identity,
including allegiance to symbols of U.S. citizenship. That citizenship
extends "the promise of freedom and equality for all," although
throughout its history "citizens have struggled to make sure that all
Americans have the rights they need to fulfill this promise."[27] A textbook series published by Houghton Mifflin that fits within the *Framework* was adopted at the state level; most districts in the state use it.

However, adoption of the series was fought by parents in urban
districts, as well as a cadre of others "who grew to include not only
racial and ethnic minorities but also Muslims, Jews, Christians, gays,
lesbians, and feminists."[28] Joyce King, an African-American scholar
who argued against the *Framework*, has pointed out that "none of the
history textbooks reviewed, including those that were eventually
adopted, received higher than 'moderate' ratings for 'cultural diversity,' one of the *Framework*'s seventeen 'characteristics' for evaluating
the texts."[29] Ultimately, adoption of this series of texts, which views
multiculturalism as a common experience of immigration and assimilation, was orchestrated by a small, largely white group of academi-
cians and political leaders including Diane Ravitch, Charlotte Crab-
tree, Bill Honig, and Lynne Cheney.[30] This *Framework* and textbook
series does not fit clearly within any of the five approaches to multicultural education mentioned earlier in this chapter since the anchoring ideas draw most firmly from the experience of European immigrants; alternative voices and perspectives are added but are truncated
and muted.

In the late 1980s New York State also began to write its own multi-cultural curriculum, but took a very different approach from that taken in California. A task force created by Commissioner Thomas Sobol drafted *A Curriculum of Inclusion*, which is a framework for subsequent curriculum development.[31] The task force was predominantly minority and drew substantively on the literature of multicultural education.[32] In 1990, *A Curriculum of Inclusion* was presented at a conference of textbook publishers in which texts were criticized for superficial multicultural content, and various speakers articulated the depth of diverse perspectives they would like to see in curriculum materials for teachers.[33] My presentation at the conference was a critique of forty-seven textbooks published in the 1980s and used in grades 1 through 8 in core academic subjects. I argued that most additions to textbooks to make them multicultural were far more cosmetic than substantive.[34]

In 1991, a second task force produced another report entitled *One Nation, Many Peoples: A Declaration of Cultural Interdependence.*[35] This report called for

the acknowledgement and study of racism and the continuing struggle to realize democratic ideals in everyday life. In so doing, the New York position recognizes structural inequities in U.S. society. Pluralism is not contained as in California, and diversity is not trimmed to fit the European immigrant experience, but neither is the conventional story of America directly confronted.[36]

To assist teachers in making their seventh and eighth grade U.S. history course multicultural, for example, the New York City school system had produced a supplementary curriculum guide of lessons and resource material that teachers are encouraged, but not required, to use.[37] The unit topics coordinate with those in standard history textbooks, but the activities help students examine events from the perspectives of many groups. Activities help students to critique policies in view of their impact on oppressed groups (such as the impact of expansionist policies on Native Americans and Mexicans). For example, in Activity 4 of Unit 4 the students are asked to contrast the Mexican viewpoint regarding Texas with that of the United States during the 1830s and 1840s. Activities throughout the curriculum guide regularly incorporate many cultural groups and multiple perspectives about events to encourage students to engage in critical thinking. The guide can be criticized for oversimplification because it suggests that there was one single U.S. viewpoint and one single Mexican viewpoint and because it fails to provide in-depth treatment of the histories of any oppressed group. Its critical stance, however, is a departure from the tendency of other history curricula to gloss over brutal policies of aggression. The New York supplementary curriculum guide illustrates the "multicultural and social reconstructionist" approaches to multicultural education.

Portland, Oregon, also published its own material to assist teachers in making their subject curricula multicultural. The first package of materials to receive distribution was the *African American Baseline Essays*, published in 1989.[38] This is a series of six commissioned essays by authors from six disciplines: art, music, literature, social studies, science, and mathematics. Each essay develops an Afrocentric perspective on the discipline, highlighting particularly the contributions of ancient Egypt to the development of knowledge in that discipline. An Afrocentric perspective means "placing African ideals at the center of any analysis that involves African culture and behavior."[39] It entails situating people of African descent within an African history and worldview. The essays provide teachers with background information they can use in their own teaching. Other baseline essays on Hispanics and Native Americans are nearing completion. These essays illustrate the "single-group studies" approach to multicultural education.

These three curricular projects, along with revisions of core curricula at several universities, have become the focus of debates about multicultural education in the 1990s. They have come into the public spotlight largely through the work of critics of multicultural education who are attempting to mobilize public opinion in support of a conservative conception of how children should be taught to regard America's diversity. In the next section I will comment on issues emerging from debates over these curricula.

Contemporary Criticisms of Multicultural Education

Although most of the literature on multicultural education in the United States supports and develops the concept, the amount of writing that criticizes it has escalated rapidly. Through a search of the literature I located two critiques published in journals in the 1970s, six in the 1980s, and fifty-one between 1990 and 1992 alone.[40]

Although critiques that take a conservative position greatly outnumber other critiques of multicultural education, the latter need to be mentioned. A handful of the critiques articulate a radical left position; these appear exclusively in scholarly literature and are written for an audience of theorists. They critique multicultural education as a field rather than targeting specific curriculum projects. Their main criticism is that the field downplays or simply ignores structural inequalities such as systemic racism, focusing instead on cultural differences and simplistic solutions to racism in education. For example, Olneck ties multicultural education to the Intergroup Education movement, arguing that both stress individualism and upward mobility of individuals rather than collective advancement of oppressed racial groups.[41] Since the criticisms of the radical left focus on theory more than on curriculum they will not be reviewed here.

Although little has yet been published, an anthropological critique of multicultural education is emerging. This criticism has been voiced mainly at professional conferences. The main concern of some educational anthropologists is that the concept of "culture" is not being used in the way that anthropologists use it and therefore much work in multicultural education offers simplistic analyses of minority students' underachievement and other problems related to race. But again, since anthropologists have not specifically targeted curriculum for criticism their views are not reviewed here.

The remaining critiques share common assumptions and concerns that will be reviewed. Some observers term these critiques "conservative," although some of the "conservative" critics describe themselves as "liberals." Other observers term the critiques "neonativist" since they echo the Americanization movement of earlier decades.[42]

What the conservative or neonativist critics define as multicultural education is not the scholarly literature on the subject, but rather specific curricular changes. Their most frequent targets are New York State's *A Curriculum of Inclusion*, New York City's first grade curriculum, Portland's *African American Baseline Essays*, Afrocentrism in general, and revisions of core curricula on several university campuses. They often uphold California's *History/Social Science Framework* as a version of multicultural education they support.

I will address here four charges made by conservative critics. First, they characterize multicultural education as the politically charged work of an extremist lunatic fringe of radicals who represent neither the public at large nor the majority of African Americans and Latinos. For example, an editorial in *U.S. News and World Report* characterized New York's *A Curriculum of Inclusion* as the product of a group of "prescreened worshipers at the altar of multiculturalism" who do not represent "the views of most blacks, immigrants, or New Yorkers in general."[43] Arthur Schlesinger, who served on and eventually dissented from the second New York task force, complained that "ethnic ideologues" and "unscrupulous hucksters" have "imposed ethnocentric, Afrocentric, and bilingual curricula on public schools, well designed to hold minority children out of American society."[44] Dinesh D'Souza described changes universities were making to accommodate diversity as the work of former radical student protesters of the 1960s who have now returned to the university as professors to complete their conquest of it.[45]

The second charge against multicultural education is that it places excessive emphasis on race and ethnicity, which conservative and neonativist critics regard as divisive and capable of tearing the United States apart. The critics view U.S. history as one of progress in learning to implement the ideals of Western political thought. These ideals champion the rights of individuals: "Class, race, religion, national origin or culture all disappear or become dim when bathed in the light of natural rights, which give men common interests and make them truly brothers."[46] Western ideals also presumably articulate universal principles of the good life, which are of a higher order than principles emanating from particular sociocultural experiences. Education should cultivate reason, enabling individuals to rise above their own particular group affiliations and participate in a common society; Western classics offer the best training for this honing of the mind and contemplation of universal principles. Some critics are worried that contemporary attention to ethnic origin reverses what they view as a progressive trend in U.S. history toward inclusion of everyone.

Some critics of writing on multicultural education are troubled by what they regard as excessive criticism of the West, which they believe calls Western political ideals into question. For example, can American slavery best be understood as a "holocaust" that needs to be examined because of what it reveals about how white supremacy was and still is institutionally embedded in social constructions? Or, should slavery be regarded as an unfortunate historic institution in which most societies participated but the effects of which have been virtually eliminated? These critics tend to take the latter position, arguing vehemently that the former position undercuts the West. For example, Schlesinger asserts: "Whatever the crimes of Europe, that continent is also the source—the *unique* source—of those liberating ideals of individual liberty, political democracy, the impartial rule of law, and cultural freedom . . . to which most of the world aspires."[47]

Few conservative critics deny that the United States is culturally diverse, and they propose a conception of multicultural education that fits with their belief in progress, individuality, and Western ideals. Diane Ravitch is perhaps the leading spokesperson for what she terms "pluralistic" as opposed to "particularistic" multicultural education.[48] Pluralistic multicultural education, exemplified by California's *Framework*, which Ravitch helped to draft, seeks commonalities across diverse groups and views U.S. history as a grand narrative of the extension of Western ideals to all Americans. Conservative critics laud its search for commonalities, contrasting it with New York's emphasis on multiple perspectives, which they regard as "private tribal truths."[49]

A third objection of conservative critics is that multicultural education is intellectually weak, substituting sentimentality and political dogma for sound scholarship. Their main target is Afrocentrism, with Portland's *African American Baseline Essays* receiving a good portion of their attention. The science essay has been criticized most strongly. Although disputing some of these criticisms, Portland is currently having the essay revised. But the larger problem critics have with Afrocentrism is that it "reject[s] European civilization outright—or take[s] credit for it."[50] They argue that this rejection is based on poor scholarship. Davidson argues, for example, that Afrocentrists are too "sunk . . . in a blanket rejection of Western civilization" to be swayed by evidence.[51] Schlesinger refers to Afrocentric curricula as "myth" passed off as "fact."[52]

New York's curriculum is also attacked as intellectually weak, a "hatchet job on existing academic standards," as Paul Gray put it in *Time* magazine.[53] Similarly, multicultural courses in higher education are also criticized as lacking scholarship. Lewis Feuer, for example, regards the aim of cultural diversity in higher education as being "to entrench a place for the superficial and mediocre," advocating "ideological apologia for backward peoples";[54] D. P. Bryden describes professors who teach multicultural courses as "dumb."[55] The problem as conservatives see it is that such courses replace what they regard as the intellectually sound study of the Great Books.[56]

A fourth criticism from the conservative perspective is that multicultural education attacks the problem of minority students' underachievement by advocating exercises in self-esteem rather than hard work and by substituting "relevance" of subjects studied for instruction in solid academics. For example, several critics point out that writers of color such as Richard Wright, Ralph Ellison, and Chinua Achebe profited intellectually from their study of Western classics, and that minority students today who are offered an intellectually

weak multicultural curriculum are not served well.[57] Ravitch faults
"particularistic" multicultural education for tracing minority students'
underachievement to lack of self-esteem and for proposing to correct
that lack by replacing the study of Europeans with the study of the
children's own ancestral group. She argues that this line of reasoning
is faulty because it places children's identity "on another continent or
in a vanished civilization" rather than in contemporary America and
because it does not emphasize achieving success by working hard.[58]
She asks whether it makes more sense to teach ancient African number systems rather than modern mathematics, suggesting that Afrocentrists' prescriptions for teaching African-American children are
flawed by their interest in ancient African culture.[59] Bilingual education is also criticized as retarding language minority children in their
acquisition of English and hence in their cultural assimilation.

The Criticisms Reexamined

The conservative or neonativist critics regard multicultural education as the work of a dangerous radical fringe group, and position
themselves as spokespersons for Americans of color as well as for
Americans in general. Herein lie serious weaknesses of their entire critique, as well as an affront to the underlying premise of multicultural
education, namely, that it emerged as educators of color attempted to
articulate their own concerns about schooling and that it is based on
sound scholarship.

The critics ignore a great deal of the literature on multicultural
education, as well as the supporting research and theory from fields
such as anthropology and social psychology. For example, a major
concern of educators of color is how to promote high achievement
among students of color. One approach they have used to explore this
concern has been to identify schools and/or teachers who are excep-
tionally successful with students of color and to find out what factors
seem to account for their success. Such studies that have been
reported in the literature are being synthesized for educators.[60]
Research findings are consistent with multicultural education literature, emphasizing, for example, (1) the need for teachers to become
familiar with students' community culture and build on that, (2) the
need to build on students' language base rather than attempting to
replace it, (3) the benefit to students of a culturally relevant curriculum, and (4) the academic value of teachers' viewing parents as a
resource from whom teachers can learn. By framing such practices

only as builders of "self-esteem," critics manufacture a straw person to tear down. None of the conservative critiques reviewed above mentioned any of the scholarly work supporting multicultural education; about half of the radical left critiques reviewed some of it. It is ironic that the conservative critics fault multicultural curricula for weak scholarship, but often display this very weakness in their own critiques.

However, the conservative and neonativist critics mask their disconnection with established multicultural scholarship including ethnic studies by name-dropping and drawing selectively on quotations by well-known scholars of color. By far most critics are white, although conservatives of color are also enjoying the public spotlight.[61] To position themselves as colleagues of Americans of color, many of the white conservatives sprinkle their writings with names such as W. E. B. Du Bois, Carter Woodson, Frederick Douglass, and James Comer who, they imply, agree with their viewpoints. Consider, for example, the following passage:

Multicultural history in its militant vein promotes fragmentation, segregation, ghettoization—all the more dangerous at a time when ethnic conflict is tearing apart one nation after another. James Baldwin once said, "To create one nation has proved to be a hideously difficult task; there is certainly no need now to create two, one black and one white."[62]

In this passage, Schlesinger implies that he and Baldwin share a common version of multicultural education. But they do not, and there is no suggestion in Baldwin's writings that he would support Schlesinger over advocates of multicultural education. Yet, by linking their arguments with quotations from prominent scholars of color, the conservative and neonativist critics suggest that those scholars agree with them.

In fact, one can marshall evidence that conservative criticisms and renderings of multicultural education contradict the interests and positions of a large spectrum of Americans of color. For example, Joyce King, who participated in the committee that created the California *Framework*, actively dissented from its defining of all Americans as immigrants and its transmutation of the problem of racism into a problem of assimilation and ethnic conflict. In a discussion of the politics surrounding California's curriculum, she notes that minority communities in several cities, including East Palo Alto, Hayward, Oakland, San Jose, San Francisco, Los Angeles, and Berkeley, objected to the curriculum. In order to probe the perspectives of the African-American communities, she convened meetings with parents from those communities and African-American multicultural education specialists. In the discussions that ensued, these groups found Sylvia Wynter's Black Studies perspective[63] to be more useful to their own understanding of race relations in the United States and the educational needs of African-American students than the perspective adopted by the California Education Department and the State Board.[64]

Conservative critics as well as most white mainstream educators differ from most scholars in multicultural education and in ethnic studies regarding the nature of racial inequality today, and how to address it. Conservatives (and many whites) tend to frame their understanding of race relations around a theory of ethnicity that is based on an analysis of the experience of European ethnic groups in the United States and mainly examines the extent to which groups retain distinct cultures while becoming structurally assimilated into the dominant society. As Omi and Winant argued in their review of theoretical perspectives for examining race in the United States, "ethnicity theory assigned to blacks and other racial minority groups the roles which earlier generations of European immigrants had played in the great waves of the Atlantic migration of the nineteenth and early twentieth centuries."[65]

In the California social sciences curriculum, all groups are presented as immigrants, retaining to various degrees different cultural customs and holidays, and the story of the United States is presented as one of progress in extending rights to all citizens. Even African Americans were immigrants, although they arrived in chains; slavery was an institution many societies practiced, and one that ended in the United States with the Civil War. Reconstruction is skipped over; African Americans are described as facing largely the same problems after the Civil War as other immigrants, including lingering prejudice and discrimination.

Ethnicity theory suggests that, over time, "successive" groups will assimilate; the process of assimilation is facilitated by focusing on commonalities among Americans; and there is no need to change institutional or political structures to accelerate this process. Thus, adherents to ethnicity theory tend to regard traditional school practices and curricula as well suited to the assimilation of diverse children. Further, the traditional curriculum's foundation in Western liberal thought enables any citizen to learn to transcend the limits of sociocultural context and participate in society objectively. As Schlesinger put it, the United States is a nation in which people "escape from origins" and go about "casting off the foreign skin."[66] From this perspective, any inequalities in the broad society will be corrected over time by adhering to tradition and continuing to expect schools to eradicate cultural differences among groups. White ethnics assimilated as did Jews; African Americans are to be next in line, followed by Mexicans and Asians.[67] The conservative or neonativist critiques of multicultural education are framed around discussion of unity versus difference, defining equality as equal rights of individuals before the law rather than as political and economic equality across groups. That perspective allows critics to regard racism as "a great national tragedy" in U.S. history that has been largely overcome: "The American synthesis has an inevitable Anglo-Saxon coloration, but it is no longer an exercise in Anglo-Saxon domination."[68]

While conservative critics seem to conceptualize ethnic and racial conflict as stemming from excessive group pride, multicultural education scholars conceptualize it as stemming largely from systemic racism and other forms of exclusion and domination. Conservatives may not regard data showing that white Americans enjoy the highest standard of living in the world while African Americans rank 31st[69] as evidence of "Anglo-Saxon domination," but Americans of color tend to see it as precisely that. Further, Americans of color increasingly voice frustration over the eroding conditions of life many have experienced over the past twelve years, as jobs have been exported, social services cut, funding for scholarships cut, and support for expressions of racism strengthened. Continuing to adhere to past traditions means, for example, continuing policies of land theft and Native American genocide, continuing to regard Mexican Americans chiefly as expendable "cheap labor," and continuing to divert economic resources away from African-American communities while regarding them as culturally and morally depraved.[70] To answer the question of how to elevate the collective status of groups and how those groups can gain more control over their own futures, ethnicity theory is helpful only to Euro-Americans; it fails to critique white racism and it presumes that time will take care of inequality.

Race- and nation-based theories conceptualize racism as an integral part of U.S. institutions and their origins in Europe's development and global expansion, as much a part of the present as the past.[71] While European immigrants were able to blend in, non-Europeans look visibly distinct and cannot melt (or "cast off the foreign skin") even if they wish to do so. In addition, non-European groups have experienced oppressive colonial relationships with Europe and the United States, which have brought about great disparities in wealth and power among races and well-ingrained racist theories that render such relationships legitimate. To understand the experiences of any given racial group, one must begin with that group, rather than adding that group's experience onto a narrative constructed around Euro-Americans.

The text *The African American Experience*,[72] for example, begins with Africans and documents struggles and achievements central to understanding the history and present status of African Americans in the United States. Portland's *African American Baseline Essays* specifically develops themes derived from a study of people of African descent, including a strong cultural connection between African civilizations, African Americans, and people of African descent worldwide, and the strengths of people of African descent in the face of continued oppression. According to race- and nation-based theories, history teaches us that the status of peoples of color will not be improved by attempting to assimilate with whites, by letting time take care of things, and by allowing the white majority to control their fate. Instead, collective advancement must continue to be a struggle in the face of persistent white resistance.

Conservative critics attempt to discredit much of multicultural education by depicting it as political and unscholarly, which they contrast with the study of Western classics. For example, Sandra Stotsky wrote: "One of the most contentious issues in education today is what the words 'multicultural education' mean and whether the content of such programs serves academic or political ends."[73] According to Western liberal thought, proper intellectual training can enable an individual to transcend personal vested interest in order to speak dispassionately for the whole society. This is an intellectual process, not a political one.

According to scholars in ethnic studies, women's studies, and cultural studies, however, Western liberal thought is not apolitical. Rather, it is tied to the experiences of a segment of humanity, and needs to be understood as such. No body of knowledge is universal and apolitical; there is no single perspective about anything. Once we understand the limitations and politics embedded within bodies of thought, we can appreciate the wisdom therein without limiting our inquiry to a single perspective. An intellectually rigorous multicultural curriculum teaches students to identify assumptions, perspectives, vested interests, and viewpoints within multiple bodies of thought.[74]

What about new immigrants who often do not line up behind established minority groups' perspectives? Indeed, many do enter the United States expecting to assimilate. But what is often ignored in discussions of new immigrants is that they are entering a society that is most definitely not colorblind, and that has a long history of complex racial dynamics. Those immigrants who are not from Europe—currently the great majority of immigrants—may not expect to become entangled in race relations, but over time they do so. For example, a colleague who is from Latin America and looks Hispanic or Indian to U.S. Anglos, came to the United States with no thought of being a "minority." However, over time many Anglo Americans have treated her as a minority (and often as uneducated). She has gradually redefined her own identity and her perception of race and ethnicity in the United States, so that her thinking has become increasingly congruent with that of "minority" Americans.[75]

Implications for Educators

This discussion has focused largely on curriculum controversies. Two central questions emerge: (1) In your own school or school district, how much serious dialog takes place among diverse sociocultural groups? (2) To what degree do those who have historically been disenfranchised have power to define education policies and practices, including curriculum?

The teaching profession continues to be predominantly white. This means that perspectives about education originating in any other sociocultural community and intimate knowledge of such communities are not often found within the corps of education professionals. I have observed that white educators tend to agree with conservative criticisms of multicultural education unless they work hard to learn alternate perspectives. Further, by regarding themselves as "experts" on educational issues and believing that their own education has helped them to view matters objectively, white professional educators often do not see much point in serious dialog and power sharing with minority communities. Instead, they make decisions about what multicultural education might mean by dialoging with each other and drawing very selectively from the literature in that field.

Educators must begin by learning to listen to and learn from the students and their parents. They must also learn about the community

from which the students come. This means inviting dialog and listening nondefensively. Sometimes students may say that they prefer
group work to individual worksheets in situations where the teacher
also sees cooperative learning as feasible and desirable. At other times,
however, a teacher's ideas may be challenged, which can require
painful self-examination or much follow-up learning. For example, an
African-American high school student recently tried to explain to a
white teacher that she was tired of reading white literature and wanted
to read African-American literature. The teacher had difficulty understanding why and conceptualizing an alternative curriculum. Instead,
she tended to dismiss the student as oversensitive. If the teacher were
to listen to and take seriously the student's viewpoint, and also to listen to other African Americans discuss the same issue, she would
begin to see a different perspective.

Luis Moll and his colleagues at the University of Arizona have
developed a project called "funds-of-knowledge," in which teachers
are trained to conduct extensive interviews with parents of their students in order to situate teachers as learners in a different sociocultural community from their own. Teachers arrange at least three visits
in the home of at least one student. The main purpose of the visits is
to enable the teacher to discover areas of knowledge the parents have
in order to develop authentic collaboration in the construction of
teaching that bridges cultures.[76] This kind of project is useful to teachers of any racial or ethnic background. My preservice students who
complete a project that is similar to, although less extensive than
Moll's, seem to learn to "tune in to" a different perspective.

Educators should make a point of systematically reading professional literature by scholars of color, addressing specific questions such
as the following: What kinds of practices have helped students of color
learn mathematics successfully? Why do Latino educators usually insist
that bilingual education is necessary and that it does not retard acquisition of English? Why do many Indian educators believe Indian children
fare better in tribally controlled schools than in mainstream white
schools? Reading professional literature does not substitute for dialog
with people of color in one's own community, but it helps develop
depth and support for what lay people know from their own experience.

Developing a multicultural school is a process of reconstructing relationships rather than adopting a program or a product. One school
that illustrates this process is La Escuela Fratney in Milwaukee, an
example of excellent multicultural education in action. It was established

182   CURRICULUM CONTROVERSIES

in 1988 through a grassroots effort, and the school has an active collaborative relationship with parents. The school's basic philosophy advocates high-quality multicultural, antiracist education; it offers a two-way Spanish-English bilingual program. The teachers create a good deal of the curriculum, which is oriented around helping children learn to examine issues from multiple points of view.[77]

Engaging in listening, learning, and dialog can help move educators beyond simplistic conceptions of multicultural education or tugs of war over "political correctness," and toward the creation of school practices that better serve a diverse society that has yet to eliminate racism, sexism, and institutionalized poverty.

I am very grateful to Joyce E. King and Ellen Swartz for their helpful and insightful comments on an earlier draft of this chapter.

NOTES

1. James A. Banks, *Multiethnic Education: Theory and Practice*, 2d ed. (Boston: Allyn and Bacon, 1988); Geneva Gay, "Multiethnic Education: Historical Developments and Future Prospects," *Phi Delta Kappan* 64 (1983): 560-563.

2. Banks, *Multiethnic Education: Theory and Practice*, pp. 30-31.

3. James A. Banks, "African American Scholarship and the Evolution of Multicultural Education," *Journal of Negro Education* 61, no. 3 (1992): 279.

4. James A. Banks, "Multicultural Education: Characteristics and Goals," in *Multicultural Education: Issues and Perspectives*, edited by James A. Banks and Cherry A. McGee Banks (Boston: Allyn and Bacon, 1989), p. 23.

5. Carl A. Grant, "Education That Is Multicultural: Isn't That What We Mean?" *Journal of Teacher Education* 29, no. 5 (1978): 45-48.

6. Jeannie Oakes, *Keeping Track* (New Haven, CT: Yale University Press, 1985).

7. Ray C. Rist, *The Invisible Children* (Cambridge, MA: Harvard University Press, 1978).

8. Carl A. Grant and Christine E. Sleeter, *After the School Bell Rings* (London: Falmer Press, 1986).

9. Susan U. Phillips, *The Invisible Culture* (New York: Longman, 1983).

10. See, for example, Shirley Brice Heath, *Ways with Words* (New York: Cambridge University Press, 1983); Luis Moll, "Bilingual Classroom Studies and Community Analysis: Some Recent Trends," *Educational Researcher* 21, no. 2 (1992): 20-24; Marietta Saravia-Shore and Steven F. Arvizu, eds., *Cross-Cultural Literacy* (New York: Garland, 1992); Barbara J. R. Shade, *Culture, Style, and the Educative Process* (Springfield, IL: Charles C. Thomas, 1989).

11. See, for example, Rodolfo Acuña, *Occupied America* (New York: Harper and Row, 1988); Paula Gunn Allen, *The Sacred Hoop* (Boston: Beacon Press, 1986); Molefi Kete Asante, *Kemet, Afrocentricity and Knowledge* (Trenton, NJ: Africa World Press, 1990); Paul Lauter, *Canons and Contexts* (New York: Oxford University Press, 1991).

12. Geneva Gay, "Curriculum Theory and Development in Multicultural Education," in *Handbook of Research on Multicultural Education*, edited by James A. Banks and Cherry A. McGee Banks (New York: Macmillan, forthcoming).

13. Geneva Gay, "Effective Teaching Practices for Multicultural Classrooms," in *Multicultural Education for the 21st Century*, edited by Carlos F. Diaz (Washington, DC: National Education Association, 1992), pp. 38-56.

14. Christine E. Sleeter and Carl A. Grant, *Making Choices for Multicultural Education*, 2d ed. (Columbus, OH: Merrill, 1994).

15. Christine E. Sleeter, *Keepers of the American Dream* (London: Falmer Press, 1992).

16. Derrick Bell, *Faces at the Bottom of the Well* (New York: Basic Books, 1992); Susan Faludi, *Backlash: The Undeclared War against American Women* (New York: Doubleday, 1991); Andrew Hacker, *Two Nations* (New York: Charles Scribner's Sons, 1992).

17. For development of this argument, see Noam Chomsky, "Domestic Policy: Change of Business as Usual," *Z Magazine* 6, no. 2 (1993): 30-42; Mahmut Mutman, "Under the Sign of Orientalism: The West vs. Islam," *Cultural Critique* 23 (1992-93): 165-198; Holly Sklar, "Crosscurrents: Young and Guilt by Stereotype," *Z Magazine* 6, no. 7/8 (1993): 52-61.

18. Ellen Swartz, "Cultural Diversity and the School Curriculum: Content and Practice," *Journal of Curriculum Theorizing* 9, no. 4 (1992): 73-88.

19. Sharon Harley, Stephen Middleton, and Charlotte M. Stokes, *The African American Experience: A History* (Englewood Cliffs, NJ: Globe, 1992).

20. *African American Literature* (Austin: Holt, Rinehart and Winston and Harcourt Brace Jovanovich, 1992).

21. Alan C. Purves, ed., *Tapestry: A Multicultural Anthology* (Paramus, NJ: Globe Book Co., 1993); Charles Tatum, ed., *Mexican American Literature* (New York: Harcourt Brace Jovanovich, 1990).

22. Louise Derman Sparks, *The Anti-Bias Curriculum* (Washington, DC: National Association for the Education of Young Children, 1989); Nancy Schniedewind and Ellen Davidson, *Open Minds to Equality* (Boston: Allyn and Bacon, 1983).

23. Catherine Cornbleth and Dexter Waugh, "The Great Speckled Bird: Education Policy-in-the-Making," *Educational Researcher* 22, no. 7 (1993): 31.

24. Catherine Cornbleth and Dexter Waugh, *The Great Speckled Bird: Multicultural Politics and Education Policymaking* (New York: St. Martin's Press, forthcoming).

25. History-Social Science Curriculum Framework and Criteria Committee, *History-Social Science Framework* (Sacramento: California Department of Education, 1988). The textbook series that was adopted is Beverly J. Armento, Gary B. Nash, Christopher L. Salter, and Karen K. Wixson, *Some People I Know*, *Across the Centuries*, and *America Will Be* (Boston: Houghton Mifflin, 1991).

26. Cornbleth and Waugh, "The Great Speckled Bird," p. 32.

27. Armento, Salter, and Wixson, *America Will Be*.

28. Cornbleth and Waugh, "The Great Speckled Bird," p. 33.

29. Joyce E. King, "Diaspora Literacy and Consciousness in the Struggle against Miseducation in the Black Community," *Journal of Negro Education* 61, no. 3 (1992), p. 322.

30. Cornbleth and Waugh, "The Great Speckled Bird."

31. Task Force on Minorities, *A Curriculum of Inclusion* (New York: New York State Education Department, 1989).

32. Leslie Agard-Jones, "Implementing Multicultural Education: The New York City Experience," *Multicultural Education* 1, no. 1 (1993): 13-15+.

33. The conference was held in Albany, New York, on January 9, 1990. The theme was "Winds of Change: A Forum on Multicultural Education."

184   CURRICULUM CONTROVERSIES

34. Christine E. Sleeter and Carl A. Grant, "Race, Class, Gender, and Disability in Current Textbooks," in *The Politics of the Textbook*, edited by Michael W. Apple and Linda K. Christian-Smith (New York: Routledge, 1991), pp. 78-110.

35. Social Studies Review and Development Committee, *One Nation, Many Peoples: A Declaration of Cultural Interdependence* (Albany: New York State Education Department, June 1991).

36. Cornbleth and Waugh, "The Great Speckled Bird," p. 35.

37. New York City Public Schools, *United States and New York State History: A Multicultural Perspective* (New York: Board of Education of the City of New York, 1990).

38. *African American Baseline Essays* (Portland, OR: Portland Public Schools, 1989).

39. Molefi Kete Asante, *The Afrocentric Idea* (Philadelphia: Temple University Press, 1987), p. 6.

40. Christine E. Sleeter, "An Analysis of the Critiques of Multicultural Education," in *Handbook of Research on Multicultural Education*, edited by James A. Banks and Cherry A. Banks (New York: Macmillan, forthcoming).

41. Michael Olneck, "The Recurring Dream: Symbolism and Ideology in Intercultural and Multicultural Education," *American Journal of Education* 98, no. 2 (1990): 147-174.

42. Cornbleth and Waugh, "The Great Speckled Bird," pp. 31-32.

43. John Leo, "Multicultural Follies," *U.S. News and World Report* 111, no. 2 (1991): 12.

44. Arthur M. Schlesinger, Jr., *The Disuniting of America* (New York: Norton, 1992), p. 10.

45. Dinesh D'Souza, *Illiberal Education: The Politics of Race and Sex on Campus* (New York: Free Press, 1991).

46. Alan C. Bloom, *The Closing of the American Mind* (New York: Simon and Schuster, 1989), p. 27.

47. Schlesinger, *The Disuniting of America*, p. 127.

48. Diane Ravitch, "Multiculturalism: E Pluribus Plures," *American Scholar* 59, no. 3 (1990): 337-354.

49. Leo, "Multicultural Follies."

50. Nicholas Davidson, "Was Socrates a Plagiarist?" *National Review* 43, no. 3 (1991): 45.

51. Ibid., p. 46.

52. Arthur M. Schlesinger, Jr., "The Disuniting of America: What We All Stand to Lose if Multicultural Education Takes the Wrong Approach," *American Educator* 15, no. 3 (1991): 28.

53. Paul Gray, "Whose America?" *Time* 138, no. 1 (1991): 13.

54. Lewis Feuer, "From Pluralism to Multiculturalism," *Society* 29, no. 1 (1991): 21-22.

55. D. P. Bryden, "It Ain't What They Teach, It's the Way That They Teach It," *Public Interest* 103 (1991): 46.

56. D'Souza, *Illiberal Education*; Irving Howe, "The Content of the Curriculum: Two Views: The Value of the Canon," *Liberal Education* 77, no. 3 (1991): 8-9.

57. Schlesinger, *The Disuniting of America*; Howe, "The Content of the Curriculum."

58. Diane Ravitch, "Diversity and Democracy: Multicultural Education in America," *American Educator* 14, no. 1 (1990): 47.

59. Ravitch, "Multiculturalism: E Pluribus Plures."

60. For syntheses of research, see Etta Ruth Hollins, Joyce E. King, and Warren Hayman, eds., *Teaching Diverse Populations: Formulating a Knowledge Base* (Albany: State University of New York Press, 1994); Beverly McLeod, ed., *Language and Learning: Educating Linguistically Diverse Students* (Albany: State University of New York Press, 1994).

61. Dinesh D'Souza is an immigrant from India. Other conservatives of color who do not support multicultural education include Linda Chavez, *Out of the Barrio: Toward a New Politics of Hispanic Assimilation* (New York: Basic Books, 1991); Richard Rodriguez, *Hunger of Memory* (Boston: D. Godine, 1981); Shelby Steele, *The Content of Our Character* (New York: St. Martin's Press, 1990); Thomas Sowell, *Inside American Education* (New York: Free Press, 1993).

62. Arthur M. Schlesinger, Jr., "Writing, and Rewriting History," *New Leader* (December, 1991): 14.

63. Sylvia Wynter, *Do Not Call Us Negroes: How Multicultural Textbooks Perpetuate Racism* (San Jose, CA: Aspire Books, 1992). Wynter's perspective can be described as "a cultural model or epistemology with the potential for transmuting knowledge by challenging the 'prescriptive rules' of the American 'public culture,' which over the centuries have rigidly maintained racial harmony." Cornbleth and Waugh, *The Great Speckled Bird.*

64. King, "Diaspora Literacy and Consciousness in the Struggle against Miseducation in the Black Community."

65. Michael Omi and Howard Winant, *Racial Formation in the United States* (New York: Routledge and Kegan Paul, 1986), p. 20.

66. Schlesinger, *The Disuniting of America*, pp. 15, 112.

67. Joyce E. King, Personal communication, June 14, 1993.

68. Schlesinger, *The Disuniting of America*, pp. 19, 48.

69. Robin Wright, "Living Standard in U.S. Diverse: U.N.," *Kenosha (Wis.) News* 16 May 1993.

70. Ward Churchill, *Struggle for the Land* (Monroe, ME: Common Courage Press, 1993); Acuña, *Occupied America.*

71. Acuña, *Occupied America*; Bell, *Faces at the Bottom of the Well*; Ward Churchill, *Fantasies of the Master Race* (Monroe, ME: Common Courage Press, 1992); Omi and Winant, *Racial Formation in the United States.*

72. Harley, Middleton, and Stokes, *The African-American Experience.*

73. Sandra Stotsky, "Cultural Politics," *American School Board Journal* 178, no. 10 (1991): 26.

74. James A. Banks, "The Canon Debate, Knowledge Construction, and Multicultural Education," *Educational Researcher* 22, no. 5 (1993): 4-14.

75. Carmen Montecinos, "Multicultural Education That Is Social Reconstructionist: What Should Teachers Know?" in *Multicultural Education and Critical Pedagogy*, edited by Christine E. Sleeter and Peter McLaren (Albany: State University of New York Press, forthcoming).

76. Luis C. Moll, "Bilingual Classroom Studies and Community Analysis."

77. Priscilla Ahlgren, "La Escuela Fratney," *Teaching Tolerance* 2, no. 2 (1993): 26-31.

CHAPTER IX

Creating Educational Opportunity for African Americans Without Upsetting the Status Quo

ROBERT LOWE AND HARVEY KANTOR

In the post World War II era African-American educational efforts redefined formulations of equality of educational opportunity to make race central to them, and those efforts inspired parallel struggles by other subordinated peoples of color. These struggles informed more sophisticated analyses of the ways inequality is reproduced along with more rigorous definitions of equal opportunity and the practices required to achieve it. What drove educational change in the postwar period, however, was not simply the demands of those denied equality of educational opportunity, but the dialectic between those demands and governmental responses that tried to address them without infringing on the privileges of whites.

The results of this dynamic have been ambiguous. By a number of measures African Americans have achieved significant long-term educational advances. In 1960, for instance, the median number of school years completed for the 35 to 44-year-old African-American males was merely 8.5 and for African-American females it was 9.0, but for 25 to 34-year-olds the median had risen to 9.8 and 10.3. By 1973, 68 percent of 19 to 20-year-old blacks had completed high school, a percentage that rose to 71 percent in 1980 and 78 percent in 1990.[1] In addition, over the last two decades African Americans made gains on many measures of the National Assessment of Educational Progress, as well as in both the number of academic courses taken by high school graduates and the percentage of students enrolled in college directly after high school. Though the chasm in educational accomplishment between African Americans and whites generally has diminished, significant

Robert Lowe is Associate Professor of Educational Foundations at National-Louis University, Evanston, IL. Harvey Kantor is Associate Professor of Educational Studies at the University of Utah.

186

gaps remain. In 1990, for example, only 9.4 percent of 24-year-old African Americans held a bachelor's degree or higher as opposed to 22.9 percent of whites, and 65.4 percent of African American 19-year-olds were high school graduates or higher as opposed to 80.2 percent of 19-year-old whites.[2] Disparities between blacks and whites, in fact, persist on virtually all other academic measures.

In this chapter we contend that postwar educational policy contributed to black achievement by providing openings for the realization of African-American educational aspirations, while that same educational policy allowed for practices that have sustained inequalities between blacks and whites. We argue further that resistance to inequitable practices has been compromised by limited political power and the erosion of resources in urban areas. Enduring inequities in part trace to the focus of policy on what Harold and Pamela Silver have called "an educational war on poverty" rather than on the economic roots of inequality.[3] But they are also rooted in efforts meant to achieve educational equality while preserving whites' privileges.

In limiting our discussion in this chapter to the education of African Americans we are acknowledging that their efforts are essential to understanding the politics of education over the past half-century. Although we recognize that the educational struggles of African Americans in some ways are analogous to those of Chicanos, Native Americans, and Puerto Ricans, we are not suggesting that the experiences of the latter are unimportant or can be reduced to those of the former. We simply recognize that a synthesis that incorporates various peoples of color in a nontokenistic manner is presently beyond our means.

The Glacial Pace of School Desegregation

During the years of World War II a precipitous decline in southern agricultural laborers—particularly African-American tenant farmers and sharecroppers—took place as a result of the military draft and the draw of decent paying jobs in war industries. Black migration to northern and western cities in the 1940s totalled 1.6 million. Despite the potency of racism in the South, southern whites understood how strongly blacks valued education and, consequently, they significantly reduced funding inequalities between black and white schools to moderate the flow of blacks from the rural South.[4] Yet the scarcity of cheap labor also spurred the mechanization of southern agriculture. The results were dramatic. According to economic historian Gavin Wright,

"The percentage of the American cotton crop that was machine harvested went from 5 in 1950 to 50 in 1960, and was over 90 by the end of the 1960s."[5] If greater opportunities initially drew blacks out of the rural South, the dramatic decline in demand for rural labor and discrimination against them in nonagricultural employment pushed them out in the 1950s and 1960s. By 1970 approximately 50 percent of African Americans resided in the North, approximately three quarters of whom lived in metropolitan areas.

African-American urbanization and migration had particularly important political consequences. In the North, garnering the vote of newly enfranchised blacks became vital to the success of the Democratic party, while in the South urban blacks had become substantially free of white surveillance and control imposed by a semifeudal existence.[6] The loosening of constraints and incipient political influence were preconditions for the Civil Rights Movement. Animating that movement was *Brown v. Board of Education*, which gave federal-level legitimacy to efforts aimed at abolishing discrimination. There followed an accelerating, many-faceted struggle for equality of which school desegregation was a modest part. From the Montgomery Bus Boycott to the lunch counter sit-ins and freedom rides, from the Albany and Birmingham movements to the Selma march for voting rights, a mobilized black population dramatized injustice and prompted passage of the Voting Rights Act of 1964 and Civil Rights Act of 1965.

Although the *Brown* decision fueled the freedom movement, the pace of school desegregation was glacial. By the time of the 1964 Civil Rights Act, only 3 percent of southern blacks were attending school with whites. After *Brown* several border cities made modest desegregation efforts, but in the absence of court decisions mandating measures to effectively end segregation, southern states resisted. The violence that accompanied the effort of nine black children to desegregate Central High School in Little Rock was rare, but the blatant acts of pupil placement to avoid desegregation and the more subtle freedom of choice plans that replaced them dramatically restricted black efforts to attend white schools in the South. In the North, demands for desegregation typically were rebuffed before the middle 1960s based on the argument that schools were not charged with the task of social engineering and that segregation was created by housing patterns rather than the practices of school officials. Sometimes busing was used to send African-American children to white schools, but the purpose was to relieve overcrowding rather than to promote integration. Cleveland and Milwaukee practiced intact busing, meaning that black students bused into receiving schools attended segregated classes. Milwaukee went so far as to return students to their home school for lunch to avoid integrating the cafeterias.[7]

By the early 1960s, suits against school districts, often but not always filed by the NAACP, were accompanied by increasingly vigorous protests—from petitions to demonstrations to boycotts—that won little more than token changes. Even when the boycotts reached massive proportions in Chicago and New York, involving as many as 224,000 students in the former and 464,000 in the latter, they wrung virtually no concessions from school officials.[8]

Compensatory Education

Spurred by the freedom movement, equality of educational opportunity became the center of federal energy and initiative, but in the beginning the federal effort was directed toward compensatory education rather than school desegregation. Social scientists created the ideological justification for such activity by maintaining that deficits in the environments of poor children—especially black children—largely accounted for their weak performance in school. What they termed "cultural deprivation" was caused, they claimed, by a lack of stimulation and interaction that retarded children's linguistic and perceptual development and created passivity and present-mindedness. Thus ill-prepared for school, they were destined to fall further and further behind.[9]

Although these social scientists rejected a biological explanation for group differences in educational achievement, only deeply held assumptions about racial difference could have supported a belief in cultural deprivation in the face of disconfirming evidence presented by the mass mobilizations of the civil rights movement. Psychologist Kenneth Clark was one early critic who warned that notions of cultural deprivation could exonerate schools from their role in causing failure:

To what extent are the contemporary social deprivation theories merely substituting notions of environmental immutability and fatalism for earlier notions of biologically determined educational unmodifiability? To what extent do these theories obscure more basic reasons for the educational retardation of lower-status children? To what extent do they offer acceptable alibis for the educational default: the fact that these children, by and large, are not being taught effectively and they are not being taught because those who are charged with the responsibility of teaching them do not believe that they can learn, do not expect that they can learn, and do not act toward them in ways which help them learn.[10]

Judgments of cultural deprivation often were made either without evidence or were dependent upon ethnocentric observations. Even characteristics that would be considered unequivocally positive in middle class children at times were seen as liabilities among the poor. Thus one scholar reduced the high educational aspirations of black children and parents to "defensiveness," "wishful thinking," and a psychological "adjustment to failure."[11] In addition, some social scientists in the early 1960s who pointed out that the poor had strengths typically focused on nonintellectual qualities. Martin Deutsch, for instance, observed that lower-class children tend to express independence. "However, this independence—and probably confidence—in regard to the handling of younger siblings, the crossing of streets, self-care, and creating of their own amusements does not necessarily meaningfully transfer to the unfamiliar world of books, language, and abstract thought."[12]

From the early 1960s several critics of cultural deprivation expressed concerns similar to Clark's and by late in the decade a more widespread critique was conjoined with a growing recognition of the cultural strengths that engendered perseverance and vitality under circumstances of subordination.[13] Yet a general acceptance of cultural deprivation in the policy arena justified the ongoing efforts of social scientists to solve the educational problems of those whose inadequacies made it impossible for them to act in their own behalf, and this acceptance shaped the ideology, practice, and location of federal intervention in education.

The extraordinary efflorescence of federal initiatives in the 1960s mainly stressed the need to compensate children for environmental inadequacies. Compensation for deprivation justified the creation of Head Start for early childhood intervention; for school-age children it provided the rationale for add-on programs ranging from Title I of the Elementary and Secondary Education Act, the most highly funded of the initiatives, to the modestly funded Upward Bound.[14] Meant to support the schools' role in acculturating students rather than to challenge the practices of public schools that might have contributed to unequal outcomes, these programs had few enemies. Aggressive federal support for school desegregation, in contrast, not only would have interfered with local practice, but also it would have antagonized working class whites and threatened the Democratic Party's coalition by violating the sanctity of racially homogeneous neighborhood schools.[15] Even though the new initiatives did represent a drastic change in federal educational involvement both in their scale and in their devotion to equalizing educational opportunity, they simply were not what African Americans had sought, and they were couched in language that increasingly was seen as offensive. This does not mean, however, that the programs have had no positive effects.

Since the middle 1960s an enormous amount of energy and expense has gone into evaluating the education programs of the War on Poverty. Hugh Davis Graham has underscored the "frustrations in teasing objective generalities from a sea of program evaluations wherein the goals of policy intervention are typically so broad, ambiguous, and contradictory that both success and failure are virtually unverifiable."[16] Yet these evaluations have yielded some consistent and easily predicted results across programs.

Situated on the periphery of schools, programs have been hindered by inadequate funds, relatively short-term contact with children, and an incapacity to reach more than a small percentage of eligible students. Early evaluations were highly critical and more recent ones generally agree with their predecessors that gains in academic achievement are short-lived for program participants.[17] Basically, evaluations have concurred that achievement gains in preschool programs wash out in the elementary grades. Chapter 1 (formerly Title I) students show greater elementary school gains than similar non-Chapter-1 students if funds are concentrated, but these gains also are lost over time.[18] In addition, graduates of Upward Bound, a high school program that prepares low-income students for college, drop out of college at the same rate as control groups.[19]

This is not the entire story, however. As limited as these interventions have been, federally funded and other major compensatory programs also have had positive consequences overlooked by early evaluations. Upward Bound programs, for instance, have been enormously successful in placing graduates in postsecondary institutions and enabling them to receive financial aid.[20] At the preschool level a number of programs have had the long-term effect of diminishing placements into remedial and special education classes, reducing grade retention, and increasing rates of high school graduation.[21]

Chapter 1 has been less successful, however. In part this has been the result of inadequate concentration of funds where they are most needed. In addition, governmental attempts to guarantee that funds are directed to low-income students rather than the general purposes for which many school districts initially used them have encouraged the practice of pulling students out of the regular classroom. As of the mid-1980s approximately 75 percent of Chapter 1 students were in pull-out programs. Instead of enriching these students' educational experience, such a policy often has substituted a tedious regimen of drill on skills for a portion of their regular curriculum.[22]

Charting gross educational effects, of course, provides no sense of program variation on the ground. Individual programs have provided employment to many idealistic staff of color who have not necessarily subscribed to formulations of cultural deprivation or compensatory educational practices. Some directors have attracted considerable private money to supplement meager federal funding. And some projects have extended the duration of their contact with young people. One that has done all three is the Educational Opportunity Program at Marquette University which enrolls students after eighth grade and in many cases sees them through to university graduation eight or nine years later.[23]

An obvious conclusion from examining the compensatory educational initiatives of the era is that ever since the creation of the Demonstration Guidance Project in New York City in 1956 the amount of resources devoted to students and the duration of the commitment have strongly influenced programs' success.[24] Yet even though well-funded, long-term experiences have been atypical, the federal programs at least in modest ways have expanded opportunities for many children.

Desegregation on Terms Favorable to Whites

Although federal initiatives in education were created as a substitute for the fractious policy of integration, the increasingly vigorous pursuit of desegregation by the Fifth Circuit Court of Appeals and the Office for Civil Rights was legitimated and extended by a series of Supreme Court decisions, beginning with *Green v. New Kent County* in 1968, which banned freedom of choice plans that did not produce desegregation. *Green* was followed by *Swann v. Charlotte Mecklenberg* in 1970, which approved busing, and in 1973 by *Keyes v. Denver*, which extended desegregation to the North and included Chicanos as well as

African Americans in desegregation plans. As a consequence of these rulings many districts in the South desegregated rapidly, as did a number of northern districts. In the nation as a whole, there was significant progress toward desegregation between 1968 and 1980. In the former year 76.6 percent of African-American students attended schools that were more than half minority and 64.3 percent attended schools that were 90 to 100 percent minority. By 1980 these figures had declined to 62.9 percent and 33.2 percent.[25]

One consequence of desegregation was that many black students were able to attend schools with resources superior to those in schools they previously attended. Yet changes accompanied desegregation that jeopardized the extent to which these students could enjoy enhanced resources. In the South, for instance, a dramatic decline in the number of black teachers and administrators initially accompanied desegregation. More than 30,000 teachers lost their jobs, and in some states 90 percent or more black principals were removed from their positions.[26]

At stake were not simply jobs for African Americans or "role models" for students. Rather the issue, powerfully addressed by W.E.B. Du Bois in an often quoted 1935 defense of separate schools, was the greater likelihood of sympathetic bonds between teachers and students of the same race.[27] A number of writers, for instance, have documented the fear and hostility with which white teachers have responded to children in inner cities. Surveying the schools of Harlem in the middle 1960s, where the teaching force had always been overwhelmingly white, Kenneth Clark likened the relationship between white teachers and black students to class war, "with middle-class and middle-class-aspiring teachers provided with a powerful arsenal of half-truths, prejudices, and rationalizations, arrayed against hopelessly outclassed working class youngsters."[28]

If black teachers have been more likely than white teachers to identify with black students, creating greater possibilities for classroom environments congenial to the risk-taking that learning requires, their presence also has influenced the degree to which African-American students have avoided penalties and placements harmful to academic success. In their study of 174 large school districts, for instance, Robert England, Kenneth Meier, and Joseph Stewart have found that the greater the percentage of black teachers in a district, the fewer the cases of suspensions and expulsions of black students, the less likely their placement in special education classes, the greater their access to gifted classes, and the higher their graduation rates.[29] By dramatically diminishing the percentage of black teachers throughout the South, desegregation contributed to forms of second-generation segregation that white teachers were less likely to contest.

Perhaps the most pronounced form of second-generation segregation is tracking. Its roots lay in educational reforms during the Progressive Era that were predicated on the assumption that students had different interests, abilities, and destinies in life. Educational leaders, therefore, believed that the increasingly heterogeneous high school population would benefit from a differentiated curriculum and ability grouping. Although the intent was perhaps benign, the consequence was to provide working class young people disproportionately with a less demanding curriculum that limited access to higher education. According to Robert Hampel, by 1930 approximately 50 percent of the high schools in the United States divided the curriculum into academic, general, commercial, and vocational tracks.[30] Matters of class rather than race initially shaped this policy, since a ceiling on educational attainment induced by Jim Crow legislation severely restricted African-Americans' attendance at high school. As blacks increasingly got access to secondary schools and began to attend them with whites, tracking was extended to them with a vengeance.

Even before *Brown v. Board of Education*, there is evidence that northern school systems managed steeply rising black enrollments by disproportionately relegating African Americans to the general track. In a study of Detroit, for example, where the African-American population increased significantly during World War II, David Angus and Jeffrey Mirel found that during the 1946-47 school year African-American students were overrepresented in the general track by 50 percent.[31] With the *Brown* decision, this trend continued. In the St. Louis and Washington, DC school systems, which both underwent a measure of desegregation in the 1950s in immediate response to *Brown*, tracking commenced in order to assuage whites' concerns that their academic achievement would be compromised by African-American students.[32] It preserved substantial segregation within schools by relegating black students to the lowest tracks.[33] Superintendent Carl F. Hansen of Washington, DC, who launched a four-track scheme later to be found unconstitutional, was clear about the rationale. "To describe the origin of the four-track system without reference to desegregation in the District of Columbia Public Schools," he maintained, "would be to bypass one of the most significant causes of its being."[34]

This practice appeared in the North as well. When Berkeley, California, desegregated its nearly all-white, upper-middle-class Garfield Junior High in the middle 1960s, black students found themselves disproportionately placed in the lower tracks of a four-track curriculum.[35] Similar imbalances existed in Berkeley's Willard Junior High which had been desegregated since the 1930s and had recently responded to criticism by creating a more equitable tracking plan. Yet 90 of 107 whites and all 13 Asians were in the upper two tracks, while 61 of 110 black students were in the lower two tracks, including all 19 of the students in the lowest track.[36]

Nationally, the Coleman Report found that grouping or tracking was experienced by approximately 38 percent of elementary school students and 75 percent of high school students in the 1960s.[37] And there is evidence that it continued to expand in the wake of court-ordered desegregation.[38] It also became more differentiated than the three or four conventional curriculum streams. Advanced placement classes, initiated in the 1950s along with the rapid expansion of other advanced courses during that decade, constituted, according to David Cohen, a new track for the top tier of students enrolled in college preparatory programs.[39] In contrast to these largely white preserves, students of color would find themselves concentrated at the other end of the spectrum—the burgeoning realm of special education. Meier, Stewart, and English have found, in fact, that for African-American students in the mid-1970s desegregation bore a positive relationship to educable mentally retarded (EMR) placements and a negative relationship to placement in gifted classes.[40]

Following the period of most rapid desegregation in the South, black students in more than 75 percent of southern districts were overrepresented in EMR classes by more than 100 percent. An already astounding overrepresentation by 330 percent in 1968, rose to 540 percent in 1974.[41] In view of these figures it is hardly surprising that a considerable body of research has found that high percentages of special education placements have been inappropriate.[42]

In summary, the increasingly aggressive court action to define *de jure* segregation more rigorously and to require positive measures to overcome segregation in violating districts had limited benefits for African Americans because they could not control the context in which desegregation took place. As a result desegregation was accompanied by practices that tended to segregate African-American students within schools. Based on presumably impartial means, tracking and special education placements concentrated them in the least desirable academic programs, allaying the fears of white parents that academic standards would decline or that much mixing of the races would take place. This special regard for middle-class whites was reflected as well in their typically being spared school closings in their neighborhoods and the concomitant burden of busing. In addition, magnet schools, created to hold middle class whites in city schools, often absorbed disproportionate resources of financially strapped urban districts.[43]

The Illusory Goal of Integration

Despite the large number of districts that underwent desegregation from the late 1960s through middle 1970s, integration remained an illusory goal. Policymakers and the public have typically viewed desegregation as successful when it has required minimal disruption and inspired little resistance. The courts, even in the most aggressive period of desegregation, were more concerned with achieving racial balance rather than academic and social integration within schools. Yet advocates of integration as early as the middle 1960s had recognized that racial balance was not enough. *Racial Isolation in the Schools*, for instance, maintained that what was needed was "to minimize the possibility of racial friction in the newly desegregated schools; the maintenance or improvement of educational standards; the desegregation of classes within the schools as well as the schools themselves, and the availability of supportive resources for individual students who lag in achievement."[44]

The contradictory research on school desegregation effects, in part, is a result of the extent to which desegregated schools have varied from authentic integration. According to Nancy St. John,

Whether for children of either race the benefits outweigh possible harm seems to depend on how desegregation is accomplished in schools—on the leadership given by the principal, on a teaching staff that is unbiased and trained in ways of handling diversity in the classroom, on the cultural pluralism of the curriculum, and—above all—on equality of status for each racial group with the school.[45]

To the extent that generalizations can be made about the relationship of desegregation to increased academic achievement, it appears, according to Robert Crain and Rita Mahard, that desegregation is most successful when implemented at the beginning years of schooling and when it is metropolitanwide in a way that includes a majority of white students yet a critical mass of black students.[46] These scenarios have a greater chance of living up to the principle of equal status for all students than desegregation that takes place in the higher grades or that includes a very small number of African-American children.

Whatever the potential benefits of metropolitan desegregation, however, such a policy has been rare. The Supreme Court, which had actively promoted desegregation with key decisions between 1968 and 1973, ruled against a metropolitan desegregation plan in Detroit in 1974. The majority in *Milliken v. Bradley* maintained that school officials in each of the fifty-three suburban districts included in the suit had to be found guilty of intent to segregate before they could be compelled to participate in the plan. This effectively ruled out mandatory metropolitan remedies in the North, and it meant that many cities, where schools were increasingly populated by African Americans and Latinos, could not attempt meaningful desegregation within their borders. Whereas in 1950 whites had been a majority in all of the nation's largest school systems except Washington, DC, by 1968, six of the ten largest school systems in the country were more than half minority, and by 1980 all were two thirds and most were at least three fourths minority.[47] Further, despite national progress toward desegregation during the period, segregation increased in the Northeast. Between 1968 and 1980 the percentage of African-American students in the Northeast who attended schools that had more than 50 percent minority enrollment rose from 66.8 to 79.9, and the percentage who attended schools with 90 percent or more minority enrollment rose from 42.7 to 48.7.[48] Finally, with the eclipse of desegregation as an instrument of educational policy in the 1980s, segregation nationwide has increased for African Americans. In 1991-92, 66 percent of blacks were in schools where a majority of the students were African American or Latino.[49]

The Demand for Responsive Schools

Frustrated by the slow pace of desegregation and by injustices faced in schools that had accomplished it, many African Americans abandoned the pursuit of desegregation at the very time the courts most actively pressed it. Activists sought greater black representation in the makeup of faculties and curricula, and in some cases viewed community control as the best means for realizing these goals. Often leaders in these efforts to make schools hospitable to black students previously had been prominent in struggles to secure desegregation, and in a sense they were now acting to realize the unfulfilled promise of those struggles. If demands for desegregation challenged the legitimacy of schools as white preserves, demands for greater influence on schools tested the legitimacy of both the conventional governance structures of education and the traditional curricular canon.

By the fall of 1968 widespread and often militant actions of African Americans at the local level involved strikingly similar demands. These included greater representation on governing boards, the firing of teachers and counselors who failed to share the aspirations of students for higher education, the hiring of more minority teachers and counselors, the abolition of tracking, and the promotion of subject matter that addressed the cultures of students.

The relative influence of community leaders, parents, college students, and high school students varied, but students were the most visible force in the protests. A congressional survey conducted by the House General Subcommittee on Education found that in 1968-69 alone, student protest took place at 18 percent of the high schools in the nation. Although many of the protestors were white and the dominant concerns were matters of discipline and dress code, approximately one third of the protests addressed racial issues, and 59 percent did so in major cities.[50] Even in majority white schools, like Bronx High School of Science and New York City's High School of Music and Art, black students often took leadership positions.

Certainly some militant students did little more than mouth the demands of the Black Panther Party and other leftist organizations of young adults, and, as activist student Donald Reeves maintained, some were more interested in posturing and avoiding final exams than advocating a serious program for change.[51] Several historians, in addition, have condemned activists for incivility, ethnocentrism, and an equity agenda pursued at the expense of educational excellence. Yet this perspective fails to take into account the incapacity of conventional "civil" protests in the first half of the 1960s to make school authorities responsive to the concerns of African Americans. It also fails to recognize that many students sincerely pressed demands that sought to illuminate and transform practices, pedagogies, and forms of knowledge that had marginalized them. Thus the prevalence of histories that excluded or distorted the lives of African Americans led to demands for classes in black history. The demand for such courses, moreover, was not simply made to correct conventional subject matter, but to transform a subject from one that was considered the most irrelevant, according to a Louis Harris Poll of students, to one invested with significance.[52] Rather than representing the collapse of excellence, the desire for courses in black studies often meant taking academics seriously, an orientation to schooling that had been uncommon for whites.[53]

For students like Donald Reeves, reading books by black authors like *Soul on Ice* and the *Autobiography of Malcolm X* led to a serious campaign of reading and learning that was not primarily aimed at extrinsic rewards and college admission, but at better understanding the world.[54] Amid the posturing and acting out that took place at both the college and high school level, there was for many activists a recognition of the relationship between knowledge and power that produced committed intellectual effort.

That many students were demanding an education of substance was also suggested by the way efforts to establish ethnic studies courses and hire African-American staff were conjoined with both demands for greater educational resources and an end to tracking and other practices that yielded insubstantial curricula for students of color. At Ravenswood High School in California, for example, an organization called Students for Higher Education staged a sit-in in the principal's office in the fall of 1968. In addition to the demands for black studies and more black personnel that are typically associated with the protests of the period, the students also sought more foreign language laboratories, a greater selection of works by both black and white authors for the library, after-school study halls, and an end to worksheets.[55] Also in the fall of 1968, 55 percent of students at Chicago's Harrison High, where the majority was black, walked out, demanding, among other things, more homework.[56] In addition, Robert Rossner, a teacher at Bronx High School of Science in New York, has written about the "sense of purpose" of black students who participated in opening the school during the strike by the United Federation of Teachers in October 1968. During that month fewer than 300 students out of 3200 were in school, but this included approximately 70 percent of the black students.[57] A number of black students from De Witt Clinton High School, which was closed during the strike, chose to attend class at Bronx Science as well.[58] Teachers and students jointly developed the curriculum. Readings chosen for Rossner's English classes were *Antigone, Manchild in the Promised Land,* and *Walden.*[59]

These struggles of African Americans to reshape schools to affirm their identities and confirm their aspirations had only limited success during the late 1960s and early 1970s. Responding to community pressure, school systems throughout the nation hired black personnel and introduced ethnic studies courses. Yet African-American teachers remained underrepresented, the addition of new courses was a change at the margins of the curriculum that had little effect on the content of the major subjects, and forms of second-generation segregation at best were more limited where black educators were highly represented.

Although black demands in the 1960s often engendered only token responses from white school boards, more recently the racial makeup of urban boards has changed significantly as whites have abandoned public schools in cities. By the 1980s African-American membership on school boards in major urban school systems had become proportional to their districtwide populations. African-American school board membership, in turn, has influenced the hiring of black administrators and teachers. Consequently, blacks also have attained nearly equal representation among administrators and teachers, despite the losses earlier brought about by desegregation in the South.[60] Nonetheless, this representation is less favorable when it is based on student attendance, since a much higher percentage of African American students attend public schools than the district percentage of the population would suggest. With black students as a basis of comparison, black administrators were 27 percent underrepresented in 1986. That year black teachers were 32 percent underrepresented as opposed to 19 percent in 1968 and 27 percent the following year (despite a 3 percent increase in the overall number of African American teachers since 1968)[61]

Despite some positive consequences associated with increased black leadership and its potential to implement more thoroughly multicultural curricula, that leadership has not been able to dismantle inequitable school practices. Sometimes these practices have taken on new forms. Protest against the disproportionate placement of blacks in EMR classes, for instance, resulted in significant reductions, but a new category of special education, learning disabled (LD), was created in the middle 1960s. Initially it was meant for underachieving white students for whom EMR was associated with children of color, but now minorities tend to be overrepresented in it. According to Gerald Coles, the condition allegedly requiring LD treatment is unproven and the students so labeled increasingly fall behind their peers academically.[62]

The use of LD placements, however, does not mean that students of color, especially African Americans, have escaped other forms of second-generation segregation, including disproportionate representation in the traditional special education classes. In their study of 174 large school districts Meier, Stewart, and England found the following:

A black student is nearly three times more likely to be placed in a class for the educable mentally retarded than is a white student. A black student is 30 percent more likely to be assigned to a trainable mentally retarded class than a white student. At the other end of the spectrum, a white student is 3.2 times more likely to be accepted to a gifted class than is a black student . . . A black student is more than twice as likely as a white student to be corporally punished or suspended. A black student is 3.5 times more likely than a white student to be expelled.[63]

In addition, The College Board found that in the middle 1980s, 33 percent of African Americans as opposed to 40 percent of whites and 52 percent of Asians were enrolled in college preparatory classes.[64]

Despite greater representation of African Americans in positions of educational leadership, school practices that reproduce inequality were prevalent in the 1980s. Furthermore, in cities where black leadership has come to predominate it has operated under increasingly impoverished circumstances that have profoundly undermined equality of educational opportunity.

Black Control over Poverty

Suburbanization historically was spurred by governmentally sanctioned discrimination—both the support of segregated housing by the Federal Housing Administration and, until the late 1940s, the provision of legal standing for racially restrictive covenants. Over time, cities have become less white and more poor, as middle-class whites have departed for suburbs that have provided racially homogeneous refuges with well-funded public schools and other services at relatively low tax rates. A report prepared for the U.S. Commission on Civil Rights found that of twelve metropolitan areas in 1950, per-pupil expenditures in city schools were greater than in suburbs in ten instances. By 1964, however, cities were being outspent in seven of the twelve cases.[65] In addition, by 1960 in all regions of the country median family income in suburbs exceeded that in cities.[66] Subsequently, the closing of many factories and the migration of other industries to the suburbs have further eroded urban tax bases and accelerated the impoverishment of city residents.

202   CREATING EDUCATIONAL OPPORTUNITY

Overwhelmingly residing in urban areas, African Americans suffer much higher rates of poverty than whites, and children especially experience this disadvantage. Even though the proportion of African-American children living in poverty has declined considerably from a 65.5 percent figure in 1959, it has increased since 1970 when 41.5 percent of African-American children under eighteen lived in poverty, as opposed to 10.5 percent of whites. In 1980, for children under eighteen, 42.1 percent of African Americans lived in poverty, as opposed to 13.4 percent of white children. For both groups conditions worsened in 1990, with 44.2 percent of African-American children living in poverty and 15.1 percent of white children.[67]

As a consequence of economic and demographic change, as well as a waning federal commitment to desegregation, many urban schools are often as segregated as were southern schools before the courts dismantled segregation. In addition, disparities in expenditures between these schools and white suburban ones resemble the inequities of the Jim Crow era. Jonathan Kozol has powerfully evoked the widespread injustice of providing the most meager resources to the most economically disadvantaged.[68]

Not only have inadequate resources limited the capacity of urban school districts to provide enriched educational environments to those students not graced by access to a few well-funded preserves for middle-class children, but also poverty, unemployment, and isolation from those who earn adequate incomes may also influence students' sense of whether schools provide access to greater economic opportunity, and consequently whether serious effort is rewarded.[69] There is evidence, in fact, that skepticism is warranted when it comes to rewards for education in the labor market. Clearly, more years of schooling tend to be compensated by higher wages and lower levels of unemployment; yet in 1980 35 percent of unemployed African American males in Boston possessed a high school diploma. This was the case as well for 28.9 percent of unemployed black males in Detroit, 28.8 percent in Philadelphia, 28.3 percent in New York, 26.6 percent in Chicago, and 24.7 percent in St. Louis.[70] Moreover, between 1969 and 1985 blacks in central cities who had completed more than one year of college experienced an unemployment rate that leaped from 3.7 percent to 13.1 percent, while for similarly situated whites it merely rose from 1.6 percent to 3.6 percent.[71] There is also evidence that black college graduates have experienced higher rates of unemployment over time. Between 1963 and 1965 1.0 percent of black male college graduates between 25 and 54 years old were unemployed for the entire year as opposed to 1.7 percent of whites. By 1985-1987, these percentages rose to 7.2 for black males and only 2.2 for white males. Furthermore, since the middle 1960s black male college graduates often have had higher rates of annual unemployment than white high school dropouts.[72]

Even for employed African Americans, returns for high school graduation and college graduation have shown signs of erosion. Black high school graduates experienced a 44 percent decline in wages between 1973 and 1987.[73] In 1979 black high school graduates with between one and ten years of work experience earned on a weekly basis only 83 percent of what whites with the same qualifications earned. Blacks who had completed college or beyond with one to ten years of experience received weekly salaries in 1979 that were 88 percent of what whites with comparable educations received.[74] John Bound and Richard Freeman estimated that by 1987-88 the typical salary of a black male with fewer than ten years of experience since graduating from college was 15 percent less than that of similarly experienced white males, though it had been 8 percent greater in 1975-76.[75]

Although gaps in educational attainment between African Americans and whites have diminished significantly, continuing inequalities are compounded by apparent discrimination in the labor market. Along with disparities in unemployment and wages between blacks and whites, African Americans have unequal access to rewarding jobs. According to research conducted by Stanley Lieberson and Mary Waters, African-American males, based on their educational attainment, are not underrepresented in the professions, but they are underrepresented in executive, administrative, and managerial jobs, as well as in positions in sales. On the other hand, they are overrepresented in the least desirable jobs.[76] Similarly, black women are very disadvantaged in labor market opportunities based on their education.[77]

Conclusion

Given the imperfect correspondence between educational attainment and economic rewards, the persistence of inequitable school practices, and the maldistribution of educational resources that provide the least to the poorest, what is remarkable is not the extent to which black students have failed, but the extent to which they have succeeded.[78] The significant percentage of African American students who have managed to achieve under adverse circumstances once again discredits formulations about cultural deficits and weak educational aspirations. Substantially broadening that achievement, given the uncertain returns of the labor market to schooling, requires that schooling makes sense to students in its own right rather than as an instrumental means to other goals. Schools that respect students through commodious facilities, ample educational resources, intellectually challenging curricula that validate their experience, and teachers who identify with students' aspirations are all expected in white suburban districts.[78] If such schools were the norm in urban districts, compensatory programs would be less necessary and fewer students could be labeled "at risk," the latest lexical effort to pin the blame for failure on students and their families.

At bottom, the Civil Rights Movement amplified an effort begun by African Americans at the end of the Civil War to fashion schools equally accessible to all members of the public. Despite the inadequacies of many of the policies and programs meant to equalize educational opportunity since World War II, what has changed significantly over the past fifty years is that the institutions of secondary and higher education have become broadly accessible. And if the terms of entry have been far from equal, it is clear that a little opportunity, given the high educational aspirations of African Americans, has resulted in advances toward equalizing results.

Yet what also has become clear over the past half century is that redistributing educational opportunity is no easier than redistributing income. As African Americans have sought entry to the public schools on equal terms, whites have resisted these efforts by trying to bar their entry, by establishing preserves of privilege within public schools, and by removing their children and money from the schools that black children attend in large numbers. More than 150 years after Horace Mann launched his campaign for public education, truly public schools remain elusive.

NOTES

1. Stanley Lieberson, *A Piece of the Pie: Black and White Immigrants Since 1880* (Berkeley: University of California Press, 1980), Table 6.4, p. 130; National Center for Education Statistics, *The Condition of Education, 1992* (Washington, DC: U.S. Government Printing Office, 1992), p. 58.

2. U.S. Department of Commerce, 1990 Census of Population, *Education in the United States* (Washington, DC: U.S. Government Printing Office, 1994), pp. 3, 5.

3. Harold Silver and Pamela Silver, *An Educational War on Poverty: American and British Policy-Making, 1960-1980* (Cambridge: Cambridge University Press, 1991).

4. Gavin Wright, *Old South, New South: Revolutions in the Southern Economy Since the Civil War* (New York: Basic Books, 1986), p. 245.

5. Ibid., p. 243.

6. Francis Fox Piven and Richard A. Cloward, *Poor People's Movements: Why They Succeed, How They Fail* (New York: Vintage Books, 1979), p. 203.

7. U.S. Commission on Civil Rights, *Racial Isolation in the Public Schools*, vol. 1 (Washington, DC: U.S. Government Printing Office, 1967), pp. 56-58.

8. For the figures on boycott participation in Chicago and New York City, see Gary Orfield, *The Reconstruction of Southern Education: The Schools and the 1964 Civil Rights Act* (New York: Wiley-Interscience, 1969), p. 162; David Rogers, *110 Livingston Street: Politics and Bureaucracy in the New York City School System* (New York: Random House, 1968), p. 26.

9. James T. Patterson, *America's Struggle against Poverty, 1900-1980* (Cambridge, MA: Harvard University Press, 1981), chapter 7.

10. Kenneth B. Clark, *Dark Ghetto: Dilemmas of Social Power* (New York: Harper Torchbooks, 1967), p. 131.

11. Irwin Katz, "Academic Motivation and Equal Educational Opportunity," in *Equal Educational Opportunity*, prepared by the Editorial Board of the *Harvard Educational Review* (an expanded version of the Winter 1968 special issue of the *Harvard Educational Review* (Cambridge, MA: Harvard University Press, 1969), pp. 66, 67.

12. Martin Deutsch, "The Disadvantaged Child and the Learning Process," in *Education in Depressed Areas*, edited by A. Harry Passow (New York: Teachers College Press, 1963), p. 178.

13. See, for instance, A. Harry Passow, "Education in Depressed Areas," in *Education in Depressed Areas*, edited by A. Harry Passow (New York: Teachers College Press, 1963), p. 343; Eleanor Burke Leacock, ed., *The Culture of Poverty: A Critique* (New York: Simon and Schuster, 1971).

14. Julie Roy Jeffrey, *Education for Children of the Poor: A Study of the Origins and Implementation of the Elementary and Secondary Education Act of 1965* (Columbus: Ohio State University Press, 1978).

15. Ira Katznelson and Margaret Weir, *Schooling for All: Class, Race, and the Decline of the Democratic Ideal* (Berkeley: University of California Press, 1985), chapter 7.

16. Hugh Davis Graham, "Transatlantic Wars on Poverty: History and Policy," *History of Education Quarterly* 33 (Summer 1993): 223.

17. For summaries, see Henry Levin, "A Decade of Policy Developments in Improving Education and Training for Low-Income Populations," in *A Decade of Federal Anti-Poverty Programs: Achievements, Failures, Lessons*, edited by Robert Haveman (New York: Academic Press, 1977), chapter 5; Nathan Glazer, "Education and Training Programs and Poverty," in *Fighting Poverty: What Works and What Doesn't*, edited by Sheldon Danzier and Daniel Weinberg (Cambridge, MA: Harvard University Press, 1961), chapter 7.

18. Harvey Kantor, "Education, Social Reform, and the State: ESEA and Federal Education Policy in the 1960s," *American Journal of Education* 100 (November 1991): 75.

19. Gary Natriello, Edward L. McDill, and Aaron M. Pallas, *Schooling Disadvantaged Children: Racing against Catastrophe* (New York: Teachers College Press, 1990), pp. 68, 74-76, 111.

20. Ibid., p. 111.

21. Ibid., pp. 66, 57.

22. See Kantor, "Education, Social Reform, and the State," note 26, p. 78.

23. College graduation rates and other successes of this program are documented in Marquette University Educational Opportunity Program, "1992-93 Annual Report to the Office of the Vice President for Academic Affairs." See also Arnold L. Mitchem, "Marquette University's Educational Opportunity Program: A Case Study of a Compensatory Education Program in Higher Education, 1968-1981" (Ph.D. Dissertation, Marquette University, 1981).

24. *Racial Isolation in the Public Schools*, pp. 123-24; Natriello, McDill, and Pallas, *Schooling Disadvantaged Children*, pp. 191-194.

25. Jennifer L. Hochschild, *The New American Dilemma: Liberal Democracy and School Desegregation* (New Haven: Yale University Press, 1984), Table 1, p. 30.

26. Estimates vary on job loss. Kenneth Meier, Joseph Stewart, and Robert England put the figure at more than 31,000 teachers and Jacqueline Irvine at nearly 40,000. Irvine also cites a study of the Association for the Study of Negro Life and History that puts the loss of black principals throughout the South at 90 percent. See Jacqueline Jordan Irvine, *Black Students and School Failure: Policies, Practices, and Prescriptions* (New York: Greenwood Press, 1990), pp. 34, 40; Kenneth J. Meier, Joseph Stewart, Jr., and Robert E. England, *Race, Class, and Education: The Politics of Second-Generation Discrimination* (Madison: University of Wisconsin Press, 1989), p. 17.

27. W.E.B. Du Bois, "Does the Negro Need Separate Schools," *Journal of Negro Education* 4 (July 1935): 328-335.

28. Ibid.; Robert Hampel, *The Last Little Citadel: American High Schools Since 1940* (Boston: Houghton Mifflin, 1986), p. 76; Clark, *Dark Ghetto*, p. 129.

29. Meier, Stewart, and England, *Race, Class, and Education*, pp. 95-103.

30. Hampel, *The Last Little Citadel*, p. 10.

31. David L. Angus and Jeffrey E. Mirel, "Equality, Curriculum, and the Decline of the Academic Ideal: Detroit, 1930-68," *History of Education Quarterly* 33 (Summer 1993): 184-186.

32. See, for instance, Carl F. Hansen, *The Four-Track Curriculum in Today's High Schools* (Englewood Cliffs, NJ: Prentice-Hall, 1964), p. 11.

33. For this phenomenon in St. Louis, see Patricia Jansen Doyle, "St. Louis: City With the Blues," *Saturday Review*, February 15, 1969, p. 92. In addition, Kenneth Clark found in the African-American Banneker District that nearly 50 percent of students had test scores that would place them in the vocational track. See *Dark Ghetto*, p. 143.

34. Hansen, *The Four-Track Curriculum*, pp. 7-8.

35. James S. Coleman et al., *Equality of Educational Opportunity* (Washington, DC: U.S. Government Printing Office, 1966), p. 477.

36. Ibid., p. 479.

37. Ibid., p. 115.

38. Kenneth J. Meier and Joseph Stewart, Jr., *The Politics of Hispanic Education* (Albany: State University of New York Press, 1991), p. 21.

39. Arthur G. Powell, Eleanor Farrar, and David K. Cohen, *The Shopping Mall High School: Winners and Losers in the Educational Marketplace* (Boston: Houghton Mifflin, 1985), p. 286.

40. Meier, Stewart, and England, p. 125.

41. Hochschild, *The New American Dilemma*, p. 31.

42. Meier and Stewart, *The Politics of Hispanic Education*, pp. 19-20.

43. Robert Havighurst was probably the first scholar to recommend the creation of what would later be termed magnet schools. He was explicit about their role in stemming "the flow of middle-class people from the central city." See Robert J. Havighurst,

"Urban Development and the Educational System," in *Education in Depressed Areas*, edited by A. Harry Passow (New York: Teachers College Press, 1963), pp. 43-44.

44. U.S. Commission on Civil Rights, *Racial Isolation in the Public Schools*, p. 154; also see Coleman et al., *Equality of Educational Opportunity*, p. 477.

45. Nancy St. John, "The Effects of School Desegregation on Children: A New Look at the Research Evidence," in *Race and Schooling in the City*, edited by Adam Yarmolinsky, Lance Liebman, and Corinne S. Schelling (Cambridge, MA: Harvard University Press, 1981), p. 99.

46. Robert Crain and Rita Mahard, "Minority Achievement: Policy Implications of Research," in *Effective School Desegregation: Equity, Quality, and Feasibility*, edited by Willis D. Hawley (Beverly Hills: Sage, 1981), pp. 61, 72, 74.

47. Gary Orfield, *Public School Desegregation in the United States, 1968-1980* (Washington, DC: Joint Center for Policy Studies, 1983), p. 23.

48. Hochschild, p. 30.

49. "Segregation's Threat to the Economy," *New York Times*, December 19, 1993, p. 12E.

50. *The New York Times Encyclopedia Almanac, 1971* (New York: *New York Times*, 1971), p. 536.

51. See Diane Divoky, "Revolt in the High Schools: The Way It's Going to Be," *Saturday Review*, February 15, 1969, p. 102; Donald Reeves, *Notes of a Processed Brother* (New York: Pantheon, 1971), pp. 65, 246-247.

52. *Life*, May 16, 1967, p. 31.

53. See, for instance, Robert S. Lynd and Helen Merrell Lynd, *Middletown: A Study in Modern American Culture* (New York: Harcourt, Brace and World, 1929), chapter 16.

54. Reeves, *Notes of a Processed Brother*, pp. 142, 147.

55. Robert Lowe, "Benign Intentions: The Magnet School at Ravenswood High" (Paper presented at the Annual Meeting of the American Educational Research Association, San Francisco, April 1992), pp. 3-4.

56. Mary J. Herrick, *The Chicago Schools: A Social and Political History* (Beverly Hills, CA: Sage, 1971), p. 363.

57. Robert Rossner, *The Year Without an Autumn: Portrait of a School in Crisis* (New York: Richard W. Baron, 1969), pp. 153, 159, 4.

58. Ibid., p. 260 and passim.

59. Ibid., pp. 177, 192. The strike ended before students read *Walden*.

60. Meier, Stewart, and England, pp. 77-78.

61. Ibid., pp. 72, 74.

62. Gerald Coles, *The Learning Mystique: A Critical Look at "Learning Disabilities"* (New York: Pantheon, 1988), pp. xiii, 205-207.

63. Meier, Stewart, and England, p. 5.

64. *Equality and Excellence: The Educational Status of Black Americans* (New York: The College Board, 1985), cited in Irvine, *Black Students and School Failure*, p. xv.

65. *Racial Isolation in the Public Schools*, p. 27.

66. For data between 1960 and 1970, for instance, see John R. Logan and Mark Schneider, "Governmental Organization and City/Suburb Income Inequality," *Urban Affairs Quarterly* 17 (March 1982): 312.

67. National Center for Education Statistics, *The Condition of Education, 1990*, vol. 1, *Elementary and Secondary Education* (Washington, DC: U.S. Government Printing Office, 1990), p. 64; idem, *The Condition of Education 1992*, p. 108.

68. Jonathan Kozol, *Savage Inequalities* (New York: Crown, 1991).

69. See William Julius Wilson, *The Truly Disadvantaged: The Inner City, the Underclass, and Public Policy* (Chicago: University of Chicago Press, 1987), chapter 2; John U. Ogbu, "Variability in Minority School Performance: A Problem in Search of an Explanation," *Anthropology and Education Quarterly* 18 (December 1987): 325.

70. John D. Kasarda, "Urban Industrial Transition and the Urban Underclass," *Annals of the American Academy of Political and Social Science* 501 (January 1989): 34.

71. John D. Kasarda, "Jobs, Migration, and Emerging Urban Mismatches," in *Urban Change and Poverty*, edited by Michael G. H. McGeary and Laurence Lynn, Jr. (Washington, DC: National Academy Press, 1988), pp. 184-186.

72. Christopher Jencks, *Rethinking Social Policy: Race, Poverty, and the Underclass* (New York: HarperPerennial, 1992), p. 156.

73. Robert B. Reich, *The Work of Nations: Preparing Ourselves for 21st Century Capitalism* (New York: Alfred A. Knopf, 1991), pp. 205-206.

74. Jencks, *Rethinking Social Policy*, p. 51.

75. John Bound and Richard Freeman, "What Went Wrong? The Erosion of the Relative Earnings and Employment of Young Black Men in the 1980s," Department of Economics, University of Michigan (1990). Cited in Jencks, *Rethinking Social Policy*, p. 243.

76. Stanley Lieberson and Mary C. Waters, *From Many Strands: Ethnic and Racial Groups in Contemporary America* (New York: Russell Sage Foundation, 1988), p. 148.

77. Ibid., p. 150.

78. Theresa Perry offers this formulation in an important discussion of African American education. See Theresa Perry, *Toward a Theory of African American School Achievement*, Report no. 16 (Baltimore, MD: Center on Families, Communities, Schools, and Children's Learning, Johns Hopkins University, March 1993).

79. On the importance of treating students as intellectuals, see Cynthia M. Ellwood, "Beyond the Basics: A Teacher-Researcher's Case Study of an Urban High School Literature Class" (Ph.D. Dissertation, Stanford University, 1990); and on the importance of schools supporting community aspirations for children, see Emilie V. Siddle Walker, "Caswell County Training School, 1933-1969: Relationships between Community and School," *Harvard Educational Review* 63 (Summer 1993): 161-182.

CHAPTER X

Minority Schools on Purpose

CHARLES L. GLENN

Thousands of public schools in the United States enroll primarily pupils of racial and ethnic minority groups, as do perhaps a thousand schools in Western Europe, particularly in nations that have experienced substantial immigration from North Africa and Asia. The concentration of minority children in American schools, however, is caused in part by immigration (primarily from Latin America and Asia) but also by internal migration of black families from the South, of Latino families from the Southwest and Puerto Rico, and of white families out of inner-city areas.

While de jure segregation by deliberate government action is no longer legal in the United States, de facto segregation (arising from residential patterns, which may indirectly result from government policies) is if anything increasing, especially for Latino pupils. A study by the Children's Defense Fund found that in 1986 one third of the Latino and black pupils in the United States were in schools with an enrollment over 90 percent minority.[1] Residential segregation of ethnic (mostly immigrant) minority groups is not as extreme in European cities as in Chicago, for example, but the high concentration of minority pupils in certain schools is generally considered a serious policy problem. While some have argued that this does not necessarily impact academic achievement, most policymakers believe that at the very least it hinders integration of minority youth into the host society.

The focus of this paper is not upon de facto segregation and efforts to reduce or eliminate it, but upon the deliberate promotion by government of separate schooling for minority pupils in what is argued to be the interest of those pupils. There are many schools in large American cities attended exclusively by black or Latino pupils;

Charles L. Glenn is Professor of Education at Boston University. He was previously with the Massachusetts State Department of Education where he was responsible for matters pertaining to civil rights, desegregation, and urban education.

they may or may not be a policy problem, depending upon state laws, the causes of the segregation, and judgments about its educational effects. It is quite another matter when a public school system sets out to create a school that is explicitly intended to serve a single racial or ethnic group and justifies this on policy grounds.

In September 1993, for example, the Washington, DC school system opened an "Afro-Centric" school with a curriculum developed by a controversial consultant who insisted upon keeping its details secret until days before school started, despite demands from local officials that they have an opportunity to review it.[2]

Proposals for ethnically oriented schools have been most notable in Detroit, where the school system in 1991 sought to open three all-male "African-American academies." Under court order, a few girls were admitted as well, but the racial focus of the schools remained intact.[3] The admission of the girls reflects what currently appears to be the greater militancy of feminist than of traditional civil rights groups in insisting upon integrated schools, as well as the fact that all-black schools are already a reality while all-male schools are extremely rare in American public education. A recent survey of public programs for black youth found no all-male schools, and only a few such programs in public schools, one of which had been shut down under challenge.[4]

Advocates for all-male schools and classes continue to press their argument that this is the only solution for the catastrophic academic and social problems of black youth, and vow that their efforts will continue around the country.[5] Nor is this a fringe opinion; an article in the venerable publication (*The Crisis*) of the NAACP reported that most authorities advocated the development of separate black schools to solve the educational difficulties of black males.[6] In March, 1993 the Savannah, Georgia, branch of the NAACP supported a local decision to establish separate classrooms for African-American boys taught by specially trained African-American men, though reserving judgment about the possible establishment of a separate black school in 1996.[7]

Other cities across the United States have taken similar measures. Milwaukee, for example, designated two public schools as "African-American immersion schools."[8] One of those advocating these schools argued that temporary segregation would be less devastating in its effects than the lifelong segregation from opportunities in a technologically advanced society that is the fate of many ill-educated black youth.[9]

The growing interest in the United States in public schools explicitly designated for minority pupils is part of a worldwide phenomenon.

In nations without our prohibition on public support of religion, government-funded minority schools are often religious in character. President Mary Robinson of Ireland recently attended the opening of a new Islamic school facility; like recently founded Islamic schools in Australia and The Netherlands, it receives public funding.[10]

Supporters of ethnically separate schooling generally contend that this is the most—perhaps the only—effective and principled way to educate minority pupils. There are four primary sources of the demand for separate education: (1) progressive academics and ethnic elites; (2) ethnic rank-and-file, especially parents; (3) conservative policymakers; and (4) a small but growing number of educators. The first group generally sees minority schooling as a basis for political mobilization, the second as a means of religious and cultural maintenance, the third as a pretext to keep ethnic minority pupils "in their place," and the fourth as a means of bolstering the self-esteem of minority pupils and thus their academic performance.

Derrick Bell, an African-American legal scholar, has called for rethinking the priority placed upon school desegregation, with more emphasis upon empowering black parents to hold schools accountable for results.[11] Arguing that it was necessary to utilize "the resources and strengths available within the black community itself," he threw his support behind a proposal, which was defeated in 1988, to carve a separate school system out of Milwaukee, a system that was projected to enroll 99 percent of the black pupils in the city.

Those who argue that separate schooling will lead to community mobilization and political power are probably deluding themselves. Political arguments for separate education based upon the home language are understandably vague in their scenarios for translating language maintenance into social justice and political power, and often must go to some lengths to distinguish themselves from conservatives who advance similar arguments. Language can serve as a rallying point for political mobilization against a dominant majority only when ethnic elites manage to inspire the masses to feel that they constitute a nationality and to act upon that feeling.[12]

Basque and Catalan separatists, the Quebecois and Puerto Rican independence movements, and the nationalisms that revived as the Soviet Union and Yugoslavia broke apart all have placed the language of schooling high on their political agenda. These movements are based upon territorial as well as linguistic claims, however, and it is difficult to see how a minority population dispersed in the cities of a

212   MINORITY SCHOOLS ON PURPOSE

host society can develop the structures to support a language-based political movement. School use of the minority language may be a crucial political goal,[13] but there is no reason to believe that such instructional use itself—as contrasted with the demand for such use—leads to political mobilization.

Sometimes a blatantly segregationist argument is advanced. Thus, a few minority ideologues, like Narayan in his book *Black England*, argue that the maintenance of minority cultural identity requires a "more racially divided society."[14]

It is not always clear to what extent ethnic elites articulate their own hope and interests and to what extent they express the priorities of those they purport to represent. Like the Hispanic population of the United States, the Finnish population of Sweden is caught between societal pressures toward assimilation and the desire of some, especially those among the educated elite, to maintain a separate identity, language, and culture. These leaders, themselves generally fluent in Swedish, insist that "without Finnish we are not Finns."[15] There is thus considerable demand on the part of Finnish organizations for all-Finnish home language classes.[16]

Immigrant parents may be less certain than are the ethnic group leaders—themselves usually successfully acculturated to the host society—who speak for them that it is best for their children to be educated apart from indigenous pupils. Advocates for sheltered home-language programs often complain that parents ask for their children to be placed in the mainstream. In Britain, for example, the Mother Tongue Project came across ethnic minority and bilingual parents who wished to raise their children as monolingual English speakers, believing that this would ensure their success.[17] Even when parents retain an attachment to their ancestral language, they are rarely fully successful in encouraging their children to retain the active use of the language.[18]

Thus, there are many examples of immigrant groups that maintain the use of their original language for various "private" functions such as family life and religious practice, but few that use their original language as the primary vehicle for effective political participation. It can be argued that the preservation of "endangered languages" is more successful in the intimacy of a family setting, even if that setting does not have a significant impact on the pursuit of political and cultural power.[19]

Further, minority leaders who call for separate schooling in the interest of solidifying their political base are perilously close to the position of white supremacists who argue against racial mixing, often claiming that their concern is for the cultural identity of both groups involved.[20]

Indeed, Bavaria, the most conservative of the German states, has been most willing to support separate instruction for linguistic minority pupils in their home language. Under the so-called "open model," parents are allowed to choose whether their children will receive an integrated education or remain in separate classes.[21] As elsewhere in Germany, this is partially a stopgap means of avoiding classes with too high a proportion of foreign pupils.[22]

Similarly, local school officials may support separate classes because of an interest in the frictionless functioning of their systems, thus becoming surprising allies of foreign parents who are interested in maintaining their language into the next generation. Still, as noted above, most foreign parents value their children's academic success over the maintenance of their native language.[23]

The demand for separate minority schools in England has grown partly out of incidents in which English parents have withdrawn their children from integrated schools, as at Dewsbury. A curious aspect of this incident, in which some parents charged that multicultural education in their local school neglected traditional Christianity, was the support they received from the separatist Muslim Parents' Association, which pointed out that their children were also at a disadvantage because the state system made no provision for Islamic teaching.[24]

Educators who argue for separate schooling of minority pupils generally claim that it will enable minority pupils to develop a more secure self-concept based upon positive ethnic identity and thus to possess the self-esteem which is expected to improve academic achievement. Maureen Stone and others have pointed out the lack of research evidence for low self-esteem on the part of minority youth or for the view that high self-esteem leads to achievement (rather than the other way around).[25] Others argue, however, that the critical factor in the underachievement of black youth is not a deficit in personal self-esteem but in a "group concept," which must be corrected through a stress upon an emerging canon of group-oriented virtues attributed to African sources but, in their pedagogical expression, owing much as well to "socialist" education in China and Cuba.[26]

Separate Schooling by Community Initiative

Public policies that encourage or support ethnically separate schooling for minority children must be put within the much broader context of schooling organized by minority communities themselves. In almost every case, the policies follow and respond to community initiatives.

Until recently, discussion in the United States has largely over-looked the quiet growth of alternatives to public schooling through initiatives in minority communities. While there was national debate over the decision by Detroit school authorities to create three schools designated for black pupils, the simultaneous creation of three "inter-faith" schools serving the same population received little attention.[27]

Supplemental schools serving the children and grandchildren of immigrants are the most widespread form of schooling organized by minority communities. There were 4,893 "ethnic schools" identified in an American survey in the late 1970s, primarily maintained by Eng-lish-speaking ethnic communities for whom language maintenance was a moral necessity. Fishman points out that the primary focus of these schools is not upon foreign-born children who do not speak English, but upon children born in this country whose first language is English but whose parents—themselves well-acculturated—wish to maintain their ethnic connections.[28]

In most nations of Western Europe, homeland governments have helped supplementary schools through recruiting and paying teachers from their national education systems. Concerns have been expressed about the potential of such arrangements simply to further the politi-cal agenda of the homeland by stressing an essentially irrelevant ver-sion of the native culture, thus fostering conservative values and a sense of alienation from Western Europe.

Further, teachers recruited by homeland governments may have difficulty relating to the special circumstances of pupils growing up as immigrants.[29] Available schoolbooks may be largely irrelevant to the experience of immigrant children, as well as too difficult for pupils who are not proficient in their home language. For many pupils, in fact, the official language of the country of origin—in which the home language instruction is given—may not be spoken in their home. Kurds and Assyrians from Turkey, in particular, may have emigrated in part because their groups and their languages were under pressure from the national government.[30]

While supplementary schools sponsored by homeland governments tend to stress culture and language in order to maintain ties with and loyalty to the homeland, those organized by immigrant communities are more likely to be religious in character, with language and culture taught as a dimension of maintaining continuity and identification with a religious tradition.[31] Indeed, parents tend to focus upon the values, behaviors, and religious beliefs and practices that they seek for the schooling of their children.

American experience demonstrates that immigrant groups can preserve their ethnic churches and associations by passing on at least some elements of their traditions and values for several generations after abandoning the use of their original language. Turkish, Moroccan, and Pakistani parents in Western Europe who stress the teaching of Islam more than the teaching of their mother tongue thus exhibit a sound grasp of which elements of identity have power to resist acculturation. Establishing and maintaining a supplemental Koran school, so often deplored by ethnic elites and mainstream educators, may be perceived as the most important element of maintaining religious practice.[32]

The strategy is exactly that followed by Catholic immigrants to American cities a century ago, building their parochial schools before their churches. Similarly today, when the supplemental instruction organized by the ethnic community does not seem adequate to counter the effects of mandatory state schooling on their children's values and loyalties, immigrant parents may begin to demand separate full-time schools that place their own goals for education above or alongside those of the host society.

For example, some Asian immigrants in England have been arguing for the right to receive government support for separate schools based upon Islam, parallel to the support given to Catholic and Protestant schools.[33]

The basis for such efforts is a growing conviction that no accommodation to Muslim beliefs and values is possible within the existing system. A government commission, on the other hand, suggested that the concerns of Muslim parents could be accommodated within the educational system by means of a broader multiracial, multilingual, and multifaith curriculum.[34] This suggestion, however, seems contrary to the same group's observation that most of the support for Muslim schools stressed the need for Islamic values in all aspects of schooling.[35] Parents seeking such a form of education for their children would not easily be satisfied with a curriculum relativizing all forms of religious expression. There is opposition within the Muslim community in Britain even to inclusion of teaching about Islam within the mandatory religious education instruction unless taught by a Muslim.

Demands for the adaptation of English schooling to minority concerns are generally opposed and often misunderstood in purely negative terms by policymakers and progressive academics alike, without acknowledgment that parents may have a legitimate interest in passing on their own values to their children. As of the start of the 1993-94 school year, no Islamic schools had been granted public funds, but it was widely anticipated that that situation would change in the near future, given the commitment of the Conservative government to parental choice of schools.

The Dutch education system is based upon a constitutional guarantee of the freedom to establish and obtain public funding for any school which is able to attract a sufficient number of pupils and meet other government requirements, but for some years authorities have not similarly encouraged the use of this freedom for the operation of schools by ethnic and linguistic minority groups.[36] As a result, although there was no question of the right of Hindu and Muslim groups to set up schools and, if enough parents selected these schools, to receive full public funding, local authorities were not eager to give approval. This resistance reflected in large part the opposition of many Labor Party leaders, who were in control of the government of most cities, to nonpublic schooling in general, as well as to the teaching of religion within the framework of formal schooling. Another frequent objection was that such schools would lead to isolation. Advocates insist that this is hypocrisy, arguing that such isolation already exists within public inner-city schools.

Despite the resistance of authorities, a publicly funded Islamic school was able to get off the ground with a hundred pupils in late 1988. Between 1988 and 1989, similar schools were founded in Eindhoven, Rotterdam, and The Hague, and enough signatures were gathered in the large cities for six to eight new schools.

These schools do not instruct pupils primarily in their home language, nor seek to shelter them from the language of the host society. The concern of the Islamic and Hindu schools is rather with the values of Dutch society and thus of Dutch schools in general, and they seek to provide an alternative schooling that is more consistent with the beliefs of immigrant parents, while equipping pupils to participate fully in the Dutch economy. These communities are seeking to reinforce their ability to socialize their children in values with which they are comfortable, to protect and isolate them in some respects from the acids of modernity. The call for Hindu and Islamic schools is not related to ethnic nationalism, but rather to the universal desire of parents to have a say in the raising of their children and to protect them from discrimination.[37]

It should be noted that the new schools in the Netherlands are Islamic rather than Turkish or Moroccan. Religion is a privileged basis for school selection, since it enjoys protection as a right of conscience.[38]

In some cases the promotion of separate schooling by ethnic community groups has owed as much to a rejection of the schools of the host society as it has to a desire to promote an alternative culture or religious tradition. In many instances, then, the problem identified by the minority community is not the insensitivity of public schools to their culture, but insufficient respect for their aspirations.

The rejection of mainstream education has been if anything even more emphatic among certain African-American circles in the United States, where it is asserted that the extreme social distress of the black underclass is directly related to public schooling.[39] Indeed, attempts to include African materials and themes in the mainstream curriculum are rejected with contempt as reflecting "a radicalized integrationalist thrust" resulting from "economic and psychic dependency."[40]

A study in 1991 identified 284 "independent neighborhood schools," most of which enrolled black pupils predominantly or exclusively; altogether this represented more than 50,000 compared with some 6.7 million black pupils attending public schools. The largest number of black pupils outside the public system—some 220,000—are in Catholic schools, including schools in the South founded long ago to serve the children of freed slaves, and schools in northern urban neighborhoods abandoned by white ethnic Catholics. Upwardly mobile black families living in these areas frequently choose a Catholic school as "a functional alternative . . . for quality suburban schools." One study found that 53 percent of the black pupils in heavily minority Catholic schools were not Catholics.[41] Considerable interest has been shown recently in indications that these schools may be particularly effective in educating pupils who would otherwise be at risk of academic and social failure.[42]

Muslim education in the United States has developed completely outside of the publicly supported sector, making perhaps its first appearance in the unorthodox form of the "Black Muslim" schools started by Elijah Muhammad's movement in Detroit and Chicago in the early 1930s. Since the mid-1970s, thirty-eight of the schools associated with this movement have become orthodox Muslim schools known as Sister Clara Muhammad Schools, with much less stress upon rejection of the majority society (and race), and much more upon Islamic teaching.[43]

The Council of Independent Black Institutions represents about thirty schools across the United States which subscribe to various aspects of an Afrocentric curriculum, including the Nguzo Saba or "Seven Principles of Blackness" formulated by Karenga in the 1960s. The purpose of this approach has been described by one principal as "to improve the self-esteem, self-worth, and self-confidence of the [black] child so he will have the coping skills necessary to merge into the broader pluralistic society and to deal with racism and some of the things he will confront as a black man."[44]

It should be noted that the emphasis of these schools is not upon educating children to live apart from American society (as might be the goal of Hasidic or Amish schooling), but to equip them to contend successfully with the pressures of life in the society as persons of color, to allow them to develop "as free as possible from the limitations imposed by racism."[45]

Although "Afrocentric transformation" may be the goal of some of the founders of black independent schools, it appears that the motivation of parents in paying tuition and sending their children to Afrocentric schools has more to do with concerns about the deficiencies of public schooling. A survey of black parents with children in thirty-six independent schools in the Washington, DC area found that "lack of Afrocentric curriculum" ranked twenty-first out of twenty-four factors in their reasons for rejection of public schools; by comparison, "lack of discipline" and "poor standards" ranked first and second.[46] Most black independent schools focus more upon academic achievement and a supportive environment than upon recovering an African heritage, though it is the latter agenda which has caused the most policy debate and has inspired efforts to create racially separate public schools.

There are some indications that pupils in black independent schools do achieve above national norms,[47] though John Witte's on-going evaluation of the voucher program under which poor children in Milwaukee may attend nonreligious independent schools has found no consistent advantage.[48]

There are a number of Protestant schools started by black churches in Los Angeles, Kansas City, Detroit, Milwaukee, Boston, and other cities. In these schools, the emphasis is much less upon Afrocentric elements and much more upon the failure of public schools to provide the moral and religious instruction that the parents who choose these schools want for their children. It is thus not the Eurocentric nature of public schools so much as their pervasive secularism and moral incoherence that give impetus to the establishment of these schools.

Separate Schooling by Government Initiative

Although demand by minority parents for separate schooling is by no means overwhelming and the evidence for its superior effectiveness is mixed, there have been a variety of government initiatives in recent years to provide separate schooling as a means of improving the academic and social achievement of minority pupils.

The most extensive form of government-sponsored ethnic segregation, though it is seldom understood in this way, has been the separate bilingual education programs developed in several nations. While initially presented as a transitional means to enable pupils to acquire the majority language quickly while continuing studies in their home language, bilingual programs have sometimes acquired a momentum of their own, in which maintenance of the minority language and culture have become the dominant concern. For example, an important study of federally funded bilingual education programs in the United States in the late 1970s found that fewer than a third of students were in bilingual classes because of their limited ability to speak English, and that few of them transferred to an English-only classroom even when they were proficient in English.[49]

State laws requiring or permitting bilingual instruction for pupils unable to perform classwork in English invariably stress the transitional and voluntary nature of these programs, but those who advocate bilingual education are often uncomfortable with the idea that parents whose children are eligible might be allowed to opt for assignment to a class in which only English is used. Lawyers for the plaintiffs in New York City's *Aspira* case argued—unsuccessfully—that assignment to a bilingual class in such cases should be mandatory,[50] and that administrators of bilingual programs have sought to make it difficult for parents to remove their children from classes taught in their home language. In Massachusetts, for example, parents were required to write a letter making this request, and school officials were warned against prompting with wording, thus creating a significant barrier for many immigrant parents.

Language minority parents are sometimes told by school officials that their children will be ineligible for any supplemental support, including instruction in English as a second language, if they are not enrolled in the bilingual program. No choice is offered between the extremes of language and academic support in a segregated program and being placed in a regular class with no attention to needs arising in the course of second-language acquisition. Children in the second situation (including those in schools where no bilingual program is offered) are often subsequently diagnosed as having learning disabilities or other needs and end up segregated in a special education program.

Bilingual education has been developed most extensively in the United States, but the example of Sweden is cited in American policy debates as evidence of the superiority of this approach. The discussion of Sweden, however, is often misleading: separate home language classes are not the norm for foreign pupils in Sweden even though several hundred are in operation, primarily for Finnish-speaking pupils. These classes represent only 7 percent of the 88,284 linguistic minority pupils in Swedish schools; nine times as many participate in supplemental home language instruction. Even among Finnish-speaking pupils, nearly four times as many take part in supplemental home language instruction while enrolled in integrated Swedish-medium classes as are enrolled in separate home language classes.

In a home language class an ethnically homogeneous group of pupils is taught primarily in their home language. In some cases Swedish instruction is not started until the fourth grade, though this has become less common because of difficulties experienced by such pupils later. In principle, the pupils are mainstreamed after the sixth grade, but there is an increasing trend toward extending the home language class through the ninth grade, the last year of compulsory schooling in Sweden.

According to Ekstrand, most research does not support such classes, nor do most immigrant groups in Sweden, other than the Finns, desire them for their children.[51] For one thing, although the classes were based upon an attractive theory of language learning, experience has been disappointing. Still, in some communities—most of them Finnish—there has been substantial pressure from immigrant associations to establish home language classes in which only pupils of their group are enrolled.

Separate public schooling in the United States, apart from that provided in the name of bilingual education, has been justified primarily on the basis of the presumed positive effects upon the self-image of minority children of a curriculum giving special stress to their ethnic identity. The two African-American immersion schools in Milwaukee, for example, have been described as drawing upon two "pools of knowledge," one filled with culturally diverse knowledge, the other drawing on an African-American world view.[52]

Single-sex programs or schools for minority pupils add the further dimension of isolating pupils to some extent from the presence of the other sex in the classroom. For boys, this may reduce the need to show off, and for girls to conform. Ascher has summarized five of the justifications given for these schools saying that they offer (1) appropriate same-sex role models and same-sex bonding; (2) formalized initiation rites for the transition into manhood or womanhood; (3) "cultural inoculation," developing identity and self-esteem as well as academic values and skills; (4) strong parent and community involvement; and (5) a safe haven.[53]

Riordan's study of single-sex Catholic schooling found negative effects for boys and positive effects for girls. However, in a sample of Catholic schools with predominantly minority populations, he found that, among Hispanics and African-Americans, both boys and girls do better in single-sex schools.[54]

Should Public Policy Promote Separate Development?

Whether public policy looks kindly upon ethnically separate schooling depends in large part upon how the society thinks of itself. For instance, Dutch society has for more than a century (though to a decreasing extent) been organized on the basis of a pluralistic model under which diverse groups negotiate to balance their respective agendas with the common good.

In the United States, by contrast, there is a lingering sense that "an American" is something that you become (like millions of immigrants) through renunciation of competing identities. Ethnicity is valued as an added spice, but it is not expected to make an American fundamentally distinctive.[55] Schooling, in particular, has been seen as the midwife of this shared identity, and most Catholic and Protestant schools serving the children of immigrants have been enthusiastic "Americanizers." There is thus an inevitable discomfort with the idea that schooling might—indeed should—become dedicated to developing an alternative identity.[56]

This folk wisdom about the role of schooling, though deeply rooted among educators in particular, ignores the actual American experience with schooling outside the public sector: although quite successful in terms of academic achievement, it has been almost completely ineffective in maintaining distinctive group identities, languages, or cultures. Graduates of Catholic or Lutheran parochial schools, for example, are just about as likely as Catholics or Lutherans who attend public schools to share general American cultural values, to marry outside their denomination, and to be woefully ignorant of languages other than American English. The development of the children of Vietnamese, Filipino, and Mexican immigrants who have arrived in recent decades suggests that American culture retains its astonishing transformative power.

The same phenomenon has been observed in other countries. North African youth in France are not culturally distinct from French youth; the problem is that they are socially and economically marginal, which has much to do with the adequacy of their education but very little to do with their acculturation.[57] The American parallels are obvious.

What does this imply for the phenomenon of separate minority schooling? One implication is that it should be judged on its merits in terms of demonstrated efficacy in improving the achievement of pupils who would otherwise be likely to fail academically and socially. Eventual social integration (what the French call "successful insertion into society") might justify such programs as the classes for black boys in a Baltimore elementary school.[58] Carefully evaluated experiments of this sort seem appropriate.

It is curious that support for deliberately Afrocentric public schools relies upon the example of a few independent schools with that focus. After all, black parents who go outside the public system to find more satisfactory schooling for their children have not generally chosen such schools. The fact that much the greatest number choose Catholic schools could be attributed to the accidental factor that these schools, abandoned by the white ethnic populations who built them, are widely available in inner-city areas, were it not for the evidence that many of them are particularly effective in serving black children as well.[59] The example of Holy Angels School in Chicago is often cited, providing what appears to be an unusually successful education to thirteen hundred black children.[60] Also in Chicago is the celebrated Westside Preparatory School, founded by Marva Collins. What these and other all-black schools of demonstrated effectiveness have in common is not an ideology of négritude but a determination to maintain high expectations and to provide a disciplined though supportive environment for learning.

The same was true of the experimental all-male class set up at Matthew Henson Elementary School in Baltimore during the 1990-91 school year. The results were very encouraging. Although all the boys and their teacher were black, the emphasis was not upon inculcating an Afrocentric consciousness but upon mentoring, encouragement, and academic and social discipline.[61]

If it is indeed time to "put the educators back into" the remedy for past discrimination against black and other minority children,[62] it will presumably be by following such examples.

A second implication of the phenomenon of separate minority schooling is that schooling based upon cultural alternatives is not a threat to a complex modern society. The Dutch willingness to accommodate the desire of many parents for schooling based upon distinctive religious or philosophical perspectives has not led to communal strife; indeed, it has reduced conflict over schooling to far below American levels. Schools that stand for something without apology, like Holy Angels and Marva Collins's school in Chicago, are likely to be more effective in every dimension of their educational mission.

Government itself, however, should not lend its authority to one or another of these perspectives. An Afrocentric public school is thus as inappropriate as would be a Catholic or a Baptist public school. The common public school should be respectful toward all perspectives to the extent that they merit respect, but partial toward none— not even the secularism or indifference that characterizes too many public schools. Achieving this balance is, of course, a matter of enormous difficulty which cannot be discussed here.

This suggests that, since schooling based upon clearly defined perspectives may be more efficacious than schooling that must scrupulously preserve its neutrality, there is a strong case for encouraging alternatives outside the public system. The desire of some educators and some parents for an Afrocentric curriculum can most appropriately be accommodated through providing funding to whatever school the parents freely select for their children, rather than through abandoning the perspectival neutrality of the common public school.

Similarly, to the extent that some Latino parents wish to entrust their children to schools in which Spanish is a language of instruction and there is a strong emphasis upon the cultures of Latin America, a scrupulous concern for liberty suggests that they should be able to choose such education without forfeiting the right to free education for their children. So long as government makes education compulsory, it must be free; but education that does not correspond to what parents consider fitting for their children is in no sense free. The parent must either pay the cost of tuition or the cost of a violated conscience. As legal scholar John Coons has argued, "[t]he right to form families and to determine the scope of their children's practical liberty is for most men and women the primary occasion for choice and responsibility."[63]

There is indeed no principled reason not to respect the right of parents to make decisions about the schooling their children will receive, and to allow the public funds for education to follow those choices, within a framework of policy that assures the adequacy of schools eligible for such funding and that protects the interests of minority, poor, and otherwise vulnerable children. There is a fundamental difference between what government may legitimately teach in its own schools and what it may allow parents to choose for their children without forfeiting a free education; the first is an establishment question, the second a question of the free exercise of conscience.

Who is making the argument for deliberately separate schools? This goes to the issue of legitimacy. Is it appropriate for the politicians and government officials of a host society to decide, on behalf of racial or language minority children, that they are better off if schooled separately from the majority in order to preserve their home language and ethnic identity? Surely not! Nor are progressive academics or well-assimilated ethnic elites qualified to make that decision.

No, the only ones who can legitimately and effectively decide whether language-minority children and youth will maintain and develop the culture and perhaps the language of their ancestors are those children and youth and the parents who act on their behalf. Many minority-group parents may choose and indeed make great sacrifices to assure that their children receive a separate education in the interest of continuity with their own identity, beliefs, and values. There is growing evidence, in Western Europe and in other Western democracies, that "countermodernization" is in full career in reaction to the high price exacted by modernity on personal satisfactions and family life, and that one of the forms it takes is the desire by parents, especially those on the margins of society, to exercise more control over the education of their children.

These parents appear determined not to accept the entire package that contemporary society offers, but to enable their children to pick and choose those elements of tradition and of modernity that will represent their own act of cultural creativity. Who can say that they are wrong? On the other hand, it is not the function of government to maintain minority cultures, any more than it is its proper role to impose the majority culture through a monopoly system of compulsory schooling. It is clear that many—perhaps most—minority parents do not place a high value upon maintaining cultural distinctiveness, except perhaps at the most superficial and sentimental level.

Lambert and Taylor found that Puerto Ricans were the most emphatic of ethnic groups in their desire to maintain their own cultural values.[64] Curiously, though, they did not show support for the idea that such cultural elements could be maintained by community efforts; instead, they wanted the schools to do it for them. Puerto Rican history, they agreed, should be given equal emphasis with that of the United States. The paradox is that it is Puerto Ricans, of all recently arrived language-minority groups, whose culture has been most deeply influenced by that of the United States, in both its white majority and black minority forms.

Puerto Ricans also had a contradictory response to the question of language maintenance. While on the one hand they responded that Spanish should be used in the home, and that it was the responsibility of the public school and not of the Puerto Rican community to assure that children could speak Spanish, their responses on a question about what it would mean for their children to be bilingual or to speak only English indicate that the two options seem equally preferable to the parents.[65] The appropriate policy would seem to be to provide public support, through parents, for schools that seek to maintain Spanish, but not to adopt a policy that Spanish should be maintained. Parents and their children should—indeed only they can—make such fundamental decisions about the continuing vitality of language and culture in their lives.

But in conceding the right of parents to make decisions about the normative content of the education that their children receive, we must not overlook the equally legitimate interest of the wider society in promoting, so far as consistent with that right, certain common goals. These goals include (1) preventing the emergence of a caste system in which ethnicity becomes permanently linked with a social class position; (2) developing habits of mutual respect and civic virtue; and (3) assuring that the future work force, particularly those for whom society will do no favors, is ready for the demands of the next century.

If we believe that it is desirable for schools to reflect and help to create a just and pluralistic society, then we should provide incentives (presumably extra funding) to schools that find ways of educating language-minority and language-majority children together that are so demonstrably effective and so respectful of diversity that parents will enroll their children voluntarily.

It may be that supplemental programs, like those maintained for many years by elements of the Chinese, Jewish, and Greek communities in the United States, are the only satisfactory alternatives for language-minority parents who wish to send their children to integrated schools but also expose them in a systematic way to their linguistic and cultural heritage. Indeed, the efforts of official educational systems to include among their goals the maintenance of minority languages and cultures have been plagued with controversy and with practical difficulties.[66]

Even if we accept the validity of allowing parents to choose schools that they can support wholeheartedly, without forfeiture of their right to a free education for their children, the troubling question remains: Are schools organized on a racial or ethnic basis consistent with constitutional principles and with sound policy? The question is by no means simple. Should public funds be provided for a school based upon a perspective—say, Afrocentric consciousness—all of whose adherents are of a single racial group? Reluctantly, I conclude that public funds should be provided; it is as perilous for government to inquire about the validity of alternative perspectives as it is for it to seek to establish one of its own.

What if the perspective is one which rejects the humanity or the common citizenship of members of other racial or ethnic groups? Here, it seems to me, there is scope for the careful use of the government's power of oversight of schools (explicit in American constitutional law and also in the international covenants that guarantee educational freedom) to rule that certain schools do not merit public funding and do not satisfy the requirements of compulsory attendance laws.

The fact is, of course, that such schools have long existed in the United States without government interference, at the expense of parents who could afford them, but have remained a marginal phenomenon. There is no reason to believe that a significant number of parents of any racial or ethnic group would choose them for their children. Policies that seek to secure freedom can never exclude the possibility of its abuse by a few.

Respect for freedom requires that we accept and support the choice by some parents of racial, ethnic, language, or religious "minority schools." For some children these schools may offer a focus that enables them to succeed academically and socially. We should at the same time provide incentives to create effective integrated schools for a society in which diversity is increasingly a fact of life and at least a potential source of strength.

NOTES

1. Donald Leake and Brenda Leake, "African-American Immersion Schools in Milwaukee: A View from the Inside," *Phi Delta Kappan* 73 (June 1992): 783-785.

2. *Education Week*, 15 September 1993.

3. Ibid., 4 September 1991; 21 October 1992.

4. Carol Ascher, "School Programs for African-American Males . . . and Females," *Phi Delta Kappan* 73 (June 1992): 777-782.

5. Jawanza Kunjufu, "Detroit's Male Academies: What the Real Issue Is," *Education Week*, 20 November 1991.

6. David Hatchett, "A Conflict of Reasons and Remedies," *The Crisis* 93, no. 3 (March 1986): 36-41, 46-47.

7. *Education Week*, 24 March 1993.

8. Leake and Leake, "African-American Immersion Schools in Milwaukee."

9. Donald Leake, "Averting 'A Lifetime of Segregation'," *Education Week*, 28 November 1990.

10. *Times Educational Supplement*, 7 May 1993.

11. Derrick Bell, "The Case for a Separate Black School System," *Urban League Review* 7, nos. 1, 2 (Summer/Winter 1987-88): 143.

12. Joshua A. Fishman, *Language and Ethnicity in Minority Sociolinguistic Perspective* (Clevedon: Multilingual Matters, 1989).

13. John Mallea, "Minority Language Education in Quebec and Anglophone Canada," in *Conflict and Language Planning in Quebec*, edited by Richard Y. Bourhis (Clevedon: Multilingual Matters, 1984).

14. Malcom Saunders, "The School Curriculum for Ethnic Minority Pupils: A Contribution to a Debate," *International Review of Education* 26, no. 1 (1980): 37.

15. As quoted in Fishman, *Language and Ethnicity in Minority Sociolinguistic Perspective*, p. 277.

16. Bertil Norbelie, *Mother Tongue Teaching in Classes Comprising Two Nationalities: Compendium of Information on Intercultural Education Schemes in Europe* (Strasbourg: Council of Europe, 1983).

17. David Houlton and Edith W. King, "Mother Tongue Teaching in Britain and the United States: Some Current Developments," *Journal of Multilingual and Multicultural Development* 6, no. 1 (1985): 45-57.

18. Fishman, *Language and Ethnicity in Minority Sociolinguistic Perspective*.

19. Ibid.

20. Pierre-Andre Taguieff, *Les métamorphoses du racisme, L'Immigration dans l'histoire nationale* (Paris: CEFISEM, 1988).

21. Gerhart Mahler, "Bildungspolitische Schwerpunkte," in *Zweitsprache Deutsch für Ausländerkinder*, edited by Gerhart Mahler and Michael Steindl (Donauworth: Auer, 1983).

22. Hans H. Reich, "Die Rechtlinien der EG-Ansätze zu einer Zweisprachigen Erziehung der Gastarbeiterkinder," in *Ausländerunterricht: Schulrechtliche, bildungspolitische und unterrichtsorganisatorische Beiträge*, edited by Michael Damanakis and Hans H. Reich (Essen/Landau: ALFA, 1982).

23. Ibid.

24. *Times Educational Supplement*, 11 September 1987. See also, Fred Naylor, *Dewsbury: The School above the Pub* (London: Claridge Press, 1989).

25. Maureen Stone, *The Education of the Black Child: The Myth of Multiracial Education*, 2d impression (London: Fontana Press, 1985).

26. Carol D. Lee, "Profile of an Independent Black Institution: African-centered Education at work," *Journal of Negro Education* 61, no. 2 (Spring 1992): 160-177.

27. *Education Week*, 4 September 1991.

28. Fishman, *Language and Ethnicity in Minority Sociolinguistic Perspective.*

29. B. Buvelot, "Tweetaligheid is gewenst van het begin tot het einde van de school," *Samenwijs* 7, no. 4 (December 1986): vi-viii.

30. Mujgan Dericioglu and Nuri Orfali, "Memorandum der türkischen Regierung zur Unterrichtung türkischer Kinder in der Bundesrepublik Deutschland," in *Ausländerunterricht: Schulrechtliche, bildungspolitische und unterrichtsorganisatorisch Beiträge*, edited by Michael Damanakis and Hans H. Reich (Essen/Landau: ALFA, 1982).

31. Mart-Jan de Jong, *Herkomst, kennis en kansen: Allochtone en autochtone leerlingen tijdens de overgang van basis- naar voortgezet onderwijs* (Lisse: Swets and Zeitlinger, 1987).

32. Driss El Yazami, "Présence Musulmane et immigration," in *L'Immigration dans l'histoire nationale* (Paris: CEFISEM, 1988).

33. John Rex, "The Urban Sociology of Religion and Islam in Birmingham," in *The New Islamic Presence in Western Europe*, edited by Tomas Gerholm and Yngve Georg Lithman (London: Mansell, 1988); Suzanne Hewitt, "Primary Purposes: 'Children Need to Develop and Express Their Own Beliefs'," *Times Educational Supplement*, 16 December 1988.

34. *Education for All: The Report of the Committee of Inquiry into the Education of Children from Ethnic Minority Groups* (the "Swann Report") (London: HMSO, 1985).

35. Ibid.

36. H. B. Entzinger, *Het Minderhedenbeleid* (Meppel: Boom, 1984).

37. Joop Teunissen, "Basisscholen op islamitische en hindoeïstische grondslag," *Migrantenstudies* 6, no. 2 (1990): 45-57.

38. Jan Rath, Kees Groenendijk, and Rinus Penninx, "Nederland en de islam: Een programma van onderzoek," *Migrantenstudies* 8, no. 1 (1992): 18-37.

39. Nsenga Warfield-Coppock, "The Rites of Passage Movement: A Resurgence of African-Centered Practices for Socializing African American Youth," *Journal of Negro Education* 61, no. 4 (Fall 1992): 471-82.

40. Kwamei Agyei Akoto, as quoted by Basir Mchawi in a book review in the *Journal of Negro Education* 61, no. 4 (Fall 1992): 570-71.

41. James G. Cibulka, Timothy J. O'Brien, and Donald Zewe, *Inner-City Private Elementary Schools: A Study* (Milwaukee, WI: Marquette University Press, 1982).

42. P. L. Benson, R. J. Yeager, P. K. Wood, M. J. Guerra, and B. Manno, *Catholic High Schools: Their Impact on Low-income Students* (Washington, DC: National Catholic Education Association, 1986); James S. Coleman and Thomas Hoffer, *Public and Private High Schools: The Impact of Communities* (New York: Basic Books, 1987).

43. Hakim M. Rashid and Muhammad Zakiyyah, "The Sister Clara Muhammad Schools: Pioneers in the Development of Islamic Education," *Journal of Negro Education* 61, no. 2 (Spring 1992): 178-85.

44. Kenneth Holt, as quoted in Kofi Lomotey, "Independent Black Institutions: African-Centered Education Models," *Journal of Negro Education* 61, no. 4 (Fall 1992): 461.

45. Mwalimu J. Shujaa, "Afrocentric Transformation and Parental Choice in African American Independent Schools," *Journal of Negro Education* 61, no. 2 (Spring 1992): 154.

46. Faustine C. Jones-Wilson, Nancy L. Arnez, and Charles A. Asbury, "Why Not Public Schools?" *Journal of Negro Education* 61, no. 2 (Spring 1992): 125-137.

47. Joan Davis Ratteray, "Independent Neighborhood Schools: A Framework for the Education of African Americans," *Journal of Negro Education* 61, no. 2 (Spring 1992): 138-47.

48. John Witte, *Second Year Report: Milwaukee Parental Choice Program* (Madison: University of Wisconsin, 1992).

49. Kenji Hakuta, *Mirror of Language: The Debate on Bilingualism* (New York: Basic Books, 1986).

50. Nathan Glazer, *Ethnic Dilemmas, 1964-1982* (Cambridge: Harvard University Press, 1983).

51. Lars H. Ekstrand, "Bilingual Learning: Problems, Results, and Theoretical Advances," unpublished paper, 1988, quoted with permission of the author.

52. Leake and Leake, "African-American Immersion Schools in Milwaukee," p. 785.

53. Ascher, "School Programs for African-American Males . . . and Females."

54. Cornelius Riordan, *Girls and Boys in School: Together or Separate?* (New York: Teachers College Press, 1990).

55. Richard D. Alba, *Ethnic Identity: The Transformation of White America* (New Haven: Yale University Press, 1990).

56. Charles Glenn, *The Myth of the Common School* (Amherst, MA: University of Massachusetts Press, 1988).

57. François Dubet and Lapeyronnie Didier, *Les quartiers d'extil* (Paris: Seuil, 1992).

58. Debra Viadero, "Baltimore Class Tests Theory of Providing 'Positive Role Model' for Young Black Boys," *Education Week* 13 February 1991.

59. Coleman and Hoffer, *Public and Private High Schools.*

60. Portia H. Shields, "Holy Angels: Pocket of Excellence," *Journal of Negro Education* 58, no. 2 (1989): 203-11.

61. Viadero, "Baltimore Class Tests Theory of Providing 'Positive Role Model' for Young Black Boys."

62. Derrick Bell, "Time for the Teachers: Putting Educators Back into the *Brown* Remedy," *Journal of Negro Education* 52, no. 3 (1983): 290-301.

63. John E. Coons, "Intellectual Liberty and the Schools," *Journal of Law, Ethics, and Public Policy* 1 (1985): 511.

64. Wallace E. Lambert and Donald M. Taylor, *Coping with Cultural and Racial Diversity in Urban America* (New York: Praeger, 1990).

65. Ibid.

66. Glazer, *Ethnic Dilemmas, 1964-1982*; Martin McLean, "Private Supplementary Schools and the Ethnic Challenge to State Education in Britain," in *Cultural Identity and Educational Policy*, edited by Colin Brock and Witold Tulasiewicz (London: Croom Helm, 1985).

Section Three
STRATEGIES FOR EDUCATING
CHANGING POPULATIONS IN
THE COMMUNITY

Introduction

We have recently come to a fuller understanding of the extent to which an individual's development is affected for good or for ill by the interaction of many environments—family, kin, peer, neighborhood, school, community, workplace, nation. As Brooks-Gunn, Denner, and Klebanov argue, the family and the neighborhood are characterized by both risk and resilience and by either an abundance or scarcity of such resources as time, income, psychological and social capital. Development is not fixed, according to these authors. It can be altered by interventions in the family and in the neighborhood.

They look particularly at the family as the first educator of children and at programs that can enhance the family's capacity to provide more and better learning opportunities for the developing child. Head Start, for example, works with families to counteract environmental conditions that can contribute to delays in the child's cognitive, social, or emotional development, particularly where the children are biologically vulnerable because of low birth weight, prematurity, cerebral palsy, or congenital difficulties. In general, program services can be center-based for groups of families or can be provided directly in the home by home visitors. There can be no argument about the face value of these programs. As these authors point out, however, we do not yet know whether a particular intervention is more effective with some groups than with others (for example, more effective with mothers from some ethnic groups than those from other groups, with teenage mothers than with older mothers, with poor families than with families not in poverty). What is more, although some programs have succeeded we do not know how much more successful they could be if they were to combine, in a more comprehensive "ecological" intervention, elements of social support, public health, and literacy with the enhancement of developmental learning experiences they already provide.

Theories about how neighborhoods or communities affect development have not been considered enough in planning interventions. The authors argue that we must consider the effects of the absence or presence of public and private services in a neighborhood; of the importance of peers and role models in influencing individual behavior; of poverty, ethnic diversity, and residential mobility on the cohesiveness of a community and its ability to control children in the neighborhood; of the competition for scarce resources in the community; and of the relative standing of the family in the neighborhood. There are programs for improving neighborhood resources, such as those providing economic opportunity and security, affordable and safe housing, and opportunities for community participation and empowerment. Community-based family resource centers function within neighborhoods to provide multiple services to families so that they can enhance their child-rearing abilities and their standing in the community. But such programs are still scarce and we know very little about whether or not they have significant effects.

In the ecology of child development, the school and the family are the most influential environments. But the schools must be linked to the community to provide social services to students, particularly if they are to educate children from high-risk families. Wang, Haertel, and Walberg examine some such programs. They acknowledge that there is research suggesting that some government programs may have long-term negative consequences (such as school-based health clinics that may lead to an increase in the number of unmarried pregnant teenagers). They call for a search for alternative ways of ameliorating the problems of at-risk families, such as the use of vouchers, tax credits, a negative income tax, and providing parental care for children. From their review of the effectiveness of collaborations between school and community to provide a variety of services to children and youth, the authors conclude that, despite the obvious appeal of the programs, there is little empirical evidence of their success. Given the current state of our knowledge, we must be careful in endorsing such efforts. As Wang, Haertel, and Walberg point out, we need more rigorous research before we can make reliable policy decisions regarding the establishment of these programs. They argue for the collection of data on accessibility to the programs, on implementation processes, on the roles of leaders in the schools and in the collaborating agencies, and on staff operations and budgets. They conclude that it is necessary first to establish that there is a link between services and academic outcomes, and that we must make sure that educational accountability systems assess the effects of school-linked services on academic outcomes.

CHAPTER XI

Families and Neighborhoods as Contexts for Education

JEANNE BROOKS-GUNN, JILL DENNER, AND PAM KLEBANOV

Development cannot be understood independent of the multiple and diverse contexts or ecologies in which individuals reside. While context is critical across the life span, it takes on particular relevance when considering development in the first two decades of life. Early development takes place primarily in the context of the family. Families themselves live in communities that have an influence on family systems as well as on the individuals within the system. In this chapter we will explore the meaning of the phrase "development in families in communities," as well as the consequences for the education of young children.

Development in Families in Communities

Even when looking at community influences upon children, such as the neighborhood or the school, we cannot leave families out of the equation. Education from preschool through high school is conceptualized as a partnership among teachers, parents, and children. Without parental cooperation or understanding, learning is severely curtailed.

The importance of parents and the family in education and schooling is underscored by the following. First, it is well known that parental education, occupation, and income are the best predictors of how well children fare in school. That is not to say that school resources and the structural, interactional, and climate variables in the school do not make a difference in the achievement of children.[1] However, family-level variables are very important in the early years

Jeanne Brooks-Gunn is the Virginia and Leonard Marx Professor of Child and Parental Development at Teachers College, Columbia University. Jill Denner is a Research Assistant at the Center for Young Children and Families at Teachers College, Columbia University, and Pam Klebanov is a Research Scientist at that Center.

of schooling, and they determine to a large extent children's subsequent educational experiences and outcomes in the adolescent and young adult years. Second, families provide the first learning experiences for young children. A significant body of research has accumulated on the importance of providing learning experiences that stimulate children's development in literacy and language. Those early experiences are important in the cognitive and linguistic domains and, to a lesser extent, in the social and emotional domains.[2] Third, the family has been labeled the first school. A recent report, *America's Smallest School: The Family*,[3] discussed the many educational dimensions of the family, including the availability of parents and their involvement in homework and school experiences, the provision of reading materials, the encouragement of reading, and the restrictions on television watching. Fourth, families often operate as advocates for their children, and, in Coleman's terms, are a source of social capital.[4] Some of the resources provided by the family that are relevant for education involve selecting schools, obtaining special services for children with a disability or risk condition, monitoring the classes that high school students take, preventing drop out, and petitioning schools for reentry. Parents who are educated and comfortable interacting with the school system tend to be better advocates for their children. For example, in one study of almost 2,000 elementary school students, many of whom had low birth weights, receiving special education services was associated with parental education. In the subsample of children with very low birth weights (less than 1500 grams), over half of whom would probably qualify for services under Public Law 99-457 (Schooling and Disability: Education for All Handicapped Children), the children whose parents were more educated were more likely to receive special services even though the children of less educated parents were more likely to have academic and behavioral problems that would render them candidates for special education services. These findings held even after controlling for school-level variables.[5] Examples from ethnographic accounts of teacher-parent interchanges document differences in placement in special education as a function of parental social class.[6] Similar findings are reported for high school drop outs.[7]

Similarly, federal policy initiatives for children cannot be considered without looking at their implications for the family. Federal programs such as WIC (Women, Infants, and Children—the nutrition supplement program), Head Start, and EPSDT (Early Periodic Screening,

Diagnosis, and Treatment—a program to identify young children at risk for health, educational and other problems and to refer them for appropriate services) are only effective when they engage parents. The success and widespread support of Head Start is often attributed in part to its strong base in the individual communities, parental control of the local boards, and parental involvement in the teacher aide programs.[8] Likewise, the difficulties that have been encountered in immunizing young children and in identifying those with developmental disabilities, especially those from poor families, are in part due to the lack of parental involvement in the design and implementation of these health services.

In this chapter, we look at the family and the neighborhood as contexts in which children develop and learn. Since other chapters in this volume focus on the school, our focus is not on school settings, even though connections exist among family, school, and neighborhood features. First we consider briefly the ways in which development is studied. We then outline some of the changing demographics of families and we review research on the influence of the family. Next, we review the limited research on neighborhood influences, where little attention has been paid to the intersection of family and neighborhood influences—how they interact to produce child outcomes and how neighborhoods influence children indirectly through their effects on families. Finally, we consider intervention efforts that target the family or the neighborhood. Many programs have been created to assist parents in the provision of learning experiences for their children. Fewer programs have been initiated at the community level to provide family-oriented services. An even smaller number seek to alter the neighborhood context itself in order to facilitate children's development. We describe prototypes of these programs.

DEVELOPMENT AS CHANGE OVER TIME

Development encompasses the personal and environmental conditions and experiences that contribute to the growth of each individual. In describing the development of children in families in communities over time, we need to understand how developmental transitions are dealt with, how experience shapes development, what the different domains of development are, and what conceptual frameworks guide relevant intervention.

Our focus here will be on young children, in particular on the period from birth to age five. We focus on this period for several reasons.

First, it is a time characterized by rapid developmental changes in physical growth, in cognitive abilities, and in regulation of emotions. Second, it is a period when parental expectations for more mature behavior are paramount. Third, it entails major school transitions that herald new sets of social, emotional, and academic demands on the individual. Entry into school often encompasses two transitions for the young child: entrance into some sort of preschool learning environment and then into kindergarten.

Perhaps the most compelling reason to consider young children and this transitional period involves the debate on the role of experience in shaping behavior throughout life. Beliefs about development downplayed environmental influences prior to 1970 and maybe even prior to 1975. The ability to alter the course of development was thought to be limited to the preschool period. It was believed that once a contextual change facilitating development was initiated, developmental changes would continue past the preschool years.[9] But we now know that experiences and the context in which individuals live are important for development from childhood to adulthood. If environmental changes are not continued, developmental changes will probably not be sustained. Perhaps the best known example involves the beneficial effects of Head Start and other preschool programs upon children's academic and cognitive well-being. The effects are usually reduced unless continued intervention is provided.[10] In addition, research has focused on intraindividual changes rather than on contextual changes or the interaction between the two. More contextually rich research, and research exploring interactions between persons and place have since become the norm.[11] Today, development encompasses the notion of change in a number of different domains that occur in a variety of contexts that also change over time.

Domains or indices of well-being are often divided by developmentalists into several categories: cognitive, academic, linguistic, emotional, social, motivational, physical health, physical growth, and identity, to name only some of the major categories. Often several larger domains of well-being are identified: cognitive/academic, emotional, social, and physical health.[12] Obviously, overlap occurs. For example, the field of social cognition arose in part because cognition is often directly related to relationships and the social situations in which cognitive abilities are applied. Different disciplines do not always agree as to where specific behaviors should be placed. Well-developed indicators exist for many of these domains, particularly for cognitive, academic, physical growth, and health. Less is known about so-called "social indicators of child well-being" with respect to motivation, emotions, social relationships, and identity.

FRAMEWORKS FOR STUDYING DEVELOPMENT

Current perspectives on the intersection of child and context include economic, human capital, ecological, family systems, and risk and resilience models. Additionally, models that include familial and extrafamilial resources are useful in understanding the role of the family and the neighborhood in children's development. These models are helpful for understanding how families provide the primary learning environment for children and how families influence and are influenced by communities that are also a context for learning. We briefly discuss here the ecological, risk, and resource models since they have guided much of the work on the family and neighborhood as contexts for learning.

Perhaps the most influential theory in the child development literature is that of the ecological system that is closely associated with the writing of Bronfenbrenner.[13] Bronfenbrenner discusses the various contexts in which children learn, including family, kin, peer, school, workplace, neighborhood, community, region, and country. The division of these contexts into various levels, the emphasis on the importance of sustained and consistent interactions, and the insistence on looking at the ways in which various levels interact with one another to produce development have had a major impact on the study of children and youth. These contextual systems focus on the interchanges among individuals, among systems, and among individuals and systems. The linkages between the family and other contexts, such as the neighborhood, set the stage for the ways in which families present learning experiences.[14]

Risk and resilience models have been built upon the idea that children (and families) are vulnerable in that they are likely to show lowered well-being in the face of certain biological and environmental conditions.[15] Environmental factors include a variety of family, neighborhood, and school factors as well. Biological factors typically focus on neonatal status and health, although other conditions such as temperament and reactivity are sometimes studied. Besides considering biological and environmental factors that may cause developmental problems, the risk and resilience models take into account the fact that not all children respond similarly or negatively to risk factors.

Resource models focus on the investments that are made in children by families and by society.[16] Several sets of resources are often identified—time, income, human capital, psychological and social capital. These types of resources may be considered at all contextual levels, but they are most often studied with regard to the family. In the family context, psychological capital may be considered parental characteristics and parenting behavior, while human capital focuses on resources like parent education and occupation. Social capital considers links between families and communities.

Families as Contexts for Education for Young Children

Families provide the primary context in which children develop in the first years of life. Generally, parents control their children's access to other contexts such as interaction with kin, child care, and preschool experiences. Parents interact with their children, provide learning materials in the home, talk to and play with their children, give a structured and consistent rhythm and routine to the child's life, and offer access to activities outside the home. The ways parents do these things constitute the educational environment of the young child.

CHANGING DEMOGRAPHICS OF FAMILIES

In the past thirty years the country has witnessed a sea change in how families form and in what constitutes a family.[17] Many of the changes are thought to have potentially negative consequences for children. Perhaps the most far-reaching changes have to do with the increase in the number of divorced and never-married parents and the entrance of an increasing number of mothers into the workforce. Divorce rates began to rise and by 1924 one in seven marriages ended in divorce. The turn of the century was also characterized by a decline in the birthrate among the middle and upper classes. Following World War II, the age at which first marriage occurred dropped while the birthrate climbed. As the rate of teenage pregnancies increased and then stabilized in the United States, the percentage of girls who were married by age nineteen dropped from 40 percent in 1960 to 15 percent in 1986.[18] Increasing opportunities for women to work and obtain a higher education are associated with the delay of marriage and childbirth.

Recent decades have seen a rise in the number of children being raised by single parents. Between 1940 and 1960, only 6 to 8 percent of children under the age of eighteen were living in mother-only families; by 1988 this figure had increased to 21 percent. One reason for this increase is the increase in rates of divorce. Of the single-parent families headed by women in 1960, 1.9 percent were a result of divorce; in 1988 that figure was 7.8 percent. By age sixteen, two fifths of European-American children, and three fourths of African-American children will have lived in single-parent households. The rise in single-parent homes is also influenced by the increasing number of mothers who are not married. In 1990 almost one quarter of all births were to unmarried women.

Households headed by single and never-married mothers are much more likely to be poor than households with two parents.[19] In addition, family income drops significantly following a divorce. Indeed, the high number of children who live below the poverty threshold today is due in large part to the number of single mothers. Step families have higher incomes than single-parent families, but not always as high as the incomes of the original two-parent families. But child poverty is not only a result of increasing divorce rates and single parenthood. It is also due in part to the high rates of unemployment and underemployment in the United States today as well as to the relatively low minimum wage, which for a full-time worker is below the poverty threshold for a family of four. Children in one-parent families are more likely to have behavior problems, need psychological help, perform poorly in school, and complete fewer years of schooling than children from two-parent families.[20] While students in two-parent households perform better on academic achievement tests than students in one-parent households, it is not clear what family processes are affecting performance.

Women's participation in the work force has also increased since the 1960s. The number of women in the work force who had children under six years increased from 2.3 million in 1960 to 7.1 million in 1988. While one third of women with babies under one year of age were employed in the mid-1970s, over half were employed in 1988. While maternal employment during infancy may have a negative effect on later cognitive and behavioral outcomes, this association varies depending on the number of hours worked and on the kind of care the child receives during this time.[21]

With the increase in the number of women in the workplace, the mother or another family member is less frequently the main provider of child care. A 1994 Census Bureau survey estimated that the number of children under age five in some form of child care was 9.8 million, up one million from 1986. In 1991, day-care centers accounted for 23 percent of the care, down from a high of 27 percent the previous year. So-called "family day care" (paid child care provided in a private home) declined slightly from 20 percent to 18 percent. In households where the father was out of work, 62 percent of the fathers took care of the children.

These changes in the family landscape have probably resulted in a redistribution of family resources allocated to children. For example, the time parents spend with a particular child is reduced when parents move into the workforce. As another example, the possible negative consequences of divorce include decreased contact the child has with the father and the extended paternal family, a dramatic drop in income, and potential conflict between the child and parents.[22]

Research on the effects of parental behavior and home environment upon children's cognitive and emotional well-being is discussed here based on the premise that the family context sets the stage for how children adapt to the school setting. Adaptation includes developmentally appropriate engagement in school, ability to regulate emotions and behavior, competence in dealing with peers, general knowledge about the world, and early verbal and mathematical skills.

THE PARENT AS PROVIDER OF LEARNING EXPERIENCES

The parent sets the context for learning in the early years. A variety of parental behaviors are relevant, including emotional tone, routines of the home, responsiveness, as well as behaviors more directly related to learning. Maternal warmth and responsiveness to young children's cues facilitate language development and cognitive and emotional growth.[23] The routines followed in the home are not studied very often, even though it is believed that they are important for young children. One parenting dimension that has been studied extensively is the firmness of discipline. Discipline that is reasoned and developmentally appropriate, rather than an overly permissive or a severely controlling style, is associated with children's better impulse control, high self-esteem, better peer relationships, and more advanced cognitive abilities.[24]

Behaviors that are more learning-oriented include actual behavior during problem-solving tasks. Mothers who assist their children without being overly directive or harsh have children with better cognitive and attentional abilities.[25] Provision of learning experiences in the home has been extensively studied using the HOME scale, an observational and interview scale for assessing parental responsivity, provision of learning experiences, punitiveness, and physical environment.

Across social class and ethnic groups high scores are associated with preschool readiness scores and a variety of cognitive tasks.[26] Reading to children and the mother's use of language are also linked to the development of children's verbal abilities, literacy, and perhaps even more important, to interest in reading.[27]

STRENGTHENING THE FAMILY'S ROLE IN LEARNING AND EDUCATION

Providing learning experiences and reading to children occur less frequently when parents are poor, young, have limited education, and are not literate. Poor parental emotional health, inflexible parental child-rearing beliefs, and low commitment to education also are associated with a less learning-oriented home environment.[28]

Various strategies have been employed to enhance the ability of families to provide learning opportunities. These strategies include helping the mother improve her teaching, her interaction skills, and her knowledge of child development as well as raising her self-efficacy, improving her mental health, and facilitating her education and employment opportunities.[29]

This list of strategies highlights the importance of considering the indirect ways that parents may promote their children's learning as well as the more direct paths such as parenting behavior and the provision of learning experiences. Increasing maternal education, a strategy often pursued in JOBS (Family Support Act of 1988) programs for teenage mothers, could have benefits through increased income, increased maternal self-efficacy and self-esteem, decreased depression—all of which may be associated with more responsive and learning-oriented interactions. Increased income could also result in a move to a better neighborhood or the purchase of higher quality child care, both of which are associated with young children's well-being.[30] Increasing knowledge about child rearing may influence parenting behavior or the organization of the home, both of which affect children. The provision of social support may be particularly beneficial for socially isolated or young inexperienced mothers. Decreases in depression as well as possible increases in self-efficacy and employment are outcomes of support programs.[31]

These examples also illustrate the importance of looking at subgroups of families. It is likely that certain strategies will be more or less successful depending on the characteristics and needs of families. Family-oriented programs have taken two approaches. One is the development of programs targeting certain types of families. Head

Start and most of the carefully evaluated programs for preschoolers have targeted families with risk factors known to contribute to developmental delays in children—poverty, single parents, teenage mothers.[32] Another approach would be programs that target children who are biologically vulnerable because of conditions such as low birth weight, prematurity, cerebral palsy, and congenital anomalies. Yet another strategy is to provide an intervention to a large enough group of families so that the efficacy of a program may be examined for subgroups of children. Three exemplars are the Elmira home visiting program, the Educational Testing Service Head Start Longitudinal Study, and the Infant Health and Development Program.[33] These program evaluations were able to examine whether or not the intervention was more effective for some groups than for others. The groups compared included teenage and older mothers, less and more educated mothers, poor and nonpoor families, African-American, European-American, and Hispanic American families, and children who were more and less biologically vulnerable at birth.

In working with individual families and children, home visitors and educators present information based on the child's developmental level and the parent's comprehension. In this sense, interventions are tailored to the individual, even though a particular curriculum or set of materials is being used. However, the point of these large-scale, well-designed interventions is to develop and evaluate the usefulness of specific programs.

Interventions vary with respect to whether they are home-based, center-based, or both. Programs vary also in terms of timing, intensity, and extensiveness of domains covered. The training of the facilitators or educators also differs greatly. Little work has compared any of these dimensions in a systematic way. We now provide a brief review of home-visiting programs and center-based programs.

Home visiting programs. Home visiting programs target child health and safety, parenting behaviors, maternal beliefs about child rearing, provisions of stimulating experiences, reading and literacy skills, social support, and referrals.[34] Most intervention programs address at least two of these concerns. Some programs begin during the prenatal period while others begin in the infancy, toddler, or preschool period.

Perhaps the best known health-oriented program is the Elmira Project, a prenatal home visitation program. Public health nurses provide an ecological approach to maternal and child health that takes into account the interaction between multiple levels of influence (biological, psychological, and economic) on maternal health-related behavior and child outcome. Positive effects include health behaviors (diet and smoking), maternal health (reduced kidney infection), informal social support, and utilization of community services.

Other programs focus more on maternal parenting behavior than on health and safety. Literacy programs have become increasingly popular. An exemplar is the Mother-Child Home Program, created in 1965 for low-income two-year-olds and designed to improve the mother's literacy and competence in improving the child's learning. For a period of two years, visitors demonstrate verbal and nonverbal play with the child. Positive effects were found for mother's verbal responsiveness and for the child's school competence as measured by test scores and behavior through age ten.[35] Another well-known exemplar is HIPPY, the Home Instruction Program for Preschool Youngsters. HIPPY is a two-year program for disadvantaged four- and five-year-olds that emphasizes parental participation in reading.

A more general educational approach is offered by developmentally oriented programs providing mothers with learning materials and the skills to use them. One of the best known is the Learning Games curriculum developed by Sparling and Lewis.[36] This home visiting program has been used in a series of interventions conducted from the Frank Porter Graham Clinic at the University of North Carolina and in the Infant Health and Development Program, an eight-site program for low birth weight children and their families.[37] Early education professionals usually provide this program, which has been developed for a wide range of families. The Learning Games curriculum has been associated with increased knowledge of child-rearing skills, increased learning experiences in the home, and decreased parental depression when children were twelve months of age in the Infant Health and Development Program. However, when center-based programming was not offered, the home visiting curriculum alone did not result in changes in children's cognitive well-being.[38] In the Infant Health and Development Program both home visiting and center-based schooling were provided for children after their first birthday, so that direct comparisons of effects of the two components may not be made after the child reaches twelve months of age. However, the number of home visits made to the children in the treatment group was associated with child outcomes at thirty-six months of age, even after controlling for the number of days of center-based schooling.[39] The number of home visits was also linked to maternal interactive patterns when the children were thirty months of age, as well as to child engagement with the mother.

Programs of a variety of types have proved successful in altering maternal behavior and in some cases also in enhancing children's well-being. A limitation of the work is that to date little attempt has been made to combine elements of support, public health, developmental learning experiences, and literacy into more comprehensive programs. Additionally, the different programs tend to focus on different age groups, rather than offering continuous services over the entire preschool period. Rather, emphasis is placed on certain domains at certain ages (for example, more on health and social support in the first year, more on developmental learning experiences in the second year, and more on reading and literacy in the third and fourth years). Finally, it is unclear whether or not professionals must provide all of these services, some of which may be provided just as effectively by paraprofessionals. Different models need to be developed and their results compared.

Center-based programs. Center-based programs have been developed for infants, toddlers, and preschoolers (although only a handful of those that have been evaluated begin before age six months or even twelve months). What is important from the perspective of families as learning environments is how early childhood educators and parents form a partnership. Almost all programs include parents in some facets of the center. It is widely believed that parental involvement is critical for children's success.[40] Unfortunately, little evidence exists to support or refute this premise. Information comparing different forms of parental involvement is needed in order to identify the best ways to engage parents (and different subgroups of parents) and to alter their behavior. Programs combining center-based and home-based programming are probably most likely to engage the parents. Parenting groups at centers are often poorly attended and parents and teachers often find it difficult to discuss parenting issues at the beginning or end of the child's school day.

Home visiting programs could provide continuity when children are changing preschools or moving from preschool to school. The Follow Through programs, which provided services for Head Start families during the first years of elementary school, seemed to increase the likelihood of sustained effects of Head Start.[41] However, the experience in the Abecedarian Project (a center-based program in which schooling was available from the first three months through five years of age) found that follow-through services did not seem to influence the pattern of sustained effects of preschool, that is, sustained effects were seen whether or not follow-through services were offered.[42]

Neighborhoods as Contexts for Education

Relatively few studies have considered how larger contexts such as the neighborhood or community may affect the development of children. However, sociologists and economists have identified at least six different ways in which neighborhoods might affect developmental outcomes:[43] (1) neighborhood resource theories that consider the importance of public and private services available within a neighborhood; (2) contagion theories that consider the importance of peers in influencing individual behavior; (3) collective socialization theories that consider the importance of role models in the community; (4) social disorganization theories that consider how poverty, ethnic diversity, and residential mobility negatively affect the cohesiveness of the neighborhood and its ability to maintain social control over its children; (5) competition theories that consider neighbors as competitors over scarce resources, and (6) relative deprivation theories that consider the comparisons that are made between neighbors in evaluating their standing in the neighborhood. The first four theories would predict positive outcomes for children living in affluent neighborhoods and negative outcomes for those living in poor neighborhoods. Competition and relative deprivation explanations would not predict that affluent neighborhoods have a beneficial effect, for in those neighborhoods individuals may compete for resources and/or may feel deprived given the high incomes of their neighbors.

Because children's developmental stage may affect their access to different contexts or ecological systems, different models of neighborhood influence are proposed. Very young children have only restricted access to contexts other than the immediate family, which provides the primary socialization influence for them, although some children who are placed in child care outside the home are exposed to other contexts.

Neighborhood resources may affect children directly. For example, children living in neighborhoods regularly patrolled by police and who have access to resources such as parks and libraries have direct access to stimulating learning experiences. Such experiences in turn have been associated with better cognitive and emotional outcomes.[44]

Collective socialization theories of neighborhood posit that children may also be influenced indirectly by neighborhoods. Children who live in neighborhoods where parents have access to jobs may grow up to be model parents with daily routines that stress good work habits and regular routines. In contrast, children of families who live in poor neighborhoods where few adults have jobs or where few jobs are located, may experience "social isolation" that may have damaging behavioral and psychological effects. Parents of these children may not follow family practices that emphasize school or work skills and may feel that they have little control over their own lives, all of which may have negative effects on children. Other possible neighborhood influences—contagion and relative deprivation—may be less likely to affect very young children because of their limited or supervised contact with neighborhood and school peers.

EFFECTS OF NEIGHBORHOODS ON CHILDREN AND PARENTS

Studies have found that young children who grew up in affluent neighborhoods had higher IQs than children in poor neighborhoods. It may be that the presence of role models in affluent neighborhoods had a positive effect on children's IQs by affecting parental behavior. At the same time, living in affluent neighborhoods may result in having more access to stimulating learning experiences.

Other studies involving older elementary school children (third to fifth graders) have found some evidence for collective socialization and contagion effects, although the effects were significant for boys, not girls, and differed by race. For white boys, affluent neighborhoods were associated with fewer absences and suspensions, higher scores on tests, and less need for special services. For African-American boys, poorer neighborhoods, that is, those with higher concentrations of jobless men, were associated with more of the behaviors that put them at risk of school failure.[45]

Few studies have found significant neighborhood effects on children's behavior problems. For example, Brooks-Gunn et al. and Klebanov et al. failed to find significant neighborhood effects on the behavior problems of three-year-old children, but did find that neighborhood poverty was associated with greater aggression (but not withdrawal or anxiety) for five-year-old children.[46] More aggressive or acting out behavior may be shown by children living in poor neighborhoods due to the lower quality of schools and child care settings available to these children. Higher adult-to-child ratios may lead to less supervision and greater tolerance of aggressive behavior.[47] However, the effects of neighborhood may operate indirectly by affecting parents' behavior toward children. It may be that mothers in poor neighborhoods learn that it is not only normative but more adaptive for them to be less amiable and warm to their children, and to others as well. Mothers may encourage their children to behave in a similar manner given the level of danger in such environments.[48]

A few studies have examined whether or not parental characteristics and behaviors are associated with neighborhood residence. Childrearing attitudes and behaviors and family routines and practices may be influenced by the neighborhood, and all these factors have been associated with developmental outcomes. If role models and monitoring are important ways in which neighborhoods influence parenting behavior, then neighborhood effects should be seen. Our findings suggest that poor neighborhoods are associated with worse home physical environment and low maternal warmth. In brief, the research findings to date indicate that both poor and affluent neighbors make a difference for the developmental outcomes of young children.

STRENGTHENING THE NEIGHBORHOOD'S ROLE IN LEARNING AND EDUCATION

The environments in which young children and their families live play an important role in the school performance of children. Improvement of the neighborhood context is essential to improving the lives of children and their families. A number of programs aim to improve the quality of life of families and children, either by moving the family to a new neighborhood or by working for change within the existing community. In either case, neighborhood-based programs are designed to assist families directly as well as to increase the social capital of the neighborhood (networks, stability, norms, and sanctions, and information). Additionally, many programs focus on improving economic opportunity, securing affordable and safe housing, and providing opportunity for community participation, personal development, and leadership for both parents and children. Some examples of programs that focus on enhancing neighborhood resources follow.

Family Resource Centers are community-based centers that focus on the immediate ecology of the young child. Located in community agencies, these centers are oriented toward prevention and tend to provide multiple services rather than a single specialization. The focus is on promoting parent competence and mental health in a way that is most likely to enhance child development. Child and Family Resource Programs (CFRP) emphasize the personal development of the parent by emphasizing self-esteem and self-control; Parent-Child Development Centers (PCDC) emphasize parenting skills. Positive effects of these types of centers have been found for children's social competence and school performance.[49] The positive effects of these parent-focused centers for children are reduced when parents need basic social services and face frequent crises. Both parent and child are more likely to benefit from programs that are continuous, intensive, and comprehensive.[50]

Another community-based program that may influence young children indirectly through their parents is Project Match, a welfare-to-work program aimed at low-income, single, African-American women. Project Match has been operating since 1985, with a focus on helping the women experience job success and on developing a relationship between workers and participants that will assist the women throughout the process of working toward better paying jobs. Little work has focused on how welfare-to-work programs influence young children.[51]

The Children, Families, and Community Initiative, funded by the F. R. Bigelow Foundation, aims to help children by strengthening families and communities from within the community itself. Sensitivity to race and culture, as well as to the family and community context of the child, are important considerations of this initiative.[52]

These neighborhood-based interventions appear to hold great promise for enhancing the lives of young children and their families.

Conclusion

The importance of the family as educator has been underscored in recent years. Growing concern about young children and the families in which they are raised is exemplified by the recent report of the Carnegie Task Force on Meeting the Needs of Young Children.[53] Entitled *Starting Points*, the report focuses on the importance of the first three years of life. It discusses what is known about young children as well as the critical role the family plays in enhancing their development. Media coverage was extensive and the responses by federal and local policymakers were enthusiastic. What accounts for this outpouring of interest?

We believe that the report struck a chord in many Americans in part because of the changing demographic face of the family. Clearly, the means by which these changes in families influence children are not fully understood. However, it is also clear that families need support in rearing children, perhaps more than ever before. The need is reflected in the new generation of educational programs that are being developed for young children. Such programs must be sensitive to the educational needs of families and at the same time reflect the structure and character of various communities and neighborhoods.

The writing of this chapter was supported by grants from the National Institute of Child Health and Human Development (NICHD) Child and Family Well-Being Network, the W. T. Grant Foundation, the March of Dimes Foundation, the Bureau for Maternal and Child Health and the Russell Sage Foundation. The authors wish to thank Fung-ruey Liaw, Greg Duncan, Kristine Moore, Linda Burton, Margaret Spencer, J. Lawrence Aber, Cecelia McCarton, Marie McCormick, Ruth Gross, and Brett Brown for their collaboration, as well as their colleagues at Teachers College and the Educational Testing Service. Also, we would like to acknowledge the support of the Research Division of the Educational Testing Service. A special thanks is due to the Leonard Marx family for their support, and to Virginia Marx for her ideas about enhancing the well-being of young children.

Notes

1. Larry V. Hedges, Richard D. Laine, and Robert Greenwald, "Does Money Matter? A Meta-Analysis of Studies of the Effects of Differential School Inputs on Student Outcomes," *Educational Researcher* 23, no. 2 (April 1994): 5-12; Michael Rutter, "Family and School Influences on Cognitive Development," *Journal of Child Psychology and Psychiatry* 25 (1985): 683-704. See also, Christopher Jencks and Susan E. Mayer, "The Social Consequences of Growing Up in a Poor Neighborhood," in *Inner-city Poverty in the United States*, edited by Michael G. McGeary and Lawrence E. Lynn, Jr. (Washington, DC: National Academy Press, 1988), pp. 111-186.

2. Edward Zigler and Kathryn B. Black, "America's Family Support Movement: Strength and Limitations," *American Journal of Orthopsychiatry* 59 (1989): 6-19.

3. Educational Testing Service, *America's Smallest School: The Family* (Princeton, NJ: Educational Testing Service, 1992).

4. James Coleman, "Social Capital in the Creation of Human Capital," *American Journal of Sociology* 94 (1988): S95-S120.

5. Pam Klebanov, Jeanne Brooks-Gunn, and Marie C. McCormick, "Early Childhood Intervention and Maternal Social and Emotional Health: The Infant Health and Development Program," *American Journal of Public Health*, in press.

6. Annette Lareau, "What Do Teachers Want from Parents?" in *Home Advantage: Social Class and Parental Intervention in Elementary Education*, edited by Annette Lareau (Briston, PA: Falmer Press, 1989).

7. Gary Natriello, Edward L. McDill, and Aaron Pallas, *Schooling Disadvantaged Children: Racing against Catastrophe* (New York: Teachers College Press, 1990).

8. Edward Zigler, *Head Start: The Inside Story of America's Most Successful Educational Experiment* (New York: Basic Books, 1992).

9. Benjamin S. Bloom, *Stability and Change in Human Characteristics* (New York: Wiley, 1964).

10. Valerie Lee, Jeanne Brooks-Gunn, Elizabeth Schnur, and Fung-ruey Liaw, "Are Head Start Effects Sustained? A Longitudinal Comparison of Disadvantaged Children Attending Head Start, No Preschool, and Other Preschool Programs," *Child Development* 61 (1990): 495-507; Zigler, *Head Start*.

250 FAMILIES AND NEIGHBORHOODS AS CONTEXTS

11. Jeanne Brooks-Gunn, Erin Phelps, and Glen H. Elder, "Studying Lives through Time: Secondary Data Analyses in Developmental Psychology," *Developmental Psychology* 27 (1991): 899-910.

12. Jeanne Brooks-Gunn, "Identifying the Vulnerable Young Child," in *Improving the Life Chances of Children at Risk*, edited by David E. Rogers and Eli Ginzberg (Boulder, CO: Westview Press, 1990), pp. 104-124.

13. Urie Bronfenbrenner, "Ecology of the Family as Context for Human Development: Research Perspectives," *Developmental Psychology* 22 (1986): 723-742; Urie Bronfenbrenner and Nan C. Crouter, "The Evolution of Environmental Models in Developmental Research," in *Handbook of Child Psychology*, vol. 1, edited by Paul H. Mussen, 4th ed. (New York: John Wiley and Sons, 1983), pp. 357-414.

14. Pam K. Klebanov, Jeanne Brooks-Gunn, P. Lindsay Chase-Lansdale, and Rachel Gordon, "Neighborhood Influences upon Young Children," in *Neighborhood Poverty: Contexts and Consequences for Development*, edited by Greg Duncan, Jeanne Brooks-Gunn, and J. Lawrence Aber (New York: Russell Sage, forthcoming).

15. Norman Garmezy and Michael Rutter, *Stress, Coping, and Development in Children* (New York: McGraw-Hill, 1983); Emmy E. Werner and Ruth S. Smith, *Vulnerable But Not Invincible: A Longitudinal Study of Resilient Children and Youth* (New York: McGraw-Hill, 1982).

16. Coleman, "Social Capital in the Creation of Human Capital."

17. Donald J. Hernandez, *America's Children: Resources from Family, Government, and the Economy* (New York: Russell Sage Foundation, 1993); Frank F. Furstenberg, Jr., "Coming of Age in a Changing Family System," in *At the Threshold*, edited by S. Shirley Feldman and Glen R. Elliott (Cambridge, MA: Harvard University Press, 1990), pp. 147-170.

18. Jeanne Brooks-Gunn and Frank F. Furstenberg, Jr., "Adolescent Sexual Behavior," *American Psychologist* 44 (1989): 249-257.

19. Sara S. McLanahan, Nan M. Astone, and Nadine F. Marks, "The Role of Mother-only Families in Reducing Poverty," in *Children in Poverty: Child Development and Public Policy*, edited by Aletha Huston (New York: Cambridge University Press, 1991), pp. 51-78.

20. Hernandez, *America's Children*.

21. Nuzli Baydar and Jeanne Brooks-Gunn, "Effects of Maternal Employment and Childcare Arrangements in Infancy on Preschoolers' Cognitive and Behavioral Outcomes: Evidence from the Children of the NLSY," *Developmental Psychology* 27 (1991): 932-945.

22. Alan Booth and Judy Dunn, *Step-parent Families with Children: Who Benefits and Who Does Not?* (Hillsdale, NJ: Erlbaum, forthcoming).

23. Lila Beckwith and Sarah E. Cohen, "Home Environment and Early Cognitive Competence in Preterm Children during the First Five Years," in *Home Environment and Early Cognitive Development*, edited by Allen Gottfried (New York: Academic Press, 1984).

24. Diana Baumrind, "Rearing Competent Children," in *Child Development Today and Tomorrow*, edited by William Damon (San Francisco: Jossey-Bass, 1989), pp. 349-378; Eleanor E. Maccoby and John A. Martin, "Socialization in the Context of the Family: Parent-Child Interaction," in *Handbook of Child Psychology*, vol. 4, edited by Paul H. Mussen (New York: Wiley, 1983), pp. 1-101.

25. Robert D. Hess and Teresa M. McDevitt, "Some Cognitive Consequences of Maternal Intervention Techniques: A Longitudinal Study," *Child Development* 55 (1984): 2017-2030; J. D. Jennings and R. E. Connors, "Mothers' Interactional Style and Children's Competence at 3 Years," *International Journal of Behavioral Development* 12 (1989): 155-175.

26. Robert H. Bradley and Betty M. Caldwell, "The HOME Inventory and Family Demographics," *Developmental Psychology* 20 (1984): 1140-48; Robert H. Bradley et al., "Home Environment and Cognitive Development in the First Three Years of Life: A Collaborative Study Including Six Sites and Three Ethnic Groups in North America," *Developmental Psychology* 25 (1989): 217-235.

27. Catherine Snow, "Literacy and Language: Relationships during the Preschool Years," *Harvard Educational Review* 53 (1983): 165-189.

28. Jeanne Brooks-Gunn, Pam Klebanov, Fung-ruey Liaw, and Greg Duncan, "Toward an Understanding of the Effects of Poverty on Children," in *Children of Poverty: Research, Health Care, and Policy Issues*, edited by H. E. Fitzgerald, B. M. Lester, and B. Zuckerman (New York: Garland Press, forthcoming).

29. April A. Benasich, Jeanne Brooks-Gunn, and Beatrise C. Clewell, "How Do Mothers Benefit from Early Intervention Programs," *Journal of Applied Developmental Psychology* 13 (1991): 311-362.

30. K. Alison Clarke-Stewart, "Infant Day Care: Maligned or Malignant?" *American Psychologist* 44 (1989): 266-272; Cheryl D. Hayes, John L. Palmer, and Martha J. Zaslow, *Who Cares for America's Children: Childcare Policy for the 1900s* (Washington, DC: National Academy of Sciences, 1990).

31. Klebanov, Brooks-Gunn, and McCormick, "Early Childhood Intervention and Maternal Social and Emotional Health."

32. Jeanne Brooks-Gunn, "Promoting Healthy Development in Young Children: What Educational Interventions Work?" in *Improving the Life Chances of Children at Risk*, edited by David E. Rogers and Eli Ginzberg (Boulder, CO: Westview Press, 1990), pp. 125-145.

33. David L. Olds, Charles R. Henderson, and Harriet Kitzman, "Does Prenatal and Infancy Home Visitation Have Enduring Effects on Qualities of Parental Caregiving and Child Health at 25-50 Months of Life?" *Pediatrics* 93, no. 1 (1994): 89-98; Lee, Brooks-Gunn, Schnur, and Liaw, "Are Head Start Effects Sustained?"; Infant Health and Development Program, "Enhancing the Outcomes of Low Birthweight, Premature Infants: A Multisite Randomized Trial," *Journal of the American Medical Association* 263 (1990): 3035-3042.

34. Benasich, Brooks-Gunn, and Clewell, "How Do Mothers Benefit from Early Intervention Programs?"

35. Phyllis Levenstein, "The Mother-Child Home Project: Research Findings and Problems" (Paper presented at the Second National Head Start Research Conference, Washington, DC, 1993).

36. Joseph J. Sparling and Isabelle S. Lewis, *Learning Games for the First Three Years: A Guide to Parent-Child Play* (New York: Walker and Co., 1979).

37. Craig T. Ramey and Frances A. Campbell, "Poverty, Early Childhood Education, and Academic Competence: The Abecedarian Experiment," in *Children Poverty*, edited by Aletha C. Huston (New York: Cambridge University Press, 1991), pp. 190-221; idem, "The Carolina Abecedarian Project: An Educational Experiment Concerning Human Malleability," in *The Malleability of Children*, edited by James J. Gallagher and Craig T. Ramey (Baltimore, MD: Brookes Publishing Co., 1987), pp. 127-140; Infant Health and Development Program, "Enhancing the Outcomes of Low Birthweight, Premature Infants."

38. Barbara H. Wasik, Craig T. Ramey, Donna M. Bryant, and Joseph J. Sparling, "A Longitudinal Study of Two Early Intervention Strategies: Project CARE," *Child Development* 61 (1990): 1682-1696.

39. Fung-ruey Liaw, Sam Meisels, and Jeanne Brooks-Gunn, "The Effects of Early Intervention on Low Birth Weight, Premature Children: The Infant Health and Development Program" (Unpublished paper, 1993).

40. Martin Woodhead, "When Psychology Informs Public Policy: The Case of Early Childhood Interventions," *American Psychologist* 43 (1988): 443-454.

41. Ruth H. McKey et al., *The Impact of Head Start on Children, Families and Communities*, Final Report of the Head Start Evaluation, Synthesis, and Utilization Project (Washington, DC: CSR, Inc., 1985).

42. Ramey and Campbell, "Poverty, Early Childhood Education, and Academic Competence."

43. William J. Wilson, "Public Policy Research and 'The Truly Disadvantaged,'" in *The Urban Underclass*, edited by Christopher Jencks and Paul E. Peterson (Washington, DC: The Brookings Institution, 1991); idem, "Studying Inner-city Social Dislocations: The Challenge of Public Agenda Research," *American Sociological Review* 56 (1991): 1-14.

44. Bradley et al., "Home Environment and Cognitive Development in the First Three Years of Life."

45. James P. Connell and B. L. Halpern-Fisher, "Direct and Indirect Effects of Neighborhood and Family Economic Risk on Urban Elementary School Children's Educational Risk Behavior," in *Neighborhood Poverty: Contexts and Consequences for Development*, edited by Greg Duncan, Jeanne Brooks-Gunn, and J. Lawrence Aber (New York: Russell Sage Foundation, forthcoming).

46. Jeanne Brooks-Gunn, Greg J. Duncan, Pam K. Klebanov, and N. Sealand, "Do Neighborhoods Influence Child and Adolescent Development?" *American Journal of Sociology* 99 (1993): 353-395; Klebanov, Brooks-Gunn, Chase-Lansdale, and Gordon, "Neighborhood Influences upon Young Children."

47. Hayes, Palmer and Zaslow, *Who Cares for America's Children*.

48. Robin Jarrett, "A Comparative Examination of Socialization Patterns among Low-income African-Americans, Chicanos, Puerto Ricans, and Whites: A Review of the Ethnographic Literature" (Evanston, IL: Center for Urban Affairs and Policy Research, Northwestern University, 1992).

49. Victoria Seitz, Laurie K. Rosenbaum, and Nancy H. Apfel, "Effects of a Family Support Intervention: A 10-Year Follow Up," *Child Development* 56 (1985): 376-391.

50. H. Weiss and R. Halpern, "Community-Based Family Support and Education Programs: Something Old? Something New?" Working paper (New York: National Center for Children in Poverty, 1990).

51. Julie B. Wilson, David T. Ellwood, and Jeanne Brooks-Gunn, "Welfare to Work through the Eyes of Children: The Impact on Parenting of Movement from AFDC to Employment," *in Escape from Poverty: What Makes a Difference for Children?* edited by J. Chase-Lansdale and Jeanne Brooks-Gunn (New York: Cambridge University Press, forthcoming).

52. Prudence Brown and Harold Richardson, "Neighborhood Effects and State and Local Policy," in *Neighborhood Poverty: Contexts and Consequences for Development*, edited by Greg Duncan, Jeanne Brooks-Gunn, and J. Lawrence Aber (New York: Russell Sage, forthcoming).

53. Carnegie Task Force on Meeting the Needs of Youth Children, *Starting Points: Meeting the Needs of Our Youngest Children*, Report of the Task Force on Meeting the Needs of Young Children (New York: Carnegie Corporation, 1994).

CHAPTER XII

The Effectiveness of Collaborative
School-Linked Services

MARGARET C. WANG, GENEVA D. HAERTEL,
AND HERBERT J. WALBERG

Since the late 1980s, Americans have been inundated with media
reports describing the increasingly dire circumstances surrounding
our nation's children. Families in the United States are beset by
urgent problems, including poverty, teenage pregnancy, single parenthood, substance abuse, limited health care, and inadequate and unaf-
fordable housing. Even though these problems are not strictly educational issues, they do impact all aspects of children's lives, placing
them at risk of educational failure. As a result, they place schools at
the center of interconnected social problems.

As they traditionally have, non-school-based service providers, including public and private community agencies, can provide services
for at-risk children and their families. These services include counseling, financial assistance, medical treatment, and job training. Increasingly, however, many of these agencies are subjected to heavy case-
loads, limited resources, and isolation from other related service
providers.[1] On the other hand, many professional groups now agree
that the complex problems of at-risk children and their families cannot be tackled by our schools alone.[2] Rather, broader social policies
must be established to protect the nation's at-risk children and their
families.

One response to the call for broad social policies has been the establishment of interagency, collaborative programs that link schools and
other service agencies, drawing upon the strengths of each in an effort
to meet the educational and social needs that neither can effectively

Margaret C. Wang is Director of the Temple University Center for Research in
Human Development and Education. Geneva D. Haertel is a Senior Research Associate
at that Center. Herbert J. Walberg is Research Professor of Education at the University
of Illinois at Chicago. All three authors are also affiliated with the National Center on
Education in the Inner Cities at Temple University.

meet alone. As a result, a variety of programs for "school-linked" health and human services delivery are being created across the country to implement innovative strategies to provide services to children and youth in high-risk circumstances. These programs reach out to those at greatest risk and mobilize resources to reduce and prevent school dropout, substance abuse, juvenile delinquency, teen pregnancy, and other forms of so-called "modern morbidity." Nearly all of the school-linked programs seek to develop feasible ways to build connecting mechanisms for effective communication, coordinated service delivery, and mobilization of the latent energies and resources of communities. School-linked programs are being developed as an effective way for schools to more fully meet the needs of the changing populations they find themselves serving.

In this chapter we summarize recent research into collaborative school-linked programs. On the basis of the results of a systematic review of forty-four school-linked programs[3] we draw conclusions about the nature, direction, and efficacy of such collaborations. In the first section we present a brief history and we summarize the current status of school-linked services. In the second section we describe six types of school-linked programs and briefly discuss their effectiveness. We conclude the chapter with a discussion of the impact of collaborative programs on students and families.

School-Linked Services

A BRIEF HISTORY OF COLLABORATIVE SCHOOL-LINKED SERVICES

Even though the attention paid to school-linked services has increased in recent years in response to the increased cost and incidence of social problems, the use of schools as a base from which a number of social ills could be remedied is not new. Since the 1890s, one of the goals of school systems in the United States has been improving the plight of at-risk children. Tyack's historical analysis of the development of school-linked services documents the waxing and waning popularity of using collaborative programs to meet the needs of at-risk students and their families.[4] He finds that the past century has demonstrated that much school reform, including the provision of health and human services, typically occurs from the top down, with advice from the community being ignored and programs intended for the poor frequently rooted in the wealthiest communities.

Reformers in the 1890s campaigned for increased services for at-risk children. They advocated medical and dental examinations, school lunches, summer academic programs, recreational activities, and school-based child welfare officers. Many of the health-oriented programs of the 1890s were based on a philosophy of improving the human capital of the nation's children and ensuring equal educational opportunity.

However, reformers were not convinced of the capacity of parents, especially immigrant parents, to provide for all their children's needs. Sadly enough, social reformers rarely sought input from parents as they designed and implemented these new services. Tyack notes that, while parents recognized the value of health and medical services (including improved nutrition, access to physical education, and academic remediation), some of them found these programs intrusive and sometimes fought them to preserve their own authority, as well as their ethnic, religious, or community values.

Other political reactions to these programs varied. Conservatives expressed concern that the school's academic mission would be diluted. Progressive educators lauded the new services and believed that without them students would drop out of school. Financial officers worried about finding money to support the new services. Despite these varied reactions, collaborative school-linked services were entrenched in the nation's public schools by the end of the 1930s.

Tyack reports that during the Great Depression budgets and staffs for school-based services increased, especially those devoted to improving children's health. By 1940, almost all cities over 30,000 had some form of public health service (70 percent of which were run by the schools, 20 percent by health departments, and 10 percent by a collaboration of both). Other services, such as lunches and mental health, reappeared after World War II although they did not enjoy such sustained commitment. During the late 1940s, school lunches became the norm, despite conservative fears of establishing a paternalistic state. Mental health programs were instituted in well-to-do school districts during the 1950s and in poorer ones in the 1960s. In the 1960s, education was viewed as the vanguard against poverty, and funding for school-based social services was increased. In general, the collaborative programs established during this period were more aware of the limitations of top-down models of reform and involved a greater degree of community participation. Such an expanded community role, however, sometimes spawned conflicts concerning program goals and operations among community groups, school officials, and service agencies. Despite these difficulties, Lyndon Johnson's War on Poverty had reached millions of children by 1970, and collaborative programs had found a niche in public schools. These programs received support from influential community groups, did not clash with prevailing instructional approaches, and met some of the needs of poor children at risk of school failure.

According to Tyack, collaborative programs were transformed as they became established in the public schools. To handle truancy, for example, some of the school social workers became part of the school's bureaucracy. This change represented a shifting of goals among school social workers. In an effort to enhance their professional status, some began to base their work on models from mental health and psychology, while others began to work with more privileged clients. To ensure the political viability of new social services, legislators often made such programs available to the general public. Services were delivered best in wealthy communities with large property tax bases. Thus, the children of both the wealthy and the poor became recipients of collaborative interagency services originally intended only for at-risk students.

During the late 1970s and early 1980s, the role of the schools shifted toward producing students who could compete in the global marketplace and maintain the nation's competitiveness. This shift, combined with significant budget cutbacks, reduced some of the social services provided. Still, the nation's schools became multipurpose institutions that looked beyond the academic performance of their students, as suggested by the fact that, despite the reduction in services, teachers accounted for 70 percent of all school employees in 1950 but only 52 percent by 1986.[5]

THE CURRENT STATUS OF COLLABORATIVE SCHOOL-LINKED SERVICES

Political reactions to school-linked services continue to vary. Not everyone views collaborative programs and school-linked services as the panacea to meet the needs of at-risk students. In the controversial book *Losing Ground*, Charles Murray argues that government services, including school-linked collaborations, have produced long-term negative consequences for recipients.[6] He maintains, for example, that raising welfare benefits increased the welfare rolls and that school-based health clinics contributed to the increase in the number of unmarried pregnant teenagers. Murray cautions policymakers of the unintended effects that may emerge as government services proliferate. In addition, Kirst has identified several alternative approaches to reducing the problems that surround at-risk children and families, including the use of vouchers, tax credits, a negative income tax, and less costly approaches (such as traditional parental care for children).[7]

On the other hand, in *Within Our Reach: Breaking the Cycle of Disadvantage* Lisbeth Schorr unambiguously sets forth the belief that today's complex social problems can be ameliorated through collaborative social programs.[8] Over the course of twenty years, she gathered information from researchers, practitioners, administrators, and public policy analysts. Basing her observations on research on risk and protective factors, she identifies risks that affect the lives of children, including premature birth, poor health and nutrition, child abuse, teenage pregnancy, delinquency, family stress, academic failure, persistent poverty, inaccessible social and health services, inadequate housing, inadequate medical treatment, and inadequate schools. She argues that these risks require a societal response, not simply a response from the at-risk child or family.

THE NEED FOR COLLABORATIVE PROGRAMS

Larson et al. describe the prevalence of children's problems across the nation, including increases in both incidence and cost.[9] They cite, for example, increases in juvenile delinquency and the need for foster care. Even some types of children's problems that have decreased in incidence, such as dropouts and teenage pregnancy, have become costlier in terms of benefit expenditures and reduced productivity.

Statistics collected on children's problems and the systems intended to deal with those problems appear to support the need for new approaches to service systems. Melaville and Blank have identified four flaws in the current methods of delivering organized services for children:

- the reliance upon a crisis-oriented system that does not prevent problems;
- the compartmentalization of problems into rigid categories;
- the lack of communication among various agencies; and
- the provision of specialized services that are not able to address the interconnected problems of children and their families.[10]

As one of many advocates calling for collaborative, integrated services to supplement the schools' role in society, Schorr argues that there is plenty of information available on both risk factors and effective interventions to guide action.[11] She identifies three ways in which collaborations can mend the flaws identified by Melaville and Blank:

1. by providing intensive, comprehensive services that address the needs of the "whole" child and the community;

2. by recognizing that the family should be supported, not displaced, by other social institutions; and

3. by shifting their efforts from remediation to early intervention and eventually to prevention.

THE ROLE OF SCHOOLS IN COLLABORATIVE SCHOOL-LINKED SERVICES

Collaborative school-linked services provide a strategy for meeting the complex needs of children and their families. Advocates of collaborative programs believe that making agency services available in one location, coordinating the goals of the agencies, and involving families, agencies, and schools in the development of the goals will improve the quality of life of at-risk students. In addition, the placement of these services within the schools, where problems can be seen before they reach crisis proportions, can help to make school-linked services more prevention-oriented than crisis-oriented. Not only can school-linked services provide economic and social returns on the investment society makes in them; they can also increase the efficiency and effectiveness with which social and health care services are delivered to students and families who are in adverse circumstances.

As a result, schools have become the location of choice for collaborative programs. Larson et al. provide a rationale for the role of the school as the central location for the multitude of agencies that provide services for children.[12] They argue that schools are enduring institutions that play a critical role in the life of communities. Further, Tyack suggests that schools have played this role in the past, and thus can deliver these services to children and their families in a less stigmatizing manner.[13]

Wang, Haertel, and Walberg describe the relationship between educational achievements and children's at-risk status.[14] Because education is a critical component in children's future economic success and personal welfare,[15] many support the location of noneducational services in the local school. These services can help guarantee the educational accomplishment of children. It can be argued that schools, which are the prime vehicle for delivering academic services, should be central locations for noneducational services as well. An example of schools functioning as centers of community services is demonstrated in some GOALS 2000 schools (formerly AMERICA 2000 schools), which highlight local communities as the heart of educational reform efforts.[16] In addition, further support for the placement of collaborative services within the schools was recently reported in the 24th annual Gallup poll that showed that 77 percent of adults polled favored using schools as centers to provide health and social welfare services by various government agencies.[17]

TYPES OF COLLABORATIVE SCHOOL-LINKED PROGRAMS

There is no single model for collaborative school-linked services.[18] Rather, experience shows that collaborative programs emerge out of the needs of children and families in local communities. Typical types of collaboratives currently being implemented include those directed at parents of young children, teenage parents, pregnant teenagers, dropouts, homeless children, and alcohol and drug abusers.

Structurally, collaborative school-linked programs can be curriculum-based, service-based, or both. Curriculum-based programs provide knowledge to recipients. For example, curriculum-based collaboratives may teach new mothers and fathers about their children's developmental stages, supply information on the effects of drug use, or provide educational activities for preschool children. Other curriculum-based programs not only provide information, but also teach new skills. For example, a drug prevention program may not only provide knowledge about the effects of drug use; it may also teach refusal and coping skills. Service-based collaborative programs, in contrast, are defined by the provision of various services to meet the needs of the targeted clientele. For example, some programs extend health and mental health care, recreation, housing, day care, treatment for substance abuse, transportation to appointments, and other services.

Collaborators vary in school-linked programs, particularly in service-based programs. Some of the first collaborative programs were those in which parents became more actively involved in their children's education. Other collaborative programs can involve health care workers, social workers, psychologists, university researchers, business people, community volunteers, and peers.

Collaboration can occur at different levels of the agencies and schools involved. Bruner identifies four levels of collaboration that apply to schools and social welfare, juvenile justice, mental health, and community services:

- Interagency collaboration at the administrative level, often at top managerial levels in state and local governments. This level of collaboration often results in the creation of task forces, coordinating councils, changes in staff organization, or incentives and job evaluation systems to promote interagency collaboration.

- Interagency collaboration between front-line service providers and school personnel. At this level, service workers develop a knowledge base about other resources in the community that can be used to meet the needs of clients.

- Intraagency collaboration, involving changes within a single agency. At this level, service workers are encouraged to sidestep established procedures and rigidly applied rules, thus increasing their capacity to collaborate successfully with clients and invoke a more diverse range of services than are typically available.

- Collaboration between the client and service workers. In this type of collaboration, the service worker and the client work jointly to identify needs and set goals in order to increase the self-sufficiency of the client.[19]

Although collaboration often occurs first at the top management level or at the fourth level reflecting worker-client relations, it can begin at any of the levels.

Review of Program Types and Effectiveness

COLLABORATIVE PROGRAMS FOR PARENT EDUCATION, SCHOOL READINESS, AND LIFE SKILLS

Parent education, school readiness, and life skills programs have received attention since the 1960s when Head Start programs were regarded as a means of opening up the opportunity system and educating poor preschool children. Among typical school-linked programs, parent education, school readiness, and life skills programs have been the most thoroughly evaluated and researched.

In the past, such programs focused on improving the ability of low-income parents to promote the skills and habits of their young children, thus helping them compete in middle-class environments. More recently, these programs have focused on family literacy, children's academic achievement, and the provision of health and social services to families. Recipients of these services tend to be low-income parents living in urban areas who have young children and little education. Some programs are directed particularly at teenage parents.

Collaborators in these programs include schools, social and health care workers, and occasionally private foundations, universities, and churches. Typically, these programs provide a combination of curriculum-based information and health and social services. The types of curriculum provided include information for parents on developmentally appropriate activities for their children, child-rearing practices, and self-help programs to develop parents' and children's literacy skills. The services most typically delivered include home visits by nurses and social workers, transportation to appointments for families, counseling, health screenings, and occasionally access to a parent resource center.

Overall, these programs tend to be successful in areas such as children's readiness for school, parenting skills, maternal development, and use of community resources. The long-term effects of these programs are more equivocal, however. Some evaluations of preschool programs, such as Head Start, have shown that, although children's academic advantages may fade over time, positive social and behavioral outcomes, such as incidence of retention, special education placement, and remaining in school, have had a more lasting impact.[20]

COLLABORATIVE PROGRAMS ON TEEN PREGNANCY AND PARENTING

During the past two decades, interest in adolescent parents, particularly teenage mothers, has greatly increased. Unlike parent education, school readiness, and life skills programs, however, teen pregnancy and parenting collaboratives have received little attention from the research community.

Pregnancy prevention programs typically provide contraceptives as well as information about birth control, sexuality, and pregnancy to teenagers in order to prevent pregnancies; these programs may also offer counseling and medical examinations. Teenage parenting programs, in addition to providing information on sexuality and birth control, most often promote mothers' completion of high school, and attempt to enhance their employability and job skills. The range of services offered in parenting programs is broad, often emphasizing medical care, including prenatal care, home visits by nurses, and well-child care, in addition to transportation to medical appointments.

While parenting programs target teenage mothers (particularly first-time, unmarried, low-income mothers and pregnant teenagers), pregnancy prevention programs are targeted at the more general population of young women who are of childbearing age. Occasionally, these programs have been designed for particular ethnic minorities, such as African-American teenagers living in urban areas.

These programs involve a diverse set of collaborators, including schools, home nurses, Planned Parenthood, and other health and human services agencies, as well as obstetricians, midwives, pediatricians, and nutritionists. Less frequently, departments of pediatrics and of gynecology and obstetrics from university medical schools participate.

Although research into the effectiveness of these programs has been limited, there is some evidence that they have been moderately successful, often showing an increase in clients' knowledge about pregnancy, reproduction, and birth control. In addition, some programs have shown a decline in pregnancy rates. However, the programs may not have a significant long-term impact on the dropout rate of pregnant teenagers.

COLLABORATIVE PROGRAMS ON DROPOUT PREVENTION

The national dropout rate has been decreasing and may be at an all time historic low.[21] However, while decreasing overall, local dropout rates are not uniformly low. Indeed, dropout rates in urban areas remain high, particularly among minority high school students with a history of high absenteeism and course failure, a fact which has focused attention on the design of programs to meet the needs of these students.

Because the factors leading to dropping out are many, dropout programs often serve clients with several problems in addition to dropping out of school. Some, for instance, are involved in criminal activity, alcohol and drug abuse, or teenage pregnancy. Still, all dropout prevention programs strive to increase attendance and reduce dropout rates. Most also attempt to increase both students' academic performance and the probability of their attending college or entering the work force. In addition, some also set goals to increase socially desirable behaviors.

Programs tend to involve schools, parents, businesses, and departments of family and child services as collaborators and, occasionally, university and college collaborators. Depending upon the particular group of students served, collaborators may also include the juvenile justice department, drug counselors or obstetricians, and other professionals providing specialized services. The curriculum in dropout prevention programs typically focuses on remedial basic skills and vocational education. Services provided in dropout programs include counseling, mentoring, health services, home visits, and telephone calls to homes as a follow-up for absenteeism. Some programs provide coordination of Job Training Partnership Act (JTPA) placements and preparation for the general equivalency diploma (GED) as well. Others are designed specifically around the needs of children who do not conform to typical school expectations.

Dropout prevention programs have had mixed effects. Most increase attendance rates as well as grade point averages and the number of credits earned. However, graduation rates, although improved, are still low; there is little evidence of students having more definite graduation plans as a result of participating in the programs.

COLLABORATIVE PROGRAMS ON ALCOHOL AND DRUG PREVENTION AND ABUSE

For the past three decades, young people, their parents, teachers, and government officials have been dealing with the problems of alcohol and drug prevention and abuse. Despite great public attention and concerted efforts to discourage alcohol and drug use, the number of youth using alcohol and drugs has increased, and the age at which they begin using these substances has decreased. Collaborative programs designed to tackle these problems seek to go beyond merely imparting information about alcohol and drugs to providing young people with counseling services, drop-in centers, and peer mentors.

Collaborative programs to prevent the use and abuse of alcohol and drugs have one overriding goal: to reduce the consumption of alcohol and drugs. Toward that main goal, many programs have a number of ancillary objectives such as increasing knowledge about drugs and alcohol, promoting skills to cope with the pressure to use these substances, teaching responsible drinking habits, and developing positive self-esteem. Because all young people are considered to be at risk for alcohol and drug problems, the programs target a wide population. Some programs, however, address the specific needs of urban minorities, Native Americans, and children of alcoholics. While some programs work with young people facing a number of risk factors, others work with students who might not be considered at risk for any other problems. Although this is not the case in most other collaborative programs, peers play a significant role in drug prevention programs, often joining community and social agencies, the media, counselors, health care workers, police, and community members, especially leaders. These programs offer information about social and decision-making skills in addition to information about alcohol and drugs. Typical services include peer and other counseling, alcohol- and drug-free activities, and support groups.

While there is evidence that students' drug use decreases as a result of drug prevention and abuse programs, the effectiveness of these programs on alcohol use is less clear. It appears that the most effective alcohol and drug prevention programs are those that provide knowledge about the effects of alcohol and drugs to students and also provide training in refusal and coping skills. Still, alcohol and drug prevention and abuse programs provide one of the clearest examples of the value of collaboration, and particularly of the value of peer counseling. The superior effects of peer programs reflect the special influence peers have on one another's behavior and the value of specific skills training. Regardless of the type of drug used, peer programs are successful at modifying student behavior. Indeed, work by Tobler seriously challenges the concept that knowledge changes alone will produce attitude changes and corresponding changes in behavior.[22] It appears that alcohol and drug prevention programs that use peers as collaborators stand a better chance of decreasing students' drug use, or at least retarding the likelihood that students will try new drugs.

INTEGRATED SERVICES PROGRAMS

Although the notion of integrated school-linked services for children enjoys great currency today, similar ideas have waxed and waned over the past hundred years. Indeed, medical screenings, inoculations, school lunches, and counseling for students have all become entrenched in public schools across the United States. Current reformers view schools as potential sites for providing an even greater variety of services ranging from welfare to job training and from child care to juvenile justice services. Proponents of such integration argue that current service systems cannot respond in a timely, coordinated, or comprehensive manner to social problems. They further argue that these integrated services should be school-linked, not only because schools are often the most dominant institutions in their communities, but because linking services to schools will promote academic achievement.

As the label implies, integrated services programs have a wide variety of goals. All programs seek to coordinate services, but often toward different ends. Thus, a single program might encompass goals as diverse as providing better health care and recreation, improving school attendance and achievement, decreasing dropout rates, and making community resources available to the schools. Integrated services programs exist in urban and rural communities, at both the local and state levels. They work to bring children and their families in contact with educational, medical, mental health, legal, employment, and other social services. A wide range of students are served by these programs. Integrated services programs, for example, have been targeted at delinquent children, children from dysfunctional homes, urban minorities, and low-achieving youth.

The list of collaborators in these programs is as great as the variety of services provided. With schools serving as the nexus, the collaborators include universities, businesses, state and local governments, foundations and nonprofit agencies, health care providers, mental health agencies, community and religious institutions, parents, and peers. Services offered by these programs include vocational counseling, health care, a wide variety of social services, and case management.

Outcomes from integrated services programs are predictably diverse, reflecting the variety of the programs themselves. In addition, because many of these programs are relatively new, it is impossible to measure their long-term effects. However, in terms of numbers of services provided to at-risk children and their families, these programs have demonstrated some success.

PARENT INVOLVEMENT IN COLLABORATIVE PROGRAMS

The idea of parental involvement in children's education is not new. As early as the turn of the century, Frederick Froebel, one of the founders of the kindergarten movement, argued that schools should involve parents in the education of their children. Since that time, parental involvement has enjoyed consistent support as a worthy idea.[23] Though such involvement encompasses a wide array of collaboration, most programs focus on family-school partnerships, encouraging parents to play a role in their children's physical and emotional development, and teaching effective parenting and child-rearing skills.

School programs to improve parental involvement have not only aimed to foster greater parental concern for children's educational achievement. Typically, they have also set goals of improving students' academic performance in school and creating or improving ways for parents to have input in their children's education. In addition, not all goals are school-based. Many programs aim to empower parents, create a more intellectually and educationally stimulating home environment, and promote closer family relations. Collaborative programs to foster parental involvement have worked with the families of children in preschool through high school. Schools and parents are the obvious collaborators in any parent involvement program. Some programs, however, also involve the wider community, including psychological and social services. Others have brought businesses, media, and universities into collaboration with schools and parents. Most programs are designed to provide information rather than services.

In general, parent involvement programs have shown weak to moderate positive effects on improving children's academic performance. Although these programs have often improved parental involvement in children's education and have led many parents to believe that school climate has improved, changes in academic achievement have been mixed. As a result, if parent involvement is advocated because it is "a good thing" or because parents have an obligation to be involved, then these findings are irrelevant. Those hoping to achieve goals such as better student performance and attendance, however, may want to consider other avenues toward those ends.

Conclusion

A variety of innovative collaborative school-linked programs are being created across the country to meet more effectively the changing educational and service needs of children and families. A central concern of these programs is how educators and others can enhance one another's efforts to improve the prospects of schooling success of children and youth from families in at-risk circumstances. Agencies of the community that badly need to coordinate efforts in service to people of the city are fractionated, uncoordinated, and disparate. Schools are part of this much disconnected nonsystem; school-linked services show some potential, both to help connect these disparate agencies and to help make schools a principal player in the effort to provide services.

One common underlying premise of the emerging "school-community connection" type of programs is that the challenges facing children and families—and thus increasingly facing schools—stem from a variety of cultural, economic, political, and health problems. Their solutions are by nature complex. They require the pooling of resources from public and private agencies such as city and state health and human services departments, businesses, religious institutions, and community-based social and medical service agencies. They also require negotiation of new forms of cooperation and coordination and new ways of mobilizing the energies and resources of communities.

Another commonly shared assumption in the design and implementation of the various approaches to providing coordinated school-linked health and human services delivery is that narrow plans and commitments to schools alone will not suffice to solve the growing problems that must be addressed to ensure the learning success of the many children and youth who have not fared well under the current systems. The challenge is to understand the problems and resources that can be drawn and mobilized thoroughly; to help raise consciousness about the opportunities in the community, especially among those who are in a position to shape policies; and to provide resources to improve the prospect of success in learning for children and youth in at-risk situations such as those in the nation's inner-city communities.

Despite the fact that the research base and practical know-how in implementing school-linked programs require application of knowledge and expertise from many disciplines and professions, no system is in place to communicate and share the growing body of related research findings and innovative developments among practitioners of the various fields and others who play major roles in influencing the conditions and process of education and health and human services delivery. Kirst and Kelley describe a number of operational strategies and tactics that support collaborative school-linked services.[24] They call for significant changes at all levels of the nation's schools, including district leadership, middle management, principals, and teachers. This chapter—and the Wang, Haertel, and Walberg paper upon which it is based[25]—outline some of the forms those changes may take.

Still, in spite of the obvious historic and current appeal of collaborative school-linked programs, the evidence of their effectiveness is slimmer than required for a confident overall endorsement. To be sure, several programs have been adequately evaluated and show some positive effects on outcomes. However, the evaluations that are made public may tend to be the ones with more positive results. Many reports merely describe programs and provide rudimentary information that affords little basis for recommending such programs in general and still less on the decisive features of successful programs. It must be acknowledged that much more rigorous research will be necessary to arrive at reliable policy conclusions.

Innovative programs evolve in stages of development, growth, and change. Procedures found useful in one city can be helpful to others who are initiating similar programs elsewhere. Strong efforts are needed to encourage exploration, to share ideas on solutions to thorny problems, to identify promising practices, to analyze program implementations, and to evaluate outcomes. There has been insufficient opportunity for persons involved with research and implementation of school-linked service programs to share understandings and discuss research questions and methodological considerations. This is yet another level of collaboration that will contribute to sustained improvements. Increased research and evaluation will yield a much-needed knowledge base on how to provide school-linked service integration that is both feasible and effective.

Evaluating collaborative school-linked health and human services remains a challenge. Direct measures of the "collaboration" are sorely lacking. Data are needed, for example, on the accessibility of programs; the implementation processes that established the programs; on the role of the principals and others in leadership positions of the various service agencies; on the changing role and modus operandi of the staff; on the ways in which agency staff are involved in the planning, implementation, and evaluation of the programs; and on the allocation and budgeting of the cost of the services. Kirst and Kelley conclude that, among the changes facing our schools, the educational accountability system must be altered to include outcomes that validly measure school-linked services.[26] In addition, educators must acknowledge the close linkage between the provision of school-linked services and academic outcomes. School-linked services should not be perceived as peripheral to the academic mission of schools, but rather as an essential component that can reduce the vulnerability of at-risk students and their families.

This chapter is based on a paper by the authors, "Dimensions of Collaborative School-Linked Services," presented at the School/Community Connections conference in Leesburg, Virginia, in March 1993. The conference was sponsored by the Temple University Center for Research in Human Development and Education. The research reported here was supported in part by the Office of Educational Research and Improvement, U.S. Department of Education, through a grant to the National Center on Education in the Inner Cities at the Temple University Center for Research in Human Development and Education. The opinions expressed do not necessarily reflect the position of the supporting agencies, and no official endorsement should be inferred.

NOTES

1. H. Chang, S. L. Gardner, A. Watahara, C. G. Brown, and R. Robles, *Fighting Fragmentation: Collaborative Efforts to Serve Children and Families in California's Counties* (San Francisco: California Tomorrow and the Children and Youth Policy Project, University of California at Berkeley, 1991).

2. Council of Chief State School Officers, *Family Support, Education, and Involvement: A Guide for State Action* (Washington, DC: Council of Chief State School Officers, 1989); Janet E. Levy and C. Copple, *Joining Forces: A Report from the First Year* (Alexandria, VA: National Association of State Boards of Education, 1989).

3. Margaret C. Wang, Geneva D. Haertel, and Herbert J. Walberg, "Dimensions of Collaborative School-Linked Services" (Paper presented at the School/Community Connections Conference sponsored by the Temple University Center for Research in Human Development and Education, Leesburg, VA, March 1993).

4. David Tyack, "Health and Social Services in Public Schools: Historical Perspectives," *Future of Children* 2, no. 1 (1992): 19-31.

5. Ibid.

6. Charles Murray, *Losing Ground: American Social Policy, 1950-1980* (New York: Basic Books, 1984).

7. Michael W. Kirst, "Toward a Focused Research Agenda," in *Voices from the Field: 30 Expert Opinions on "AMERICA 2000,"* edited by the William T. Grant Foundation Commission on Work, Family, and Citizenship and the Institute for Educational Leadership (Washington, DC: William T. Grant Foundation Commission on Work, Family, and Citizenship and the Institute for Educational Leadership, 1991), p. 43.

8. Lisbeth Schorr and Daniel Schorr, *Within Our Reach: Breaking the Cycle of Disadvantage* (New York: Anchor Books, 1988).

9. Carol S. Larson, Deanna S. Gomby, Patricia H. Shiono, Eugene M. Lewit, and Richard D. Behrman, "Analysis: School-Linked Health and Social Services," *Future of Children* 2, no. 1 (1992): 6-18.

10. Atelia Melaville and Martin J. Blank, *What It Takes: Structuring Interagency Partnerships to Connect Children and Families with Comprehensive Services* (Washington, DC: Educational and Human Services Consortium, 1991).

11. Schorr and Schorr, *Within Our Reach*. See also Chang et al., *Fighting Fragmentation*; H. L. Hodgkinson, *The Same Client: The Demographics of Education and Service Delivery Systems* (Washington, DC: Institute for Educational Leadership/Center for Demographic Policy, 1989); National Commission on Children, *Beyond Rhetoric: A New American Agenda for Children and Families* (Washington, DC: National Commission on Children, 1991).

12. Larson et al., "Analysis."

13. Tyack, "Health and Social Services in Public Schools."

14. Margaret C. Wang, Geneva D. Haertel, and Herbert J. Walberg, "Educational Resilience in Inner-Cities," in *Educational Resilience in Inner-City America: Challenges and Prospects*, edited by Margaret C. Wang and E. W. Gordon (Hillsdale, NJ: Erlbaum, 1994).

15. Herbert J. Walberg, "Learning over the Life Course," in *Cognitive Functioning in Social Structures*, edited by Carmi Schooler and K. Warner Schaie (Norwood, NJ: Ablex, 1987).

16. U.S. Department of Education, *AMERICA 2000: An Education Strategy* (Washington, DC: U.S. Department of Education, 1991).

17. *New York Times*, 28 August 1992.

18. Janet E. Levy and William Shephardson, "Look at Current School-Linked Service Efforts," *Future of Children* 2, no. 1 (1992): 44-55; L. C. Rigsby, Maynard C. Reynolds, and Margaret C. Wang, editors, *Schools/Community Connections: Exploring Issues for Research and Practice* (San Francisco: Jossey-Bass, forthcoming).

19. Charles Bruner, *Thinking Collaboratively: Ten Questions and Answers to Help Policymakers Improve Children's Services* (Washington, DC: Education and Human Services Consortium, 1991).

270   COLLABORATIVE SCHOOL-LINKED SERVICES

20. Irving Lazar, Richard B. Darlington, Harry Murray, Jacqueline Royce, and Ann Snipper, *Lasting Effects of Early Education*, Monographs of the Society for Research in Child Development 47, nos. 2-3 (1982). Serial no. 195.

21. Gary G. Wehlage, Robert A. Rutter, Gregory A. Smith, Nancy Lesko and Ricardo R. Fernandez, *Reducing the Risk: Schools as Communities of Support* (Philadelphia: Falmer Press, 1989).

22. N. S. Tobler, "Meta-analysis of 143 Adolescent Drug Prevention Programs: Quantitative Outcome Results of Program Participants Compared to a Control or Comparison Group," *Journal of Drug Issues* 16 (1986): 537-567.

23. Karl R. White, Matthew J. Taylor, and Vanessa D. Moss, "Does Research Support Claims about the Benefits of Involving Parents in Early Intervention Programs?" *Review of Educational Research* 62, no. 1 (1992): 91-125.

24. Michael Kirst and C. Kelley, "Collaboration to Improve Education and Children's Services: Politics and Policymaking" (Paper presented at the conference on School/Community Connections—Exploring Issues for Research and Practice, sponsored by the National Center on Education in the Inner Cities, Temple University, Philadelphia, 1992).

25. Wang, Haertel, and Walberg, "Dimensions of Collaborative School-Linked Services."

26. Kirst and Kelley, "Collaboration to Improve Education and Children's Services."

Questions for Further Study

Since its founding in 1901, the Society has had as one of its purposes the encouragement of the "study of education." Its publications are intended to provide a background as well as a stimulus for such study.

To give further emphasis to this purpose the Board of Directors has requested the editors of the two volumes of the 94th Yearbook to prepare sample questions that individuals and study groups can use to guide further inquiry into issues raised by the books. Accordingly, the editors have prepared the following list of questions which they hope will encourage readers to probe more deeply into the important problems with which this volume deals.

The basic argument that permeates all the chapters of this Yearbook is that since World War II, America has experienced striking changes in demography that have affected every aspect of life and every major institution, including schools, families, communities. While few would argue with these observations, there are serious debates about the meaning and impact of the demographic changes and, more importantly, their impact on a specific school or community.

Certainly some states and some communities have been impacted more than others. Urban schools have always experienced diversity—cultural, racial, ethnic, socioeconomic, and linguistic. Until recent years suburban and rural schools have tended to be more "homogeneous" along these dimensions.

In *your* school and community, how has the demography changed and how is it continuing to change? How have these changes impacted your school(s)? To what extent and in what ways has the changing demography been considered in your educational planning?

The alarming and distressing statistics regarding the social climate in which children and youth are being raised—unstable families, high divorce rate, child abuse, drug and alcohol abuse, high suicide rates, AIDS and venereal disease, growing incidence of crime and violence, the continuing expressions of alarm over "crises in education," declining achievement, high dropout rates, school-based violence and vandalism, and youth alienation—are reported as national or state data. What is the situation in your own school or community? What are the

271

implications locally for dealing with the local conditions, as differentiated from national trends?

1. In your own community or school, are there a "new and bewildering set of challenges" and, if so, what are they and how are they being met?

2. Are the so-called "new students" really new? In what ways?

3. Is Grubb right when he suggests that the problem is with the "responses" the schools have made—the curricula, teaching strategies, grouping processes, instructional resources—rather than with the "new students?" How should a school deal with his recommendation for *differentiated curriculum and pedagogy* in order to enable students to meet *undifferentiated standards?*

4. Pallas, Natriello, and McDill argue that the changing social and political contexts for schooling—"accountability, changing patterns of centralization and decentralization, and a changing institutional context for schooling"—are significant. How important is the cultural context in the school's functioning? What are the most important aspects of the cultural context that need to be dealt with?

5. Pallas et al. and Passow appear to view ability grouping and issues concerning instructional differentiation quite differently. Are these differences real? How do you and your colleagues view these issues? What provisions are made for developing talent potential in the diverse population of your school?

6. How do the unresolved policy tensions regarding child care and education, as pointed out by Kagan, "play out" in your community?

7. Does the recent reauthorization of Title I of the Elementary and Secondary Education Act hold promise for dealing with the problems of unfulfilled mission raised by Flaxman, Burnett, and Ascher?

8. What "second-chance" programs are available for students in your community? How successful are they? What problems do they pose?

9. Flaxman, Ascher, and Berryman observe that most students, including those considered nontraditional, are overlooked by educational policy because of the attention given by the school to its most severely disadvantaged and its most gifted and talented students. Are there students in your school who are "forgotten?" Are the disadvantaged and the gifted and talented students being dealt with adequately?

10. Sleeter discusses a variety of concepts that guide the design and implementation of "multicultural education" and argues that multicultural education is achievable and has meaning only when it empowers unempowered groups. What concept of multicultural education guides your school and its staff?

11. Lowe and Kantor analyze reasons why desegregation and racial balance have been significant issues for schools for some time without significant progress. They describe integration as an "illusory goal." Where does your school stand with respect to their charge that "truly public schools remain elusive?"

12. In many schools, so-called "minorities" constitute the majority of the school population. De facto segregation, combined with white and middle-class exodus and with religious or ethnically based schools, has resulted in a plethora of "minority schools." Glenn discusses the deliberate and legal establishment of separate schools for minorities based on their "best interests." What is your position on this issue and on what do you base your position?

13. No one denies the importance of the family as the child's first school. Few, if any, will argue that the changes in family structure and functioning can be ignored. In what ways do your school and community programs reflect these changes?

14. Wang et al. examine the effectiveness of a broad range of collaborative school-linked services, primarily as they relate to at-risk children and their families. In fact, of course, community agencies provide services for *all children*. What collaborative school-linked services for at-risk children function in your community? How effective are they? How could they be strengthened?

Name Index

Subject Index

Ability grouping, 41: studies of, 47-48; trends in schools that support, 13-14

Academic and vocational education integrated programs: barriers to implementation of, 152-58; benefits of, 146-48; need for different approach to in-service training of teachers for, 156; need for expanded vision of guidance and counseling in, 156-57; policy problems in implementation of, 157-58; skills needed by teachers in, 155-56

Accelerated Schools, 19, 23

Accountability, increased demands upon schools for, at national, state, and local levels, 36-37

Add-on programs in compensatory education, advantages and limitations of, 108

Advanced placement classes: as a new form of tracking, 195; increased participation of minority students in, 71-72

African Americans: demands of, for participation in school governance, 198; earnings of, 203; migration of, to northern and western cities, 187-88; political consequences of migration of, 188; unemployment rates among, 202-3

African-American students: ambiguous results of equal opportunity policies for, 186-87; demands of, for an education of substance, 199-200; increased nationwide segregation of, 197; limited response by schools to demands of, 200; overrepresentation of, in special education classes, 195, 200; proportion of, living in poverty, 202

Age grouping, studies of, 50

Aid to Families with Dependent Children (AFDC), 126

American Youth Commission (1937), statement of regarding inadequacy of vocational education to meet needs of "new students," 10

At-risk children: collaborative school-linked programs for, 254; need for broader social policies to protect, 253

Black leaders in schools, consequences of increased numbers of, 200-1

Brown v. Board of Education, 188, 194

California History/Social Science Framework, opposition to approach of, to multicultural education, 169

Career Education Movement (1970s), 143

Career magnet schools and career academies: advantages of, for disadvantaged students, 150; features of, 149-50

Center for Employment Training (CET), San Jose (California), 134

Centralization/decentralization, contrasting trends in schools, 37-38

Child care and early education programs: causes of restricted access to, 89; changing nature of demand for, 86; developmental vs. curricular approaches in design of, 90-91; differences in expectations of parents and providers of, 90; eight tensions inhibiting advancement of, 89-96; funding of, 87; increased demand for, 85; increased diversity in school population as a challenge to, 94-95; lack of continuity and coherence in support of, 93; lack of effective constituency for, 96; limited access of poor children to, 93-94; low participation rates of poor children in, 88; need to develop infrastructure for, 95; nature of present supply of, 87; parents' expectations of, 86-87; parents' preferences for different types of, 86; proposed actions to address tensions in, 96-98; service to children vs. service to families as issue in, 92-95; special needs for among poor children, 85; studies of quality of, 88; subsidized programs for, 87

Child development, frameworks for study of, 237-38

Civil Rights Movement, 188, 204

Coalition of Essential Schools, 12, 19

Collaborative school-linked programs: challenges in evaluation of, 267-68; complexity of problems addressed by, 266-67; evaluation of various types of, 260-66; history of, 254-57; levels of collaboration in, 259-60; need for new approaches to, 257-58; opposing views of value of, 256-57; school as central location for, 258-59

of, 105-14; criticisms of, 102; criticism of use of norm-referenced tests in, 105, 111; critique of actual operation of, 117-18; difficulty in securing parent participation in, 112; emphasis in, on instructional processes, rather than curriculum, 110-11; federal, state, and local responsibilities in, 103-4; focus of, on basic skills in reading and mathematics, 110; heavy use of teacher aides in, 114-15; problems with funding mechanisms and accountability in, 103-5; purposes of, 102-3; two models for parent participation in, 113-14; weak in-service training of teachers in, 115

Tracking: Advance Placement courses as new form of, for college preparatory students, 195; criticism of, 71; increased segregation as a result of, 194-95; studies of, 45-47

Upward Bound program, 190, 191

Ventures in Community Improvement, 130

Vocational education: expansion of, in high schools, 9-10; inadequacy of, to meet problems of "new students," 10. See also,

Academic and vocational education; TechPrep program; Work preparation

War on Poverty, 66, 102, 256-57

Well-being, indices of, 236-37

Women, increased participation of, in the work force, 239-40

Work-based education: problems of standards and evaluation relating to, 154-55; various organizational approaches to, 146-52

Work experience, disappointing effects of subsidies for, 129

Workplace learning: difficulties in making satisfactory arrangements for, 154; quality issues arising in, 154

Work preparation, for students: economic factors contributing to concern about, 144-45; increasing importance of cognitive skills in, 145-46; lack of curriculum structure for, in comprehensive high schools, 145; renewed interest in (1980s), 144

Youth apprenticeships: dangers of, 151; essential components of, 150

YouthBuild, 130

Youth Incentive Entitlement Pilot Project (YIEPP), 129-30

INFORMATION ABOUT MEMBERSHIP IN THE SOCIETY

Membership in the National Society for the Study of Education is open to all individuals who desire to receive its publications.

There are presently two categories of membership: Regular and Comprehensive. The Regular Membership (annual dues in 1995, $30) entitles the member to receive both volumes of the Yearbook. The Comprehensive Membership (annual dues in 1995, $55) entitles the member to receive the two volume Yearbook and the two current volumes in the Series on Contemporary Educational Issues.

The Series on Contemporary Educational Issues is to be discontinued after 1995. The Comprehensive Membership will therefore not be available after the end of calendar year 1995 (December 31, 1995).

For calendar year 1995 reduced dues are available for retired NSSE members and for full-time graduate students *in their first year of membership*. These reduced dues are $25 for the Regular Membership and $50 for the Comprehensive Membership.

Membership in the Society is for the calendar year. Dues are payable on or before January 1 of each year.

New members are required to pay an entrance fee of $1, in addition to annual dues for the year in which they join.

Members of the Society include professors, researchers, graduate students, and administrators in colleges and universities; teachers, supervisors, curriculum specialists, and administrators in elementary and secondary schools; and a considerable number of persons not formally connected with educational institutions.

All members participate in the election of the six-member Board of Directors, which is responsible for managing the affairs of the Society, including the authorization of volumes to appear in the yearbook series. All members whose dues are paid for the current year are eligible for election to the Board of Directors.

Each year the Society arranges for meetings to be held in conjunction with the annual conferences of one or more of the major national educational organizations. All members are urged to attend these sessions. Members are also encouraged to submit proposals for future yearbooks.

Further information about the Society may be secured by writing to the Secretary-Treasurer, NSSE, 5835 Kimbark Avenue, Chicago, IL 60637.

RECENT PUBLICATIONS OF THE NATIONAL SOCIETY FOR THE STUDY OF EDUCATION

1. The Yearbooks

Ninety-fourth Yearbook (1995)

Part 1. *Creating New Educational Communities*. Jeannie Oakes and Karen Hunter Quartz, editors. Cloth.

Part 2. *Changing Populations/Changing Schools*. Erwin Flaxman and A. Harry Passow, editors. Cloth.

Ninety-third Yearbook (1994)

Part 1. *Teacher Research and Educational Reform*. Sandra Hollingsworth and Hugh Sockett, editors. Cloth.

Part 2. *Bloom's Taxonomy: A Forty-year Retrospective*. Lorin W. Anderson and Lauren A. Sosniak, editors. Cloth.

Ninety-second Yearbook (1993)

Part 1. *Gender and Education*. Sari Knopp Biklen and Diane Pollard, editors. Cloth.

Part 2. *Bilingual Education: Politics, Practice, and Research*. M. Beatriz Arias and Ursula Casanova, editors. Cloth.

Ninety-first Yearbook (1992)

Part 1. *The Changing Contexts of Teaching*. Ann Lieberman, editor. Cloth.

Part 2. *The Arts, Education, and Aesthetic Knowing*. Bennett Reimer and Ralph A. Smith, editors. Cloth.

Ninetieth Yearbook (1991)

Part 1. *The Care and Education of America's Young Children: Obstacles and Opportunities*. Sharon L. Kagan, editor. Cloth.

Part 2. *Evaluation and Education: At Quarter Century*. Milbrey W. McLaughlin and D. C. Phillips, editors. Paper.

Eighty-ninth Yearbook (1990)

Part 1. *Textbooks and Schooling in the United States*. David L. Elliott and Arthur Woodward, editors. Cloth.

Part 2. *Educational Leadership and Changing Contexts of Families, Communities, and Schools*. Brad Mitchell and Luvern L. Cunningham, editors. Paper.

Eighty-eighth Yearbook (1989)

Part 1. *From Socrates to Software: The Teacher as Text and the Text as Teacher*. Philip W. Jackson and Sophie Haroutunian-Gordon, editors. Cloth.

Part 2. *Schooling and Disability*. Douglas Biklen, Dianne Ferguson, and Alison Ford, editors. Cloth.

Eighty-seventh Yearbook (1988)

Part 1. *Critical Issues in Curriculum*. Laurel N. Tanner, editor. Cloth.

Part 2. *Cultural Literacy and the Idea of General Education*. Ian Westbury and Alan C. Purves, editors. Cloth.

Eighty-sixth Yearbook (1987)
Part 1. *The Ecology of School Renewal.* John I. Goodlad, editor. Paper.
Part 2. *Society as Educator in an Age of Transition.* Kenneth D. Benne and Steven Tozer, editors. Cloth.

Eighty-fifth Yearbook (1986)
Part 1. *Microcomputers and Education.* Jack A. Culbertson and Luvern L. Cunningham, editors. Cloth.
Part 2. *The Teaching of Writing.* Anthony R. Petrosky and David Bartholomae, editors. Paper.

Eighty-fourth Yearbook (1985)
Part 1. *Education in School and Nonschool Settings.* Mario D. Fantini and Robert Sinclair, editors. Cloth.
Part 2. *Learning and Teaching the Ways of Knowing.* Elliot Eisner, editor. Paper.

Eighty-third Yearbook (1984)
Part 1. *Becoming Readers in a Complex Society.* Alan C. Purves and Olive S. Niles, editors. Cloth.
Part 2. *The Humanities in Precollegiate Education.* Benjamin Ladner, editor. Paper.

Eighty-second Yearbook (1983)
Part 1. *Individual Differences and the Common Curriculum.* Gary D Fenstermacher and John I. Goodlad, editors. Paper.

Eighty-first Yearbook (1982)
Part 1. *Policy Making in Education.* Ann Lieberman and Milbrey W. McLaughlin, editors. Cloth.
Part 2. *Education and Work.* Harry F. Silberman, editor. Cloth.

Eightieth Yearbook (1981)
Part 1. *Philosophy and Education.* Jonas P. Soltis, editor. Cloth.
Part 2. *The Social Studies.* Howard D. Mehlinger and O. L. Davis, Jr., editors. Cloth.

Seventy-ninth Yearbook (1980)
Part 1. *Toward Adolescence: The Middle School Years.* Mauritz Johnson, editor. Paper.

Seventy-eighth Yearbook (1979)
Part 1. *The Gifted and the Talented: Their Education and Development.* A. Harry Passow, editor. Paper.
Part 2. *Classroom Management.* Daniel L. Duke, editor. Paper.

The above titles in the Society's Yearbook series may be ordered from the University of Chicago Press, Book Order Department, 11030 Langley Ave., Chicago, IL 60628. For a list of earlier titles in the yearbook series still available, write to the Secretary, NSSE, 5835 Kimbark Ave., Chicago, IL 60637.

2. The Series on Contemporary Educational Issues

This series is to be discontinued after 1995.
The following previous volumes in the series may be ordered from the McCutchan Publishing Corporation, P.O. Box 774, Berkeley, CA 94702-0774. Phone: 510-841-8616; Fax: 510-841-7787.

Academic Work and Educational Excellence: Raising Student Productivity (1986). Edited by Tommy M. Tomlinson and Herbert J. Walberg.
Adapting Instruction to Student Differences (1985). Edited by Margaret C. Wang and Herbert J. Walberg.
Choice in Education (1990). Edited by William Lowe Boyd and Herbert J. Walberg.
Colleges of Education: Perspectives on Their Future (1985). Edited by Charles W. Case and William A. Matthes.
Contributing to Educational Change: Perspectives on Research and Practice (1988). Edited by Philip W. Jackson.
Educational Leadership and School Culture (1993). Edited by Marshall Sashkin and Herbert J. Walberg.
Effective School Leadership: Policy and Prospects (1987). Edited by John J. Lane and Herbert J. Walberg.
Effective Teaching: Current Research (1991). Edited by Hersholt C. Waxman and Herbert J. Walberg.
Improving Educational Standards and Productivity: The Research Basis for Policy (1982). Edited by Herbert J. Walberg.
Moral Development and Character Education (1989). Edited by Larry P. Nucci.
Motivating Students to Learn: Overcoming Barriers to High Achievement (1993). Edited by Tommy M. Tomlinson.
Radical Proposals for Educational Change (1994). Edited by Chester E. Finn, Jr. and Herbert J. Walberg.
Reaching Marginal Students: A Prime Concern for School Renewal (1987). Edited by Robert L. Sinclair and Ward Ghory.
Research on Teaching: Concepts, Findings, and Implications (1979). Edited by Penelope L. Peterson and Herbert J. Walberg.
Restructuring the Schools: Problems and Prospects (1992). Edited by John J. Lane and Edgar G. Epps.
Rethinking Policy for At-risk Students (1994). Edited by Kenneth K. Wong and Margaret C. Wang.
School Boards: Changing Local Control (1992). Edited by Patricia F. First and Herbert J. Walberg.

The two final volumes in this series are:

Improving Science Education (1995). Edited by Barry J. Fraser and Herbert J. Walberg.
Ferment in Education: A Look Abroad (1995). Edited by John J. Lane.

These two volumes may be ordered from the Book Order Department, University of Chicago Press, 11030 S. Langley Ave., Chicago, IL 60628. Phone: 312-669-2215; Fax: 312-660-2235.